The Carey Formula

The Carey Formula

Your Ideas Are Worth Millions

Barbara Carey

The Carey Formula: Your Ideas Are Worth Millions

Copyright © 2006 by Barbara Carey

Published by

CAREY
PRESS

ISBN 13: 978-0-9778052-0-4
ISBN 10: 0-9778052

Cover Design: Karla Dominguez
Interior Book Design: Lisa Liddy, The Printed Page

Contact information: Carey Press
19 Orinda Way, Suite L
Orinda, CA 94563

(925) 254-8610
barbarac@TheCareyFormula.com
www.TheCareyFormula.com

for Mom, my best friend
and Dad, my hero

Contents

Chapter 1. The Evolution of an Entrepreneur · · · · 11

An Alternative Point of View· · · · · · · · · · · 12
An Early Realization · · · · · · · · · · · · · · 12
A Foundation for Success · · · · · · · · · · · · 13
My Guiding Angels · · · · · · · · · · · · · · · 15
The Allure of Independence · · · · · · · · · · · 16
Is That All There Is? · · · · · · · · · · · · · · 17
Don't Be the Angel, Be the Charlie· · · · · · · · 18
A Nurturing Environment · · · · · · · · · · · · 19
Finding a Daemon in the Rough· · · · · · · · · · 23
Fourteen Percent or Bust! · · · · · · · · · · · · 24
Meanwhile, Back At the Reality Hotel . . . · .· · · · 24
The Mother of Invention· · · · · · · · · · · · · 25
A Further Revelation · · · · · · · · · · · · · · · 27
All Good Things · · · · · · · · · · · · · · · · 28
A Connection Made · · · · · · · · · · · · · · · 30
The Simple Secrets to Success: · · · · · · · · · · 30
Key Signs on the Road to Entrepreneurship: · · · · · 32

**Chapter 2. Time-Out—Lessons in Product
Selection · 35**

KISS Me You Ordinary Fool! · · · · · · · · · · · 36
Keep It Simple Smart-Gal/Guy · · · · · · · · · · 37

Temptation, Thy Name is Dyson · · · · · · · · · · · 38
  Carey's Reminders · · · · · · · · · · · · · · · · · 39
The Truth: This May Sting a Little · · · · · · · · · 39
Strap Yourself In: We're Time Traveling· · · · · · · 40
  You Don't Have to Be an Expert in Every Field · · · 42
From Ideation to Product Selection · · · · · · · · · 43
Assembling the Team · · · · · · · · · · · · · · · · 44
Making the Leap from Concept to Reality · · · · · · 45
A Swiss Near Miss · · · · · · · · · · · · · · · · · 46
Lessons Learned · · · · · · · · · · · · · · · · · · 49
Meanwhile, Back Under the Blankets · · · · · · · · 52
¡Viva Mexico! · · · · · · · · · · · · · · · · · · · 53
¡Viva Visa! · 54
The DCH Mask of Troy· · · · · · · · · · · · · · · 54
Getting to Yes With a Little Help from My Friends · · 58
Combining Products to Maximize Success · · · · · · 61
From Idea to Reality: Water Talkies · · · · · · · · · 62
And That's Not All· · · · · · · · · · · · · · · · · · 64
  The Eye of a Turtle · · · · · · · · · · · · · · · · 65
Barbara Carey's Simple Secrets of Success: · · · · · · 71

Chapter 3. Prison and Perseverance · · · · · · · 77
Odd Birds and Eccentric Redheads· · · · · · · · · · 78
Don't Do—Delegate! · · · · · · · · · · · · · · · · 80
Truth and Trepidation: Going Your Own Way · · · · 81
Doing Unto Others... · · · · · · · · · · · · · · · · 83
  Un-Edited Commentary· · · · · · · · · · · · · · · 84
Working Smart: Knowing When and How to Adapt
  Your Methods · · · · · · · · · · · · · · · · · · · 87
The "P" Word · 88
Equestrian Dreams· · · · · · · · · · · · · · · · · · 89
What Are The Chances? · · · · · · · · · · · · · · · 90
The Beat Goes On · · · · · · · · · · · · · · · · · · 93
  A Horse Story—A Father's Point of View · · · · · 94
Another Lesson in Hard Work· · · · · · · · · · · · · 95

Another Lesson in Hard Work · · · · · · · · · · · · · 95

Retail Lessons · 96

College and Crisis · · · · · · · · · · · · · · · · · · 97

School Daze · 99

A Plan Takes Shape · · · · · · · · · · · · · · · · · 101

College: A Review for the Real Test · · · · · · · · · 102

But I Thought You Said All I Had to Do Was... · · · 105

An Aquatic Acquaintance · · · · · · · · · · · · · 107

IBM Sales Boot Camp · · · · · · · · · · · · · · · 108

Barbara Carey's Points to Remember: · · · · · · · · 110

    The Apple Doesn't Fall Very Far From

      the Tree—Even When It's Pushed · · · · · · 113

**Chapter 4. Barbara Carey's Characteristics
of a Successful Entrepreneur** · · · · · · · · · · **117**

Start With Yourself · · · · · · · · · · · · · · · · · 118

One Family's Story of Giving · · · · · · · · · · · · 119

The Genius of Creativity · · · · · · · · · · · · · · 121

Multiple Intelligences · · · · · · · · · · · · · · · · 122

Know Yourself · · · · · · · · · · · · · · · · · · · 123

    I Knew Her Way Back When... · · · · · · · · 128

Being Observant · · · · · · · · · · · · · · · · · · 132

    Book of Knowledge: Recording Your Thoughts · · 133

Being Empathetic · · · · · · · · · · · · · · · · · · 135

Being Knowledgeable · · · · · · · · · · · · · · · · 136

Being a Visionary · · · · · · · · · · · · · · · · · · 136

    Why I Write in Longhand · · · · · · · · · · · 138

Being Passionately Independent · · · · · · · · · · · 139

Being Self-Confident · · · · · · · · · · · · · · · · 140

Being Persistent · · · · · · · · · · · · · · · · · · · 140

Being Realistic · · · · · · · · · · · · · · · · · · · 140

    A Friend and Colleague Responds · · · · · · · 141

Being in the Moment · · · · · · · · · · · · · · · · 143

Thinking Globally, Acting Locally · · · · · · · · · 143

The Role of Luck · · · · · · · · · · · · · · · · 145
Seeing Change · · · · · · · · · · · · · · · · · · 146

Chapter 5. Creating Successful Products· · · · · 149
  IDEATION: Inspiration and Early Trials· · · · · · 150
    Inexpensive Research and Development · · · · · 151
  Forget R&R; I'm Doing R&D · · · · · · · · · · · 153
    Depending on Patents · · · · · · · · · · · · · 155
    China and the "Hubba Hubba" Program · · · · · 159
    Beam Me Up, Scottie—Electronic vs.
      Print Direct Response · · · · · · · · · · · 163
  What a Concept · · · · · · · · · · · · · · · · · 165
  Switching Channels:
    Claire's Boutique and the Price Point· · · · · · · 167
  Barbara Carey's Simple Secrets of Success: · · · · · · 172

**Chapter 6. Preparing for and Getting a
Sales Meeting · 175**
  Befriending the Buyer · · · · · · · · · · · · · 183
  Don't Just Research, Me Search· · · · · · · · · · 184
  The Key to the Kingdom · · · · · · · · · · · · · 185
    Planograms · · · · · · · · · · · · · · · · · · 186
  An Almost Certain Dead End· · · · · · · · · · · 188
  Strategic Dialing: Getting Your Finger in the Door· · · 188
  Barbara Carey's Simple Secrets of Success: · · · · · · 190

**Chapter 7. Selling Yourself and Your Product—
A Recap · 191**
  Know Your Buyer· · · · · · · · · · · · · · · · · 193
    Guaranteed Sales—A Guaranteed No Thank You · 195
  Figuring Out Your Buyer's Type · · · · · · · · · · 196
  Pre-meeting Thoughts: A Checklist· · · · · · · · · 198
  Negotiating Points · · · · · · · · · · · · · · · · 201
  Anticipate and Solve Their Problems · · · · · · · 205
  Plan to Move the Meeting from Sales to
    Merchandising · · · · · · · · · · · · · · · · 205

When Things Went Wrong at Longs · · · · · · · · 206
    Sell-Through · · · · · · · · · · · · · · · · · 206
Ask for the Order · · · · · · · · · · · · · · · · 208
Barbara Carey's Simple Secrets of Success: · · · · · 210

Chapter 8. Passion of PINK— The Dittie™ Story · 211
    A Post Script · · · · · · · · · · · · · · · · 214
Defining Your Sales Approach: How I Made the Sale · 226
A Picture is Worth a Thousand Words · · · · · · · 230
Moving On to Marketing · · · · · · · · · · · · · 233
Marketing that Matters · · · · · · · · · · · · · · 235
Marketing in the Potty · · · · · · · · · · · · · · 237
    Helping Women in Need · · · · · · · · · · · 241
    Coming Soon! · · · · · · · · · · · · · · · · 244

Chapter 9. Zen and the Art of Balance · · · · · · 249
Balance as a Buzz Word · · · · · · · · · · · · · 251
Build a Balanced Foundation · · · · · · · · · · · 252
A Pace of Grace · · · · · · · · · · · · · · · · · 254
Drink Water · · · · · · · · · · · · · · · · · · 255
A Good Deep Breath · · · · · · · · · · · · · · · 256
Mind and Spirit · · · · · · · · · · · · · · · · · 258
Balance with Business · · · · · · · · · · · · · · 260
Keeping It All in Perspective · · · · · · · · · · · 262
    Fun · 267
Balance and *The Carey Formula* · · · · · · · · · 270
The Carey Formula CD Library · · · · · · · · · 275
Photo Gallery · · · · · · · · · · · · · · · · · · 276
Roadmap to Success · · · · · · · · · · · · · · · 287

Acknowledgments · · · · · · · · · · · · · · · · · 295

Index · 299

Foreword

Every year there are 68,000 books launched. You don't want to miss reading this one.

When I first agreed to write the foreword for Barbara Carey's book, I really didn't know what to expect. I did know, however, that Barbara is one of the most charismatic and successful business people I've met, and her book would be no less.

But when I started reading, it was much more.

A story about a female inventor—that's going to be good.

A story about a female inventor who's also an entrepreneur—that's going to be really good.

A story about a female inventor/entrepreneur who made over $40 million with only $6000 after getting back on the horse from near bankruptcy—now that's going to be an *amazing* story.

But what makes this book even more amazing is its rich detail and how personally involved you become with a multimillionaire dynamo at her lowest lows and at her highest highs. This book is personal like no other business book I have read. Failures, feelings, insights, anxieties, and joys all shared with no holds barred. She's real, she's personal, and she shares everything.

If you're someone chasing a dream, you'll undoubtedly take away these five points and more:

1. Don't take no for an answer.

2. There's no such thing as luck.

3. Don't let money get in your way; you don't need a lot.

4. Fall in love with your business plan, not your product (here's the *Formula*).

5. Passion counts.

I once read a book about why certain people make the sale, why certain people get paid more, and why things succeed. Beyond the basics, what tips the scale in your favor is passion. If you're excited about a product, then others will be, too. Passion is infectious.

Persistence is what separates the inventor from the entrepreneur. Knowledge is what separates the successful from the rest (after you've read this you'll have even more knowledge with *The Carey Formula*). But passion is the essence of Barbara Carey, the person, and Barbara Carey, the businessperson. Passion is the essence of the American dream.

Are you ready to stop *chasing* your dream and begin to start *living* your dream?

You're just a few pages away.

Mark Hughes
CEO, Buzzmarketing
Author, *Buzzmarketing: Get People to Talk About Your Stuff*

Introduction

Based on the fact you picked up this book to read, I'm willing to bet you and I already have a lot in common. Like me, you probably have an active and inquisitive mind and you chafe under the constraints others always seem to be imposing on you. In other words, you have a great deal of passion for ideas and innovations and, most likely, you love your independence.

Oh, yes—one other thing. You probably enjoy already or want to enjoy even greater success and everything it can bring you and your family.

I know that some of you don't really know exactly who I am (I'll fill you in as we go), but I'm also willing to bet that at some point in your life you've come across one of my product inventions in a retail store—whether it was Hairagami®, Motivation Mirror, Dittie™, or Friendship Bracelets, you've either seen or perhaps even purchased one of these products.

The one thing you and I may not have in common yet is that you've not yet been able to successfully bring to market and sell hundreds of thousands of units of your invention. I have. If you apply the principles of this book, work diligently and smartly, you will one day be able to say the same.

I don't mean for my statements about my past successes to sound too boastful, but the truth is, over the last twenty years I have established a track record of success in conceiving, manufacturing, and selling a wide variety of consumer mass merchandise products in national chain stores, regional outlets, and on national television. The very first item I produced earned me an initial order that resulted in eventual total earnings of more than $1,000,000. That project, from idea conception to selling the product to a national retailer, took less than four weeks. You'll get the full details of that story in Chapter Two, but be forewarned: I offer that example as much as a cautionary tale as I do an example of what to do. Call it fate, call it luck, call it whatever, that experience was born more out of desperation and a "What Have We Got to Lose" bravado than it was born of adhering to a sound business model and strategic planning.

While I don't recommend setting a goal to emulate my first sale's feat in the same amount of time, I also want you to know that such a success is possible—and this book shows you how. But keep this important principle in mind: sometimes you can catch lightning in a bottle; other times retail chain buyers will tell you to go fly a kite.

I also want you to know that I am someone in whom you can place your trust. My first venture was no flash-in-the-pan success. In the last twenty years as an inventor and entrepreneur, I have brought more than 100 products to market, launched seven companies, and have been awarded several patents. My methods have changed somewhat, but the one constant has been that I get the sale.

Admittedly, I'm not the only person who has enjoyed this kind of success in the mass merchandise arena. What makes my success different is how I attained it, not what I attained.

You've probably heard one of these two statements dozens and dozens of times:

You have to have a product before you can sell it.

Or

It takes money to make money.

I'm here to tell you that neither of those statements is true to the degree you probably believe today. By the time you complete this book, I'm confident that you will share my point of view. One of the reasons why I have been successful is that I don't accept the kind of conventional wisdom expressed in those two statements. Consequently, I have made a very nice success of my business ventures for my family and myself by defying the logic of those so-called "rules".

I call the strategy I employ to avoid those two pitfalls in thinking *The Carey Formula*. I devised this strategy in the course of twenty years of working with some of the nation's top retailers. The book you hold in your hand is evidence of the success of my strategy. At its heart, using *The Carey Formula* allows you to accomplish an important mission.

By following *The Carey Formula*, you will be able to:

- Sell your ideas first.

- Then produce and market them with the proceeds from your initial orders.

How many times have you had a brilliant idea and stopped yourself from acting on it by saying, "If only I had X number of dollars, I'd produce my idea of a better and simpler television remote control"? (I use this as an example because many of the best minds in the industry have tried and failed.)

The truth is, you don't need to sink thousands or even hundreds of dollars into research and development before you make your first move toward sales. This book is evidence of that fact. Before I'd sat down to pen a single word of this book, I'd already sold several distributors on the viability of the book. I wasn't going to proceed with the writing until I had some assurance of its success.

You don't believe that you can do something similar yourself? Well, the proof that you can is in these pages. By the time you're through reading *The Carey Formula*, you'll benefit from my success as I share with you the time-proven secrets that have evolved from work I began many years ago. I lift the veil of secrecy on the wisdom I learned from the time I was a nine-year-old wannabe entrepreneur to the lessons I learned in closing my latest multi-million dollar deal only a few days ago.

In *The Carey Formula* you will learn:

- How to identify the kinds of products that will succeed in the mass market.

- Where you can find the inspiration for mass market ideas.

- How to evaluate your product idea.

- Why it's important to pursue ideas that have low production costs and, thus, high profit margins.

- Which retailers/merchants are best suited to buying and then reselling your product.

- Who the decision makers are at hundreds of retailers and how to reach them.

- How to craft an irresistible sales pitch.

- How to find quality manufacturers and packagers who can help you bring your dream to reality.

- Why sell-through and customer care can make or break your venture.

Most important, you'll learn how to do this with very little or, in some cases, no upfront cash.

The Carey Formula is a multi-part process or set of steps you will take to go from what I call ideation to customer care and sell-through. In between those framing steps you will learn about:

- Market Research

- Product Development

- Preparing for the Sales Meeting

- Getting the Orders

- Monitoring Sell-Through and Tailoring Marketing to Meet Demand

Along the way, I hope we'll share some laughs about some of my failures as well as the more inventive steps I've taken to get my products in front of those who ultimately make a decision about whether or not a product is offered to consumers—the retail outlet's buyers. I guarantee that you won't find a complete summary of these tips and strategies in any other book, nor will you learn them in a business class at your local junior college or find them on the syllabus at any college or university.

I really can't stress enough that despite any difference in our backgrounds, our ages, our genders, our educational experiences, or most any other factor, you can accomplish what I've done. If nothing else, I want to impress upon you this fact—that as Thomas Edison once said, "Genius is one percent inspiration and ninety-nine percent perspiration."

While my formula for retail success doesn't require you to have a boatload of cash, you do need some skills. Remember your high school chemistry class when you learned a lot of formulas? Don't worry; you won't have to know what Avogadro's number is or what ATP or molality mean! I do want you to remember this: some compounds act as a catalyst. They cause a reaction. In order for *The Carey Formula* to really work, *you* are the catalyst. *You* are the compound that sets the chain reaction of success in motion.

To be perfectly honest, I don't care what your motivations are for finding success as an inventor/entrepreneur. Whether you are hoping you can achieve the dream of a situation-comedy-like-get-rich-quick-scheme (think Fred Flintstone, The Honeymooners, Laverne and Shirley, etc.), want to get revenge on a former boyfriend/teacher/parent who said you'd never amount to anything, or have a burning desire to be the next Martha Stewart or Bill Gates, you will have to have a passionate desire to succeed.

That said, one of the other key ingredients that has helped me in my career is integrity. Though some of my suggested methods may be unorthodox, unusual, or outside your comfort zone, I have never done anything unethical, illegal, or immoral in order to get ahead. While I don't like rules and regulations or traveling the beaten path that others have tread, I do have to look myself in the mirror each morning and like who I see.

Give me a moment while I step off my soapbox.

Thanks. Let's move on.

I was writing about *you* as the catalyst for this great undertaking. More specifically, a couple of key ingredients inside you are crucial to *The Carey Formula* working for you. One of those is persistence. Having the dogged determination to persevere is so crucial that I devote an entire chapter to it. Maybe you'll be more fortunate than I have been and never experience failure. I learned a lot from my failures and I'm hoping that this book will short-circuit yours or at least be less costly and less emotionally draining than mine were.

Friends ask me all the time when I'm going to slow down and take it easy. They tell me that I could just as easily be spending my days at a spa or sipping a glass of merlot at one of the nearby vineyards in California's wine country. The truth is, I don't want to slow down. I love what I do and I am so much more interested in building the proverbial "better mousetrap" than I am in lunching at a luxury resort. In fact, just a few years ago, I was with my friends at a nearby hotel. It was girls' day out and we were there to enjoy a day of spa treatments. I was wishing I were back at my office, but went along because my friends are so important to me. They were selecting various treatments to undergo, but I'm generally not that into being pampered, so I was wandering among the various rooms when I saw a sign for a threading treatment. I asked one of the spa's employees what threading was, and she told me it was an Indian hair removal method.

Something clicked in my brain. I was no longer a lady who lunched but an eager entrepreneur investigating a possible opportunity. I knew that the hair removal industry was huge—a six billion dollar a year industry. I had to know more. I knew that women spend their dollars on shaving products, waxing, laser removal, depilatories, and the like, but I'd never heard of threading. When I was told that it was much like waxing in that the body hairs are plucked out from the brow, bikini line, and other areas, I blanched a bit.

I knew I would find those kinds of treatments painful, and as much as I wanted to learn more about how the process worked, I wasn't about to undergo the treatment myself. I scoured the hallways until I found a delightfully cooperative woman who was willing to undergo the treatment while I watched. I gave her fifty dollars for her trouble and paid for the treatment, which cost another fifty dollars. I assured her that I was an inventor and businesswoman and not someone who enjoyed watching another undergo moderately painful beauty treatments!

I sat in the room with her while the threading technician took thin strands of thread, wrapped them around the offending hairs, and with a sharp tug on both ends of the thread, plucked them out. The subject reported that threading was far less painful than traditional plucking with tweezers or yanking with wax, and the technician moved with such speed that I had visions in my head of a weed-whacker.

That vision only lasted a little while. As soon as I got back to the office, I started sketching. I thought that if women were willing to spend fifty dollars on the spa threading treatment, they'd be willing to spend $19.95 for a do-it-at-home tool. Thus, the Flax was born. I came up with the tag line, "Don't Wax It, Flax It—With a Gentle Squeeze Remove Hair With Ease" (see image page 282). The product was sold nationwide. It wasn't a stellar success, but I learned a lot from the venture.

In many ways this story illustrates perfectly how simply paying attention to your surroundings, understanding the needs of consumers, and using a little imagination and ingenuity can set you up for success. Maybe I'm more driven than most, maybe I feel more like I have a calling than most, but I don't think that's entirely the case. Truth be told, I have so many ideas swimming around in my brain that I'll probably never get to half of them. The reason I have so many ideas constantly percolating is the other key ingredient so necessary to success—passion.

I'm especially passionate about bringing products to market that will improve the quality of women's lives. Given the frantic pace of our daily existence—and as a mother I know just how hectic women's lives can be—I'm constantly innovating and inventing products that will save women time. That passion never ebbs; it's always high tide in my office.

Without the two P's—passion and persistence—I don't know where I'd be or when I'd finally achieve the success I've wanted for myself for so many years, since I was a little girl, in fact.

So what's your passion? What's your favorite pastime? Believe it or not, lots of people have made millions based on their hobbies. They've been able to turn their leisure time into productive and profitable time, and so can you.

Speaking of time, we should get started. We're going to take a look at that little girl I was, and I'll show you how my parents played a crucial role in the earliest formative stages of my and *The Carey Formula*'s development.

The Evolution of an Entrepreneur

One of the questions most frequently asked of me is where I get the inspiration for my ideas. As you've just read in the introduction, I feel that I have so many product ideas that I can't possibly ever get to them all in this lifetime. In Chapter Two on product selection, I'll get to the nuts and bolts of idea evaluation and generation. My short answer to this question concerning where I get my ideas from is that I'm an introspective and observant person, so I pay close attention to what goes on around me and inside me. It would be my bet that you may have similar qualities or you would not be reading this book. Based on those thoughts and observations, I come up with the majority of my ideas. That's the simple answer. There's a far more complex one I want to explore as well.

An Alternative Point of View

In this chapter, I'm going to examine this frequently asked question from a slightly different perspective—would you expect any less from me? Instead of simply thinking about where my ideas come from, I'm going to tell you about my background and experiences growing up and my eventual evolution into an inventor and entrepreneur. In doing so, we'll be looking at *why* those ideas come to me, *what* experiences I had as a young person that shaped me to be both a generator of and conduit for ideas, and what you can do and where you can go to foster your own growth as an idea creator. Along the way, I'll examine in greater depth the ingredients I mentioned in the introduction that are necessary to succeed in this endeavor—passion, persistence and independence. I'll also talk briefly about the differences I see between being an inventor and an entrepreneur. In addition, I'll include another key component of *The Carey Formula*—creativity.

An Early Realization

Everybody has to have a dream. My father, perhaps inadvertently, inspired one of my earliest dreams. Ron Kraft worked as a seismic engineer in quake-prone California. The firm he started was headquartered in a high-rise in San Francisco. Every now and then, I'd get to see him at his office when my mother brought me there. I can remember strolling the hallways, feeling the thrill of activity and importance that seemed to beam down from the overhead lights. Most especially, I remember his office, and the nearly floor-to-ceiling windows that offered views of the city's spires (like the rising TransAmerica Building, which was still under construction) and the bay.

Strangely, even at an early age, I sensed I didn't want to work in an office like that one day. As beautiful and well-appointed as my father's office was, I sensed intuitively that an office with a dominating glass barrier would prevent me from being "out there" in the streets, prevent me from really being a part of the ebb and flow and energy of daily life. What mattered to me more than the outward signs of success was an inner sense of peace. That meant to be out there actively engaged with people. As I grew older, working in a glass-walled corner office or a particle-board cubicle seemed to me to be a stifling kind of work environment.

I have no real factual evidence to support my contention that I wanted something unique, just a recollection that even as a little girl I had a strong sense of where I didn't think my future might lie. I did see one thing very clearly about work, however. My father worked very hard and believed that, like the old saying, hard work was its own reward. He made sure that my brother and I understood and lived out the truth of that statement.

A Foundation for Success

While I definitely enjoyed the visits to my father's office for their novelty, I loved—far more—having him come home from the office. Looking back on it now, I realize that I was lucky enough to have lived a nearly *Leave It to Beaver* or *Brady Bunch*-like childhood. My mother, Margie Kraft, was a schoolteacher who left the profession to raise her two children—my brother Scott and me. She was a wonderful mother and wife. Just like I'd seen in those '50s and '60s television shows, at around five-thirty, shortly after starting dinner, my mother would retreat upstairs. Fifteen minutes later, she'd come out of her bedroom with a lovely dress on, her face made up, and her hair neatly coiffed. At six-thirty, when my father came home from the office, she'd greet him at the door looking radiant. They'd exchange a brief kiss, and then my father was all mine until dinnertime.

I would be waiting for him behind the bi-fold doors that separated our family room from the kitchen. I could hear his footsteps on the tiled floor of the kitchen. When he got close to the door, I would open it and yell, "Prizes, Daddy-Boy!" Without fail he would hand over a special gift to me that I just knew he had searched the entire city to find. It's impossible to explain how much I loved and looked forward to those gifts. I grew to expect my prize every day. It wasn't so much the prize I looked forward to, but it was the huge grin that animated his face and the sparkle in his blue eyes when he handed me my gift. What I remember most is his Santa-like laugh and his voice calling me "Kitten" when he handed over the treasure.

Now in reality, Dad didn't go shopping for me every day, but the Greyhound bus station where my dad began and ended his daily commute into and out of the city had a vending machine and Dad never forgot to put his nickel in to get my prize.

Generally, I was a very shy child, but somehow that reluctance to talk and socialize melted away whenever I was with my dad. I would snuggle up to him as we sat together in his favorite chair and I'd tell him all about my day. I'd also chat about what I wore that day. I would describe how I put my outfit together and the colors and textures of the fabrics that I chose to wear together. I loved the art of fashion and my mother swears my first words were *haute couture*.

Without interrupting us, Mom would bring in a plate of snacks for us to munch on and tide us over until dinner. During those evening sessions, my dad made me feel like I was the only person in the world who really mattered to him. He seemed to care solely about my needs and me. That sense of being the primary focus of his attention and affection is a feeling I'll never forget. It offered a valuable lesson that I put into practice when I had my own child. I have to admit it was a fairly idyllic home life—and one for which I grew even more grateful when I went to school and learned that most of my classmates spoke so negatively about their parents.

My Guiding Angels

Fast-forward a few years to 1976. This time, the four of us have eaten dinner, and Dad and I are alone in the family room watching television. I'm just about sixteen at this point, and I am completely and totally captivated by the television show *Charlie's Angels*. I love Kate Jackson for her brains, Farrah Fawcett for her persuasive charm, and Jaclyn Smith for her cool-under-pressure demeanor. I also love the fact that these three are take-charge women who lead glamorous and adventurous lives—and wear the most fabulous clothes, as well.

During a commercial break I turned to Dad, looked at him with 100% commitment and conviction, and said, "Dad, one day I am going to be a Charlie's Angel."

He turned to me, his brow furrowed, and said, "Now why would you want to be a Charlie's Angel when you could be Charlie?"

The program came back on, and instead of getting caught up in the show, I thought about what my dad had said. I realized, after a few minutes, that he was so right. Ever since then I have wanted to be Charlie—the person with the plan, the person who makes things happen. The boss. As much as I loved the three women and their lives they portrayed, I realized that most of the time, they were just following Charlie's orders. They weren't setting their own agenda, they always had to report back to someone else, always had to wait for the call to come before they could spring into action. Was that what I really wanted from my life?

The Allure of Independence

I tell this story because I realize that one of the impulses that frequently motivates entrepreneurs is the desire to be the boss, to be the one who establishes the ground rules, the person chiefly responsible for the results, the one who gets the blame or the credit at the end of the game. Since my dad was an entrepreneur himself, it's likely that I inherited some traits from him that led me in this direction. My father did work for another engineering firm before starting his own, but he never talked about his work or his dissatisfaction with working for someone else. Based on statistical evidence, it's a pretty safe assumption that he wasn't fully happy working for someone else. A recent poll by The Conference Board (a New York-based business research group) revealed that in the spring of 2005, fifty percent of American workers surveyed were dissatisfied with their jobs. Imagine that. Fifty percent!

Not surprisingly, the figures were tied to income levels—those earning between $25,000 and $35,000 had the highest rate of dissatisfaction, while those making more than $50,000 expressed the highest level of satisfaction—and yet of those surveyed, *only fourteen percent claimed to be very satisfied with their work*. A sad state of affairs, don't you think?

A similar pattern emerged when accounting for the age of the respondents. Those over sixty-five were the most satisfied with their jobs—you'd almost *have* to be to work beyond normal retirement age—while those from the ages of thirty-five to forty-four were most unhappy with their jobs.

A closer look at those numbers and the age breakdowns is quite revealing. As I mentioned earlier, you would expect those at age sixty-five to be the happiest with their jobs. In all likelihood, those sixty-five and above are the senior-most people at their place of employment and thus likely to be high salary earners. They are nearing retirement, can see the proverbial light at the

16

end of the tunnel, and as a result are less likely to complain. Also, if they are still working at sixty-five, chances are they are highly motivated and in good health.

Is That All There Is?

What I find troubling is the fact that those who are in their prime work years, the thirty-five to forty-four crowd, are the least satisfied group. We might be able to chalk some of this up to the restlessness of that age—these workers have been on the job for a few years and the novelty has worn off a bit. In addition, members of this group are still a long way off from retirement age and looking at the long road ahead doesn't quite thrill them.

Regardless of how you read the results, one half of all those surveyed are dissatisfied. If I had that rate of satisfaction among my customers, I'd be out of business in no time. Somehow, though, these people manage to slog through their days. Have you encountered anyone lately you would categorize as a disgruntled worker? Don't answer that one. I think I know what you'd have to say.

And what might be the source of their dissatisfaction? Might it be a boss with whom they don't get along or respect? Might they be tired of having to be at someone else's beck and call? Are they tired of adhering to a schedule that doesn't jive with their own internal clocks? Are they frustrated by the lack of accountability as they see others doing less, but being paid the same or more? Are they infected by the negativity that permeates some places of work? And yet somehow these sorry souls drag themselves into work each and every day.

While on one level we might admire these people for their persistence in showing up everyday, I truly wonder what their level of passion is for their work. Additionally, I wonder where and how they might really want to be expressing their desire for satisfaction.

Don't Be the Angel, Be the Charlie

As I pointed out in the introduction, one of the required attributes of a successful inventor/entrepreneur is the desire to be the Charlie, the independent person who answers primarily to oneself. The other trait is the passion that I fear is lacking in most of the dissatisfied workers out there. But that begs the question: where does this passion come from? If you don't have it, where do you find it?

One trait that all entrepreneurs seem to share is a desire to be independent. That's certainly one form of passion, but I've always felt it took more than simply the longing to not be told what to do by someone else to be a truly innovative and effective entrepreneur. That doesn't mean I dismiss the importance of independence. The language of the office is filled with words which struck me, as I was growing up and still strike me today, as harsh. I don't think anyone should have to report to a "superior" or even to a "supervisor." I'm a competent adult, thank you very much, and I don't really need supervision.

Think about that word for a moment. "Supervision." The images of George Orwell's Big Brother from his novel *1984* and all those horrible associations come prominently to mind. Literally, the word means to see from above, and that recalls an image of a god-like being controlling your destiny, or worse, an over-seer and all its connotations associated with slavery. I don't think I'm making too much of this issue; after all, I've frequently heard the term "wage slave" bandied about. Most distressing, neither the speakers/writers nor the listeners/readers seem to register much of a response to such an awful term. Is there anyone out there who has not sung along out loud, "Take this job and shove it; I ain't workin' here no more"? I suppose that's because we've all grown so accustomed to thinking of work as a grind, the "old salt-mine," and someplace that spawned the acronym TGIF.

Well, I use TGIF as much as anyone, but to me it has nothing to do with Fridays; instead, it stands for Thank God I'm Free! Autonomy is something I value to such a great extent that it nearly heads my list, lingering immediately behind family, faith, and integrity.

In reality, I have someone else to thank besides God for my freedom—my mother and father. I've already told you a little bit about each of them, but I need to let you know more about my mother's contributions since she was so instrumental in helping me become the person I was destined to become—an independent, passionate, and creative person.

A Nurturing Environment

Just as I'm often asked about the source of my ideas, my mother is often asked how she and my father raised such successful children. Rather than filter her answer through my own sensibility, I'll let her speak for herself:

One of the most influential happenings for me in clarifying childrearing concepts was my first reading of *The Prophet* by Kahlil Gibran. Barbara's father and I subsequently read it together and felt that it not only reflected what we already felt in our hearts, but that it also helped to solidify our goals for our children. Here is a portion of Kahlil Gibran's thoughts on children:

"Your children are not your children
They are the sons and daughters of Life's longing for itself
They come through you but not from you,

And though they are with you, yet they belong not to you.
You may give them your love but not your thoughts
For they have their own thoughts.
You may house their bodies but not their souls
For their souls dwell in the house of tomorrow. . ."

The main lesson we gleaned from Kahlil Gibran's thoughts was that each of our children was on a path that was unique to that child. The important thing for us as parents was not to block that path by expectations that were not in harmony with that child's true self. That concept became our guiding light in most of our decisions regarding our children, and now our grandchildren.

Barbara, from an early age, saw beauty in the world and her eyes were often wide with the wonder of it all. She seemed to want to see it all and then to somehow recreate it in her own way. I don't recall any day that Barbara did not do something creative, inhaling ideas from the world around her with every breath. She drew and sketched constantly, she wrote poetry, she sculpted, she found a dead bird in our backyard and proceeded to make anatomical drawings of the contents of its skull, she grew flowers and then pressed them into wondrous gifts—the list could go on forever, for her curiosity was insatiable. The point is that she was a child of fantasy and wonder, and she was not headed to be an accountant or a person who dealt mainly in black and white. She was a child of many hues, and the world just wasn't big enough for her huge appetite for discovery.

Barbara's exploration of the world, of course, launched her into an exploration of the people who inhabited that world. She sought out friends and the house was usually full of classmates and, sometimes, complete strangers—perhaps a lonely child from her school whose parents had to work late. She always had a special instinct for knowing when a person was crying out for help or support, and the interesting thing to us was how she would hear the softest whimper that the rest of us might miss. She loved giving of her time—herself—to her family and friends, and we all knew that she would be there for us through thick and thin. She was and is a person you can count on, and to this day I hear stories from her now grown-up friends of how she was there for them in some long ago crisis.

I recently ran into one of Barbara's old school chums who had returned to our area after a long absence. We met for lunch, and she revealed to me something that she said everyone knew about "Barbie". She said "Barbie" could juggle all her friends easily because she didn't label them or place them in artificial groupings. She said "Barbie" had this special integrity about her—she was a friend that everyone could trust, and she didn't care if they belonged to the "popular" group or some other group or no group at all. She looked at each person as an individual and saw the best in him or her. Barbara's friend said she saw that as the highest integrity a person can possess. She said she had never forgotten "Barbie," because this now very lovely, fabulously successful young woman had felt like an outsider until "Barbie" took her under her wing and changed her life as a young teenager. I, as a mother, was so gratified to hear that story, because integrity has always been a key word in our family. Our children used to laugh and tell us they could tell us they did anything, as long as they convinced us they did it with integrity!

"Seek not to make them like you," said Kahlil Gibran. Let them be who they are. Of course Barbara would become an inventor. Did we know that? No, we did not. But we encouraged the path she was on and did our best not to put up any blockades that would send her off to the wrong fork in the road. We also tried to reveal alternative paths for her to choose when we felt she might hit a stumbling block. We pointed out obstacles, but we tried to let her make her own choices. She in turn was an interesting combination of an unusually sweet, gentle flower child in love with the world and everyone in it, and a strong determined person, charging full ahead, always goal oriented. She was a person who decided what she wanted and went after it with the confidence that she would make happen whatever it was she needed to make happen. Barbara is definitely a make-it-happen kind of a person—she always was—and I think it is her most unique quality. Her secret is that she believes 100% in whatever she strives to do.

'They are the sons and daughters of Life's longing for itself,' said Kahlil Gibran. Barbara epitomizes life longing for itself, and Barbara gives back by longing for life, giving it her all."

Margie Kraft, Barbara's Mom

As a former schoolteacher, my mother may have had a head start when it comes to nurturing a child's inner spirit. She recognized early on my penchant for creativity and fostered it in every way possible. Providing me with drawing paper, crayons, an easel, watercolors, finger-paints, and a space of my own in which to be creative was merely the first step. The second, and possibly more important step, was that she exerted no pressure on me to use those materials. She simply provided them and let me explore and discover after she recognized my natural inclination toward creative expression. Similarly, once she recognized my brother's preference for numbers and puzzles and the like, she provided him with the materials he wanted and needed to feed his inner urge. Again, no pressure, just opportunity.

Finding a Daemon in the Rough

I really do believe that I was born to do what I do. I was so fortunate to have parents who agreed on how I should be raised and who provided me with everything necessary to develop my skills. I don't want to carry on too much about this notion of an inner spirit or guiding force in our lives. I've done a lot of reading on the subject, and I have a few favorite books. One of which I will mention is James Hillman's book *The Soul's Code* which explores the Greek concept of a *Daemon*—that guiding spirit or presence inside you that leads you on your intended path in life. It is, of course, up to you to follow it or not. I'm convinced that many of those members of the Fifty Percent Dissatisfied Club are experiencing a conflict between their inner compass and their chosen direction in their work life.

The fact that you picked up this book says a lot about your desire and your intended path. Having known what I wanted to do and what I was meant to do from such an early age, I often struggle to identify with those who haven't been guided as I've been in this regard. That doesn't mean that I can't empathize with those people; I know it must be horrendously difficult to honor that inner guiding spirit when the demands of putting food on the table and a roof over the heads of your family are daily distractions. I can only hope this book offers some relief and insight for those of you in the throes of figuring this all out.

Fourteen Percent or Bust!

Why have I made such a point about aligning your intentions with the guidance system you may not yet have fine-tuned? Because I'm hoping that you will be one of those fourteen percent of people who are really satisfied with their jobs. More pragmatically, when your passion is channeled in the proper direction, you are more easily able to overcome the obstacles that you will inevitably face. When your passion connects with your output, it creates a more productive and efficient problem solving you.

A desire for independence can take you places. Autonomy and passion can take you further. Freedom, devotion, and acceptance of the advice your *Daemon* provides you will lead you to the promised land of your dreams.

Meanwhile, Back At the Reality Hotel . . .

I'm not going to mislead you; downsides to working for yourself do exist. Of course, I believe that the benefits far outweigh the detriments by a wide margin. I would hate for you to exchange one brand of dissatisfaction for another. While there are no guarantees in life, I do believe that you will greatly enhance your chances of succeeding if you are in touch with the source of your desire. In my case, it is because I am so passionate about making the lives of women easier that I'm able to dip into the wellspring of ideas I can access so readily.

Obviously, I was privileged to be surrounded at an early age by an incredibly supportive family. Some of you may be thinking that you don't have the background that I do, but I can't emphasize enough this point—others will believe in you and support you when they see how much *you* believe in yourself.

I also understand that most of you won't be able to just chuck it all, tell your boss to take this job and shove it, etc. You will have to wrestle with the transition from full-time employment to independence. That's why *The Carey Formula* was designed with low or no upfront costs and why I so actively encourage budding entrepreneurs to keep it simple in the early stages of their career.

The Mother of Invention

I don't know exactly when I decided that I was going to become an inventor/entrepreneur. All I know is that I had an experience early in life that I return to time and time again as a source of inspiration and wisdom. This occurred when I was nine years old. My brother was a Cub Scout, and as a part of his enrollment in that organization, he received *Boy's Life* magazine. Curious about just what was in a magazine with that title, I used to sneak a peek or two at it when I found issues lying around the house. I'd casually flip through them, giggling at the notion of my brother as a tender foot, but genuinely interested in how what the Boy Scouts taught differed from my experiences in the Girl Scouts.

I flipped to the back of the magazine and found there a kind of classified section with advertisements for pocketknives, rucksacks, and the like. I was about to shut the magazine when another advertisement stabbed my eye:

"Want Your Own Job and Financial Independence?"

They had me hooked. Of course I wanted financial independence. Who doesn't? Sign me up!

The next line sealed the deal:

"Make Money and Start Your Own Business."

All I had to do was send them $19.95 for supplies, and I would receive a kit that could yield me $100.00. This $19.95 was the start-up funds I needed to start my own business selling metal cards the size and shape of a credit card with the customer's Social Security Number embossed on it. My head swam with the possibilities. To a nine-year-old in 1969, $19.95 was a formidable amount of capital to raise. I may not have known exactly what assets were, but I knew I didn't have any. How could I raise the cash to get my venture off the ground?

I explained the situation to my mother, and, as was the firmly established tradition in our household, she told me I could work for the money. We agreed that thirty-five cents an hour was a fair wage for vacuuming and polishing silver. Fifty-seven hours later I had my start-up capital. I sent the money into the company and three weeks later my kit arrived. I set out going from door to door asking neighbors if they wanted the card. I had enough raw materials to make at least 50 Social Security Cards, and I owned the machine with which to do the embossing. I was set. I was determined to build an empire in no time. The last few minutes of the school day were interminable. When the school day finally ended, I sprinted straight home so I could get started selling.

With no prompting from anyone—I didn't bother to read the selling tips that came with the instructions for the embosser— I soon learned how to sell. I decided I would go to the neighbors and tell them all the reasons why a metal Social Security Card would make their lives not only better, but easier too. I kept track of these reasons and tried them out in many different ways. Soon

I knew exactly what I needed to say to sell this item. The cute factor of being a child must have helped as well, since I made a number of sales my first day out. The gleam in Dad's eye when I told him was almost as great a reward as the profit I earned on my selling trips.

A Further Revelation

Not satisfied with a single sale, next I learned to 'up-sell' by offering a second card for another family member at half price. I also realized I needed to offer further incentives to my customers. I figured I'd hit them where it really mattered—their gut. I next made brownies and offered a multi-pack of four cards with the incentive of a free brownie. If they bought the multi-pack, I would throw in a free brownie made from my mother's fabulous secret recipe. That sales strategy worked, too. After only two weeks of pounding the pavement, I had earned ninety-seven dollars and had worked only a few hours. Selling was turning out to be much more profitable than vacuuming.

Next it was time to invest in more raw materials. I contacted the company and sent them another $19.95. But this time I got more material, because the embossing machine was already paid for from my first order. I was disappointed to learn I had to wait three weeks for my new raw materials. I couldn't lose that many days of sales—I had an empire to build, after all. After thinking about the problem for a while, I realized that a lack of goods didn't have to keep me from making sales. Even though I only had one sample card left to show prospective buyers, I went out every day and relentlessly took orders promising my customers a four-week delivery time. To my delight, I discovered many had no problem committing to future delivery. This accelerated my ability to keep the goods flowing in and eventually became the first component of *The Carey Formula*.

Goods can be sold (booked) even before they are available. I still employ this strategy with every product I market today. I never go into the production phase until I have confirmed orders. Remember: keep those upfront costs as low as possible.

All Good Things

My Social Security Card business lasted until I exhausted every doorbell in my neighborhood. After all, I was only nine and I could only walk and bicycle so far. I wanted to expand my operation, but Mom wouldn't let me stand in front of the grocery store. I didn't agree with her decision, but I had to agree to her ruling—after all, not only was she the Inter-Neighborhood Commerce Commissioner, she was the Director of Transportation I had to rely on to get me to the local Safeway!

Looking back at my *Boy's Life* magazine experience, I realize that I loved the venture so much because it was basically a selling and marketing enterprise. The labor involved in embossing the cards was negligible at best. In my opinion, selling and marketing ventures are always the easiest and generally the most profitable. You'll hear more about the reasons for this later on. I also enjoyed the card selling project so much because I was successful. Even though I was a shy youngster, I had no real problems speaking to strangers and trying to sell them something. I had a knack for understanding how to incentivize customers, and an almost innate understanding of their needs.

I applied the lessons learned from this venture to another important area of my life—Girl Scouts. For most people, the mere mention of Girl Scout Cookies sets off a Pavlovian response. Samoas, Thin Mints, and Trefoils create a cascade response that begins in the brain, and rattles down to the taste buds and olfactory centers, prompting the salivary glands to go to work. I counted on customers having that response system built in whenever I began to sell cookies for our fundraiser. I didn't need to convince them of the benefits of the product; they already had an inner desire for them! If only every product I ever brought to market could produce such a visceral response in my potential customers as those Girl Scout Cookies did!

Those annual fundraising sales reinforced another lesson. I didn't have to have a product in order to get sales. I suppose it was my competitive nature that prompted me to put a new spin on that idea. I realized that not only did I not need a product to sell those cookies (after all, that's what every other Girl Scout in the country *had* to do), I came to the realization that I could get a jump on my cookie-selling competitors if I didn't wait until the cookies came in. (Nowadays I don't think they allow you to do this.) With repeat customers, I could rely on them asking for boxes of their favorites annually. In addition, there was little variation from year to year on the types of cookies we offered, so who needed to scan the list before deciding? Whether I was cruising the halls of my dad's office, striding purposefully down the sidewalks of my neighborhood, or staking out the best territory in front of the various Safeway and Vons grocery stores in and around Orinda (Mom was a Girl Scout leader as well as Inter-Neighborhood Commerce Commissioner, so she approved of this sales venture), I was getting orders in advance of my troop-mates. Also, I never tried to sell just a box of cookies. I would ask, "Do you have any friends, family, or people that you work with who might enjoy a box? Imagine the look on their face when you give them the gift of cookies." I didn't sell just cookies—I sold the cookie DREAM. I sold the feeling behind the cookie. I sold the relationship between the cookie and the customer. I sold a lot of cookies.

A Connection Made

Somewhere in the part of my brain that was designated for the storage of these nascent business plans, a seed was planted in the fertile soil of my life's purpose, fed and watered by passion and hard work, nurtured and brought to fruition by my creativity. When you love your work, it becomes so much a greater force and influence than any source of dissatisfaction that so many people experience, and for me it became a source of joy and a source of fulfillment (and profit!) that persists to this day. In the next chapter, we'll take a look at how the product selection process is the key to unlocking the door of joy and fulfillment in inventing and selling.

The Simple Secrets to Success:

I believe now that, in part, I was able to be successful because of my upbringing. My mom and dad repeatedly told me I could do anything I put my mind to. They stressed that communication with people was extremely important. I was taught to be polite, to look people in the eye, and speak clearly and pleasantly.

My formative years taught me three basic principles that have stayed with me throughout my life:

- First and foremost I learned that I didn't always have to have a product in my hands to be able to sell it. Even without the item I could keep selling without wasting valuable time waiting for reorders to arrive.

- Secondly, I discovered that by not putting money up front my cash reserves increased more quickly.

- Thirdly, I learned that offering incentives to buyers resulted in accelerating sales. A $20 sale is no harder to make than a $5 sale.

I also learned the importance of knowing my assets and liabilities:

- When I started my pre-teen business I had no money for anything so I had no choice but to be creative.

- I had to sell something small so I could carry it door to door in my backpack. My distribution channel was me; my territory was limited to safe walking distance.

- Because I didn't have the inclination or the facilities to produce anything, as of yet, I had to buy something at a low price that I could sell at a higher price.

- The product had to be something I could sell at a fairly low price so my customers would more easily trust me to later deliver the goods.

- Keeping initial costs low meant profits were high.

These are concepts that I wasn't aware of when I started my first business. I learned them along the way. I also learned to sell with passion. My only cause was my dream of working creatively on my own. I took this very seriously and found that I was able to engage and captivate my customer. My customers shared my dream with me. I very rarely had anyone say no. Why?

- I came across as sincere and passionate about what I was doing, because I truly was so.

- I told my clients I wanted to start my own business and they responded by giving me the time I needed to pitch my product.

- I learned that I could close any sale when I spoke to people sincerely and passionately and presented them with a detailed plan that made sense.

- I had a good product and was a sincere, hard working person. With my drive and determination I was able to communicate my dream to my customer.

Time and time again over the last 25 years, I have gained my customers' dedicated support. They not only have stepped over to my side of the fence, but they have been like cheerleaders to me. They believe in not only my product, but they believe in me. Many times a buyer will invest in people before product. It might be because I have always been the underdog in my endeavors and everyone likes to see the underdog win. Or it might be because I start with a good product that I believe in. Or it is because I have built a relationship based on respect with a customer. Most likely it is because the combination of all of the above is a winning formula. And remember you can have the best idea in the world, but if you cannot orchestrate the business you have nothing.

Key Signs on the Road to Entrepreneurship:

- **Broad Shoulder**—You've surrounded yourself with helpful people who can give you good advice and keep you on track.

- **Dangerous Curve Ahead**—You're aware of and can anticipate the problems that may lurk ahead of you.

- **School Speed Zone**—You're entering a place where you can learn valuable lessons. Don't be in such a hurry to get to your destination that you don't appreciate everything the journey has to offer.

- **No U-Turns**—Don't be so afraid to fail that you turn around at the first sign of trouble.

- **U-Turn Permitted**—Don't be so stubbornly committed that you plow ahead no matter the costs—personal, financial, emotional.

- **Scenic Route**—While it's important to stay focused on your destination, remember that not only do you have much to learn, you have much to enjoy when you work with passion.

Time-Out—Lessons in Product Selection

When we last left the Girl Scout she was still selling cookies and in her Charlie's Angel phase. We'd seen that she had some keen instincts for selling and a real desire to be independent, but she hadn't yet created and brought a product to market. In order to get to that phase in my life, we're going to have to skip ahead a few years. Don't worry, I'll return now and again to those really early years, but in order to talk about the issue of product selection, it's better that I stop talking about cookies and embossed Social Security Cards. After all, given today's concerns about identity theft, I don't think you'd have much success in convincing folks to turn over their Social Security numbers to you, tell them that you'll be back in three weeks with a duplicate but durable stand-in for their paper card, and—oh by the way, thanks so much for paying me up front!

We need to turn to a more practical example of how *The Carey Formula* came to be.

For now, we're also going to shift our attention slightly. Rather than concentrating on the inner world of you and your desires and your predispositions exclusively, we're going to widen our gaze to take in the products that you might need and bring to market. Remember that you are still definitely in the picture. When I gave you my short answer for where my ideas come from, I said that I examine myself and observe the world around me very closely as sources of inspiration for products. I can't stress enough how important it is to be observant and self-reflective. For me, those two places—inner world and outer world—are the origination points for an exploration into product viability.

KISS Me You Ordinary Fool!

Even though you may think that my experiences are far different from yours and yours are far different from everyone else's, the truth is that we all have a lot more in common than we might want to admit. We all want to believe that we are unique, and that our friends all love to say about us, "Well, after they created you, they threw out the mold!" First, let me say, as a business-woman, I would be appalled if any of my manufacturers ever threw out any molds! They're expensive to create and I might find another use for it down the line! Second, if you are truly that unique, the kind of mass market merchandising that I'm talking about may not suit you well. In many ways, I am an ordinary run-of-the-mill (don't you just love that manufacturing metaphor?) woman, and I can use my ordinariness to my advantage.

What? How can being ordinary be an advantage?

If, in your everyday experience, you encounter some issue that needs solving and you can think of a product that will help solve that issue for you, you could make millions off that product—all by virtue of your so-called ordinariness. How? Well, think about it for a minute. If you are in the ordinary category, then there could be 100,000 others just like you out there in the marketplace with the same problem needing to be solved. What *will* set you apart is that, rather than simply gripe about the problem, you put your brains to work and come up with a unique solution. That's where the whole passion and persistence part of the you equation comes into play. You can transform your ordinary experiences into an extraordinary opportunity.

So, here's a corollary to *The Carey Formula*: Ordinary = Profitable. Now, be careful here. I don't mean an ordinary solution or an ordinary product in terms of quality or concept. Think of this corollary as subset of the KISS principle as well.

Keep It Simple Smart-Gal/Guy

I cannot tell you how many inventors/entrepreneurs come to me with concepts for amazingly complex products that they want to market. They have fallen head over heels in love with their idea.

I, too, have been guilty of falling in love with my ideas, as you shall soon see, but no matter how much I love the idea, I have learned from painful experience to be more passionate about the business formula behind the idea. The business formula has always outweighed even the product concept. I am sure you have heard the old adage "Product is King," but in street terms your product ain't nothin' without a solid business model behind it. So, first get passionate about *The Carey Formula* and then freelance from there.

If you are someone who is just becoming an entrepreneur and believe you have an amazing idea that is the next best thing to sliced bread, look at your potential product again very closely. If the product is complex, has high tooling needs, and costs more than a buck or two to make, take the advice I have given countless times: put your big idea on hold for a while. Think of something that you can be passionate about that is **simple, unique, and inexpensive to produce.**

Repeat After Me: I will fall in love with my practical business plan, not my product.

Temptation, Thy Name is Dyson

I know the temptation is great to be the person who comes up with the next wonderful and astounding big thing. I know the Dyson new and improved vacuum guy has a great accent, and I agree it would be really cool to be on television as he is, doing those ads and talking about how much time and effort you invested in your revolutionary and vastly improved method for solving one of those ordinary household problems. (By the way, good for him and thanks to him for providing us with an example of the importance of moving from the inner world of his own needs and curiosity to the outer world of others' needs by tackling this one.)

What he doesn't tell you, and what I don't know but can only guess at, is how much money he had to sink into research and development in order to spend those several years to produce the final product that is currently on the market. Do you have that kind of cash around? I know I didn't. Besides, what do you know about this guy? Does he strike you as someone who had an at-home workshop he labored in and had to shove aside his brother's-in-law Great Figures of the Civil War Action Collection in order to conduct his suction tests? Not likely. Before you start emulating someone and their business plan, be sure you do your homework and get the real story.

Carey's Reminders

We should remember two important points here about our buddy Mr. Dyson:

1. He tackled an ordinary problem that millions have.

2. He took an existing product/methodology and improved upon it.

Please keep these two points in mind, particularly the last one. You don't always have to select a product that is a brand-new-never-been-seen-before type of advice. There is no shame in building a better mousetrap or reinventing the wheel if in fact you are making real improvements or finding a better or less expensive or more efficient version of a concept already on the market.

The Truth: This May Sting a Little

Sure, I'd love to tell you to dream big and go for the home run. I'd love to be the girlfriend who gives you the big thumbs up and a hearty, "Go for it!" when you come to me all excited about the new guy you're seeing. You know, the one who's in a band? The one who wants you to quit your job and join him (and fund) your round-the-world motorcycle trip? The one who has an, ahem, sort-of-ex-wife and possible child back in Fresno who'll need some cash to live on while the two of you are gone? The one who is as gorgeous a hunk of a man as I've ever seen and who's more thrilling than any E ticket ride at Disneyland, Six Flags, and a Mid-town Manhattan cab ride in the rain all rolled into one?

I could be that girlfriend, but you'd end up hating me.
How do I know that? Trust me. Better yet, learn from me.

Strap Yourself In: We're Time Traveling

Eventually, you'll learn a bit more about what I've come to think of as the "Lost Years" of my life. For now all you need to know is that I graduated from high school and college, met, married, and had a son with the man who was my first serious boyfriend, and at the age of 24, was living in the Denver area. I loved being a mom, but I couldn't shut off that active and roving mind of mine. I think my son, Rich Jr., named after his father, has the same insatiable spirit as I did. I wasn't as resourceful as my mother, so occasionally Rich Jr. and I would run afoul of one another and I had to reprimand and discipline. That was never easy for me, and I wasn't about to employ corporal punishment on him, so I did what has become a modern-day staple: I gave him a time-out.

I socialized with a group of young mothers and the concept of timing-out our children was a frequent topic of our conversation. We each had our own styles and amounts of time—some employed a specific piece of furniture as the Time-Out Chair or a room as the Time-Out Room. The one thing that we all had in common was that we wondered about the method's effectiveness. Did our toddlers really understand what it meant when they were going to have to take a time-out for X number of minutes?

I became obsessed with this question and wondered about children and their concept of time. I knew that there were other contexts in which I questioned whether or not my son, or any toddler, had a firm grasp on the concept of time. You have FIVE MINUTES to get that stuff put away and then we're going to Grandma's. We'll be at Grandma's in FIFTEEN MINUTES, sweetie, and then you can have a drink. The list is endless.

I knew that at some point in a child's development she or he would come to an understanding of how to tell time and what time meant and what it felt like, but as far as I was concerned that time wouldn't come soon enough. Wasn't there something that I could do to help my child (and due to the ordinary nature of this experience, hundreds of thousands of other children in his age range) come to a better understanding of the concept? I realized that since these children were not yet reading, I had to do something that provided a visual cue, but didn't require them to recognize or mentally manipulate numbers or letters.

I spent hours and hours reading scores of books about this concept as well as Jean Piaget's concepts of child development and how it relates to abstract temporal imagery. (I was so engaged by the topic that the hours didn't feel like hours!) I learned that most children develop a full sense of abstract temporal imagery by the age of nine. That means that they can't just tell time by looking at a clock, but they have a sense or feeling for amounts of time and their passage. At this point, my son was three and I saw a real opportunity to help him, potentially millions of other parents and children, and me. An idea was born.

The first product I was determined to market I named the Time-Out Watch (see image page 278) in honor of the time-tested, mother approved, psychologically friendly discipline strategy. I decided to build this watch so that children could turn a bezel—a circular raised ring, such as the one on the iPOD—to one of sixty stops. Each stop corresponded to a minute. As you turned the bezel it would click at each stop, and a channel of light on the face of the watch would illuminate. Picture a sundial in reverse; instead of the dial casting a shadow, you saw a wedge of light glowing in pie-shaped segments. This way, children could see a graphic representation of the time going by. Each time the minute hand on the watch advanced, one section of the channel would dim.

I was totally absorbed by the concept of the Time-Out Watch. I was certain it was a sure-fire winner and would so thoroughly solve a pesky problem that millions of mothers would one day wonder how they ever lived without it. I had spin-offs running around in my head like kindergartners at recess—Time-Out Clocks, Time-Out Sippy Cups (how long till empty?), Time-Out Rugs, Time-Out Chairs—all with built in Time-Out time tracking devices.

The whole concept sounded great to me, and a few discreet inquiries of my friends and sister mothers confirmed my suspicions. This was a product whose time had come!

Let's take a Time-Out from the Time-Out Watch story to highlight another key component of *The Carey Formula:*

You Don't Have to Be an Expert in Every Field

We love to romanticize the notion of the wild-haired genius inventor who dabbles in everything from nuclear physics to shoeing horses. I'd have to say that the Doc Brown's types from the B*ack to Future* movie series mostly exist in the movies. While it would be wonderful if you could be the idea generator, the builder, salesperson, intellectual property administrator, marketer, inventory control manager, shipping coordinator, and cashier/bagger for your product, that's practically impossible. You can't be all things to all your product ideas.

A lovable jack-of-all-trades is charming, but fallible because at some point, he or she is going to get in way over his or her head and be forced to call in an expert for bail out at a critical juncture. That's going to be an expensive call—both in terms of cash and time. Remember this: TIME=MONEY. You would be better off surrounding yourself with people who are already experts at a task rather than trying to get up to speed yourself on these various processes. Better to spend your time refining your pitch to the buyers.

Get your orders, get your cash flow going. Love the formula!

From Ideation to Product Selection

Coming up with the product concept is what I call the Ideation phase. At this point, the watch was little more than idea. It was an abstraction, just like time. How to concretize that concept? I knew that my vision called for a watch, but how would I make a watch with hands that would synchronize with a series of lights? I am no electrical engineer, but I knew that some people are. What I really needed was to find someone who specialized in watches and their design to help make my dream a reality. Before I could think of hiring someone to help design the inner workings of the watch, I would need to raise some capital. Hiring anyone was likely to be expensive, though I had no real sense yet of how expensive.

I was 26 by this time, with one year of what some would call "real" work experience under my belt. I had been helping out our family by negotiating my husband's contracts. He was a defensive lineman for the Denver Broncos, and he didn't have an agent. Actually, he did; it was me. I wasn't particularly interested in being an agent. I liked the intricacies of contracts and negotiations only to the extent that the better job I did, the better off we were financially. That personal stake is what kept me at it. I had gotten proficient enough at it that other players had utilized my services, but I wasn't driven to do the work and I lacked the love of the game that is necessary to really do well at the task. Now that I think about it, I was one of those Fifty Percenters from Chapter One—doing my job for the sake of the paycheck but certainly not loving it.

Assembling the Team

One real benefit of negotiating those contracts was that I came in contact with a lawyer with whom I partnered. He was amazing. Not only was he an excellent communicator, but he would make sure all the legalese was structured properly. His name was Patrick Seidler, and in addition to being a very fine attorney, he was an entrepreneur who is one of the founders of Wilderness Trail Bikes in Marin County, California. I told him about my idea for the Time-Out Watch and Patrick's eyes lit up at the idea. He knew a number of influential and powerful business people in the community because of his work, and he promised to find another person to help me get this idea off the drawing board and into production.

Patrick introduced me to Art Gunther who had been a division president for PepsiCo, heading the Pizza Hut arm of that vast enterprise. Fortunately for me, and as Patrick astutely knew, Art and his lovely wife Sharon both had a passion for childhood education, having founded the BOOK IT Program that champions childhood literacy. Given the nature of the watch and its intended use for the education of children, Art agreed to come on board. He declined a salary and worked solely on a percentage basis. I hoped to reward him handsomely through lots and lots of sales of the Time-Out Watch. Together, we raised a total of $100,000 from five venture capitalists to get our newly christened company, Quantum Leap, bounding into the arena.

Making the Leap from Concept to Reality

Through lots of research and mining, we eventually hired a French engineer formerly with the high-end watchmaker Tag Heuer. Together, Francois and I mapped out a logic array on a microchip whose circuitry would electronically create the illuminated time channel, pixel by pixel, to mark past, present, and future time. This three-part concept was crucial to a child's developing understanding of the nature of time. We developed the technology and believed it could be a basic option for any watch. Our final vision of the watch included a stopwatch function, that merged digital and analog displays, for timing events at a touch of a button, and standard analog watch functions with traditional hand movement. If that sounds a little complicated to you for a watch intended for children, you're right.

I'd been smitten, and smitten hard by this idea. I think that the power of my passion, combined with that of everyone else in the project, turned our heads and had us ignoring some red flags. Our dream was to license the Time-Out Watch design to a major watch company. After developing the concept and strategy, our team of three flew to Switzerland to meet with the head of SMH, the largest watch conglomerate in the world (and marketers of the Swatch Watch). How cool was this going to be? And where else but Switzerland could you possibly want to go to discuss a watch project. This was my trip to Cooperstown to play baseball, traveling to Italy to meet the Pope, or Paris to pitch a clothing line. Okay, you get the idea. I was excited! I couldn't stop talking or thinking about the watch. If I was pouring pancake batter in the pan, I'd make a little watch out of it. Driving along anywhere, I'd be thinking about and eventually rehearsing my presentation. This was going to be the best.

The night before the flight my best friend Isabel Hamilton invited me over to do my nails. At first I didn't want to go, thinking I'd be too nervous about my first big trip overseas, but eventually I saw the wisdom in Isabel's thinking. I needed to do something to keep my mind occupied and Isabel was one of the few people who really understood how important this mission was to me. As I walked into her house, still mumbling to myself the opening lines of my presentation, I was met with a huge cheer and shouts of "*surprise!*" Like I said, surround yourself with supportive and positive people. My going-away party was the perfect way to remind me that no matter how things turned out, I still had a wonderful group of friends and family to come back to.

A Swiss Near Miss

We arrived in Switzerland three days early. Though this was my first trip outside of the US and I'd already been rehearsing my pitch for months, I hibernated in my hotel room and practiced my presentation over and over. I had it down. The bats in my stomach were performing an aerial circus. I was so worked up that I could only sit and push my food around my plate and watch while Patrick and Art devoured their meals. I had never had a dream so big, and I was completely obsessed with getting my presentation perfect. I slept fitfully the night before the meeting, tossing and turning and twisting my blankets into a knot.

We arrived at SMH headquarters in Biel, Switzerland. The ride over was a revelation. I'd spent so much time in the hotel room that I'd barely had a chance to appreciate that I was in a foreign country. That didn't matter; there'd be some time for exploring the culture after the meeting. When we arrived at the SMH office, my knees went weak as I stepped out of the car. The ride up to the 3rd floor seemed interminable. Patrick and Art tried to keep the banter light, hoping I'd join in, but I was just so focused on the task at hand they could have been speaking a foreign language, for all I knew. I kept taking deep breaths, and soon my fears were transformed into anticipation. At SMH, we were introduced to its president, Dr. Ernst Thomke.

I had been privileged to communicate with him over the past several months as we moved toward a final concept. Dr. Thomke was a brilliant and gracious man and he held my hand warmly in both of his and welcomed us. The introductions were brief and to the point. I remember sitting in this high-powered boardroom and having him give me the floor. I stood up and gave my skirt a quick and discrete press with both of my trembling hands. The next thing I knew I was in the middle of the presentation that I had choreographed and practiced for the last several months. Every word and every gesture was planned. It came off with the precision the Swiss are known for. That kind of precision is ideal for a timepiece, but not a presentation about a timepiece. I had so over-rehearsed that the presentation came out lifeless. Memorizing and practicing over and over every nuance of the presentation was a huge mistake. I happen to be really good on my feet, but the moment I formalized my messages into a preplanned pitch I became robotic, not dynamic. While I needed to convey passion, I'm afraid I presented panic. The ever gracious Dr. Thomke patiently listened to me. I think he was trying hard not to laugh, but out of respect for my effort, he let me finish.

Despite my stiffness, I communicated the technology well enough to earn an appointment with Dr. Jean Gresset, the company's patent attorney and engineer. The meeting also allowed us to meet Jacques Mueller, one of the designers of the highly successful Swatch.

After several days of more meetings we flew home. The folks at SMH indicated they wanted to set up more meetings down the line, so we thought we had found a partner. We were stoked. I was so happy I could have flown home without the jet. I felt so vindicated by everything that had happened. Where were the naysayers? I can tell you now—they were waiting patiently on the sidelines waiting for their moment to spring into action. The euphoria lasted a few days after my return, but after several months of conversations with SMH and American watch companies, all the decision makers agreed that as wonderful as the technology was, the manufacturing costs were far too high for any of the companies to make a commitment. For that reason, despite our amazing technology and a clearly demonstrated need for the product, we failed. After fifteen months of agonizing and exhilarating roller coaster climbs and descents, twists and turns, we stalled on an upside down section of the ride, and all our money fell out of our pockets. Our funding and our spirits exhausted, we folded the business with no licensing deal anywhere in sight. It took fifteen months to go from final ideation to failure. Maybe I should have thought of a watch that kept track of the hours of effort and the dollars that go into a project and then self-destructs when the bottom falls out on you.

Obviously, at the point at which the SMH deal collapsed I was devastated. This was my first major failure in life. I didn't think about there being other opportunities in the future. My youth and inexperience warped my perspective on life. I thought I had been given my only shot and had failed. I was depressed and thought I should live in a dark room the rest of my life. I once had visions of myself as the unsinkable Molly Brown, but this was the first time I'd taken on water (except for when I was pregnant!) and I'd foundered and then slipped quietly beneath the waters of despair. Woe was me!

Lessons Learned

In the intervening years, I've been able to look at the experience more objectively. Here's a list of what I learned, good and bad, based on the Time-Out Experience:

1. This was a great example of falling in love with a concept and not assessing its viability realistically.

2. I did not consider sufficient tooling costs (how much it would cost to make the machines, molds, etc. to make the parts to make the watch) into the equation because I was so focused on the novelty of the idea.

3. I made the Time-Out time teaching element too complicated. Looking back on it today, I could have accomplished the same goal—teaching kids about the abstract nature of time with a 98¢ watch from Hong Kong and added a story book on tape.

4. I shouldn't have tried to license the idea to anyone. My advice to everyone who wants to make a lot of money with their simple idea is to keep your ideas for yourself; do not license them. With a licensing agreement you will make pennies on the dollar compared to what you would earn if you found your own manufacturer and got the orders from retailers yourself.

5. Don't allow anyone exclusivity. We offered several companies, who asked for it, time when they alone could evaluate our proposal. In other words, we let them have our idea for a period of time and didn't show our work to anyone else. This came back to bite us in the end when a very interested company underwent a management change at the very end of a promising negotiation. Not

only did we lose the deal, we lost valuable time. And, just in case you forgot, Time=Money.

6. Don't sit on your heels and wait. Stay proactive. We waited for months for news from SMH because they were the best and we were so certain they were going to sign a deal with us. In the meantime, our funds were running low and we should have been seeking additional capital, pursuing other deals, etc.

7. The best presentations are those that evidence the greatest amount of energy. As someone later told me, "People will tend to forget what you say, but they will be persuaded by how you said things." Genuine enthusiasm adds dollars to your bottom line.

8. Learn something about the culture of a foreign land *before* you visit. At a lunch meeting with Swiss executives, I was chatting away when I noticed that no one had touched their meal. Only when I finally started to eat did the rest of them commence to eat. Swiss etiquette dictates that no man begins his meal before a woman. Maybe I could have used that information to a better advantage.

9. Remember that not getting a deal doesn't doom the rest of your life. I should have thrown another party rather than sulk. I had a lot of good friends and family in my corner, and I should have relied on them instead of popping the balloons of my own little pity party.

10. Traveling outside the US for the first time was a great opportunity regardless of how things turned out. I should have counted my blessings and moved on more quickly.

Another lesson learned during that time period came as a result of another venture my husband Rich and I took just before Quantum Leap took off. Rich had the idea that identity theft was a real concern even before nearly every financial transaction and piece of personal data about us was recorded in some computer's memory. Remember the old days when a credit card transaction was imprinted on a slip with carbon paper sandwiched between the printed copies? At first no one thought a lot about what happened to those sheets of carbon paper. You got your copy, the store kept theirs, but what happened to the carbon which had your card number on it? Well, first, savvy crooks figured out they could collect those carbon copies and use the information to bilk you and stores.

After a while, smart shoppers started to ask for the carbon copies back from the cashier, but how convenient was that? So Rich came up with a great idea. Why not create a credit card plate machine that had a shredding device attached to it. We started working on creating one, but soon realized that someone had beat us to the punch by creating carbonless forms to fit on the machines already existing, thus eliminating the need to tear up or hand over the carbon sheets to the customer.

Not only was our idea rendered unnecessary, Rich and I realized that their solution was much more elegant—no need for stores to buy new machines, the forms would have to be constantly replenished while the machines were a less frequent purchase. Another lesson in the KISS model. Remember, Keep It Simple Smart-gals/guys! I can't even begin to imagine how much the tooling charges would have been for that device. At least we didn't sink much else besides our thought labor into that one.

Meanwhile, Back Under the Blankets

Six days after the final word came down from SMH, I had still not seen the light—literally and figuratively. My husband Rich brought me soup. I didn't want it but I ate it as long as he didn't turn on the lights in the bedroom. It was not dark only in the room; I felt the light in my life was out, too. I only felt a deep dark sadness in the pit of my belly. I had no tears left for crying. I really thought this feeling would be with me forever. This was going to be my one chance to be an entrepreneur. But at that point all I felt about myself was that I was a great big nothing.

Yes, I was pouting and someone should have given me a Time-Out; fortunately, Rich realized that the last thing I needed was another negative in my life. At the depths of my despair, Rich had had enough. He broke into my room and violated my pity party rule by turning on the lights.

"What are you doing?" I yelled.

He waved a credit card at me and replied, "There is an institution in this country for people like us."

I panicked momentarily thinking he was suggesting I be institutionalized, then I realize he said "us." So I mumbled past my chapped lips, "Oh yeah, what is it?"

He said, "It's called bankruptcy. Honey, I just opened a 14th credit card." The other 13 were used to keep Time-Out alive. "And we are going to Mexico and having a last celebration. Then we're going to come home, file for bankruptcy, and move forward. Barbara, you are not living in this dark room anymore." Pointing, he said, "Look, your bag is packed."

I didn't have the energy to say no, so I headed to Mexico with Rich.

¡Viva Mexico!

We landed in Cancun at 10 P.M. and went immediately to the hotel. Rich made sure that I didn't fall back into my post-Swiss blues routine, and threw open the curtains at 9:00 A.M. the next morning. Daggers of sunlight stabbed my eyes and I wrapped a pillow around my head before Rich snatched it away and prodded me toward the shower. By 10, we were sitting at a beachside restaurant with a platter of fish tacos sitting between us. Their scent was heavenly and mixed with the Caribbean breeze; the combination stimulated my dormant appetite. From my dark room to a dark drive to the airport to the dark flight and arrival, and finally to the colorful beach scene, the contrast was almost too much to bear. But in a good way.

While we ate, some darling children were running around selling masks cut out of old rubber tire tubes. I bought some of them because they were so cute. So were the children. The masks reminded me of the kind the Lone Ranger used to wear. Suddenly a vision jumped into my brain. Little Rich Jr. was a big fan of the Teenage Mutant Nina Turtles. They wore masks just like these!

I suddenly had an idea. I jabbed Rich in the ribs and said, "Hey, I could make these in fun shapes and in bright colors and sell them to chain stores like Wal-Mart and Kmart."

Rich mumbled something through a mouthful of fish taco and then began nodding his head up and down vigorously. Then it dawned on me: Halloween was less than a month away.

"Rich, let's go home. I need to claim a victory."

In reality I had already won, thanks to Rich. He knew the Mexico trip would rekindle my positive attitude and renew my spirit. Little did he know it would also cut short our vacation. We took the next flight home.

¡Viva Visa!

Because cash is king in any new business venture, we immediately held a garage sale to gather as much money as we could. I don't have a tally of the number of unsuspecting venture capitalists that event attracted, but the fund-raising effort was a success. After the sale, I had, including the rest of my available credit card balance, a total of about $6,000 to use to get this venture up and running. I immediately bought a stunning new Donna Karan suit for $4,000.

Just like you, Rich thought I was nuts. I didn't. I wasn't. Yes, I had just spent 67% of our available capital on one suit, but I knew exactly what I was doing. I felt like a million bucks in that suit and it only cost me four grand to get the jolt of adrenaline that produced the look of success I needed if I was going to convince anyone I meant business. And I did. I was in business. I had a new dream. I had a life.

This phase was what I call New Beginnings. Whenever I need to start something over I conceptualize it as New Beginnings. And after how I felt as a result of the Time-Out Watch failure, *new* plus *beginnings* made exactly the prescription I needed.

The DCH Mask of Troy

As soon as we got home from Mexico, I went to work on the new idea. I always love the beginning phase of any venture. It's when the excitement of something fresh and mysterious dominates. I'm not certain where the journey will take me, but I have a clear vision of where it is I want to go and what it will look like once I get there. I set my sights on Troy, Michigan—the site of Kmart's World Headquarters. I was going to climb the walls of that fortress and get inside and somehow tell them about my idea and sell them on it.

I almost have to laugh at my naiveté. That really was the extent of my business plan. I had a design concept in mind for what the masks should look like. I knew that Halloween was coming so the masks would be a desirable item for retailers. I knew that Kmart was one of the largest retailers and lots of people would shop for Halloween costumes there. I knew where they were headquartered. Brilliant, right? Other than looking up the address of the national headquarters, the only other research I did was to find a rental car outfit that would allow me to rent a car with unlimited miles. I was on a tight budget, after all, and I knew I'd be on the road for a while, so I had to find the most cost effective means of traveling.

I made a car rental reservation in St. Louis, Missouri, and four days after returning from Mexico, I flew to the city of the fabled Arch, the one time gateway to the west. Back in the 1980s most car rental companies charged for each mile, so this was a rare find that I took advantage of gratefully. I was able to rent a Honda Civic for $14.99 per day and only had to pay for gas. Rather than spend money I didn't have on hotels, I decided to sleep in my rental car, wash up at service stations, and move on to my next stop. A far cry from farewell parties and flying overseas and staying in nice hotels in Switzerland, but I didn't care. I was a woman on a mission!

My first stop was Kentucky where I found a manufacturer that would produce my Halloween disguise. While on the road, I'd made a few calls and found out that my masks could be produced by a number of different processes. One expensive option was to have them stamped. Stamping adds greatly to your costs because you have to find a tool and die maker to make the die that would be used in the stamping process. Depending upon the complexity of the designs, and mine were relatively simple, the cost of the die alone could have been somewhere between $5000 and $7500. I didn't have that kind of cash, and no tool and die company was likely to work on the terms that I would need if I were to choose that option—ninety days until payment. Their upfront costs were too high to let an unknown like me get generous credit terms like that. They would want their payment immediately.

I also learned that the masks could be cut out of their plastic material with something called a water jet cutter. In this process, a great deal of water is forced through a tiny hole in a nozzle. It is under such high pressure as it goes from the tank to the nozzle that the stream is powerful enough to cut through a finger. (I know this because when I went to visit just such an operation the first time, I was about to put my hand in the stream when the plant foreman who was showing me the facility pulled my hand away before I sustained a serious injury.) It wasn't that I was so impressed by the process that I had to use it for the masks, but that the price was well within my budget.

The next thing I needed to learn on this trek toward Troy was what material would be ideally suited to this application. Fortunately for me, the water jet cutter people had a forty-foot long boxcar of DCH foam on the premises. They told me it would be a great choice of material for what I was trying to do. Plus, they had it on hand which meant no transportation or delivery fees and they had it in a variety of colors. Cool. DCH. Very cool.

In reality, I had no idea what DCH meant, but I assumed it was Dioxy Carbonate Hydrologized something or other. I let them throw the term around for a while, but when I saw these huge square chunks of it, my innate curiosity won out over my desire to not appear ignorant. So I asked what DCH stood for.

The foreman, most uninterested, replied, "Drink Cup Holder." Those big squares of foam were eventually turned into the soft, rubbery, insulating cup holders that we've all seen. I fought back a giggle, and nodded thoughtfully, hoping I did not look as uninformed as I felt.

"So how do we get that DCH," I pointed to the chunk as big as a mattress, "to look like this?" I next pointed to the drawing I had in my hand of a mask. They showed me. The water jet cutter went to work on that giant slab and sliced it into 1/8" slices. The term they used was that they skived it. You say slice, I say skive, let's call the whole thing *on*. I didn't have the cash for a major tooling operation and this seemed like the most cost-effective manufacturing process for this application, so I went with it.

They took my drawing, scanned it digitally into the computer that controlled the water jet cutter, and a few minutes later I had an orange prototype of my mask (see image page 279). I thanked them and told them I'd be back with a big order in a matter of days.

Next I had to find someone who could design a package for the mask. When searching for a designer, it makes sense to see samples of their work, find out if they work in the category of your product (in this case, toys), how many sample designs they'd be willing to produce, how many revisions/edits they'd allow as a part of their basic design fee, how quick their turn around time would be, etc. I only had one question: "Would you work on 90-day terms?" I had no money to pay a designer up front.

I finally found a packaging designer who would agree to my terms, met with her, and had the design completed the next day. I took the mock-up of the packaging, inserted my sample mask, shrink wrapped it, and was back on the road. My next stop was Troy, Michigan: Kmart World Headquarters.

Getting to Yes With a Little Help from My Friends

An all-night drive from suburban Lexington got me to Troy early the next morning. I parked in the lot of a Kmart and got two hours sleep and hoped that by osmosis, I'd gotten some good karma from my choice of campgrounds. Maybe to you sunrise over the Grand Tetons or Midtown Manhattan would be an idyllic view. For me, the sunrays poking through the gap between the "m" and the "a" on the store's sign was an inspiring sight. I knew I needed more than inspiration that morning. I scanned the horizon and noticed an open auto body shop. I walked in while the employees were all standing near or slouching on the counter before getting started. They gave me that look that only men can give. I smiled and asked, "Hey guys, do you mind if I use your electricity to iron my suit?" I pointed to the parking lot and my dew-drenched Civic, "I just slept in my car. I'm out here from California and it's my dream to sell these Halloween disguises to Kmart."

Not only did they show me where the nearest outlet was, they fed me donuts and coffee. After surviving on a jar of peanut butter and a loaf of bread the past four days, those packaged donuts tasted like the most buttery croissants, and the instant coffee they served up was as wonderful as a cup of the finest Kona. They let me use their restroom to wash up and sent me on my way with their best wishes for success.

My belly now full, I set about getting a Kmart buyer on the phone. I'll fill you in later on some tricks for getting through the maze of extensions and departments at a large retailer. To be honest, I don't even remember everything I said in order to get a meeting with the buyer. I probably sounded something like this. "Hello, I am Barbara, and I was in Mexico just the other day when I decided to make these disguises. I didn't have any money so I held a garage sale to raise funds for this venture. I have been sleeping in my car so

I could talk to you. I am here to sell you the very best Halloween masks you have ever seen. May I come see you?"

The buyer, later referring to me as "a piece of work," probably figured that at the very least I would provide some comic relief on a slow day, so he agreed to see me. At that very moment I thought I had the order. I was that confident. In retrospect I was that naïve. Incidentally, I hope you've been able to figure out that this stumbling approach is NOT an example of my following *The Carey Formula*, even though the lessons I learned eventually led to my first great success and helped me develop the formula.

I found my way to the corporate headquarters. I wore my $4,000 suit like a suit of armor—nothing was going to keep me from completing my quest. I don't know if it was because I had less than fifteen days invested in this project compared to the more than fifteen months I invested in the Time-Out Watch venture, but I was amazingly relaxed. Certainly the financial stakes weren't as high in terms of investor cash, but my family and I were on the verge of bankruptcy. Strangely, that thought comforted me. What did I have to lose? And you know what, I thought there was NO WAY I was going to lose, anyway.

I thought my presentation went well. The buyer had sat stoically throughout it, his arms propped on the armrest of his chair, his chin resting on his hands folded as though in prayer. After my dog and pony show, he squinted at me and said, "no." Not just a regular "no" but an ear-ringing "no" that pushed me back into my chair. His resounding "noooooooooooooooo" gradually dissipated into infinity. Well, I was in no position to take no for my answer. I needed a yes not only to make our next mortgage payment, but also to claim the victory I felt was destined to be mine. I needed to take my life back. After the buyer said no, I just sat for a moment figuring out my next steps. Then I came up with a brilliant question:

"Why?"

"You're here two months too early for us to buy in for Halloween *next* year. Besides, I would get fired if I did something like this in this short a period of time. Things just don't get done this way." He pushed himself back from the desk and stood to escort me out. My chances of success were nearly gone, so I asked him if he really liked the disguises.

"Yes, I love them. They are cute and priced right and they would sell."

"Then what's stopping you? What would your boss think? Would you do this deal if your boss said yes?"

He couldn't hold my gaze after that. A few more moments passed. Finally, he took a deep breath. He said, "Yes, let's go see him."

The same thing happened with the next man up the line. So I asked, "Would you, could you buy these if your boss said yes?" Once again, this manager said, "yes."

So, now the three of us went striding off to see the head buyer. I felt a little bit like Dorothy from *The Wizard of Oz*. I was with two guys who had brains and hearts that could recognize the value of my product, but so far neither of them had the courage to buck the system. Finally, after doing my presentation in front of Mr. Wegscheid, I heard him say the magic word. "Yes!" I love you, Mr. Wegscheid, wherever you are today. That little three-letter word, delivered by him with heartfelt appreciation for my creation, provided me with an unbelievable and lasting jolt of energy.

We weren't done yet. I got my yes, but what he wanted to negotiate was what this was going to cost him. I hadn't thought all of that through at that point, so I flipped the question around and put the burden on him. I figured the perceived value of the masks was $2.99. I asked Mr. Wegscheid what percentage he needed to make. And that's how we arrived at a figure of their paying me $2.19 per mask. My production costs were low at 32¢, so I was set to earn $1.87 per mask ordered. I eventually sold

Kmart 299,000 Halloween disguises for a total of $654,810. They cost me $95,680 for a net profit of nearly $560,000. I was ecstatic when Kmart gave me 10-day terms meaning they would pay within ten days of delivery. They printed the purchase order and handed it to me within ten minutes, pending my securing of product liability insurance. Completing the purchase order depended on my filling out and filing the necessary vendor forms with Kmart. They were in the next day. I was in business again.

Combining Products to Maximize Success

Another way to keep tooling costs down is to utilize products that are already in existence, but combine them in a unique way.

One of my favorite ways to create exciting new products is to combine two product concepts to make an entirely new product. I call this the 1 + 1 = 3 concept. By starting with two proven technologies, you decrease your risk of failure and increase your chance of getting a patent for your invention. I only like to market products that have some level of patent protection. The perfect example is when my ten-year-old son decided he wanted to talk underwater. Once again, interestingly enough, it was travel experiences that lead to the discovery of a wonderful idea and project. This time, we were in Hawaii.

We were on a family vacation and for the first time my water-loving son was snorkeling in the clear warm water of the South Pacific. He was snorkeling with his father and, to his utter surprise, a family of turtles passed under him. He started yelling and gesturing underwater for his dad to look, but his dad was focused on another undersea vision. Dad never got to see the turtles! Rich Jr. got out of the water and decided right then and there that there had to be a way to talk under water. On the airplane trip home, he began sketching out on a napkin some ideas for an underwater communication device.

61

From Idea to Reality: Water Talkies

When we got home, Rich Jr. went to work. He took soda pop cans and cut holes in them. Then he plugged the holes with his fingers and tried many different bathtub experiments. I remember coming home from work in my suit and he couldn't wait another second. I had to lean over the bathtub and immerse my head in the water to see if I could hear him.

Rich Jr. researched underwater sound travel and to his fascination he discovered that since sound already traveled underwater, he did not need electronic amplification. What he needed was a container to talk into that would keep water out of his mouth while releasing the extra air that entered the container. He went shopping at the local Ace Hardware store in Lafayette, California. They helped him find parts, materials and components. A week later Rich Jr. had a prototype. He used a small orange soccer cone for the container to talk into—its megaphone-like shape was conducive to sound travel. He covered and sealed the big end. He then purchased two snorkels and cannibalized the two blow valves as well as the mouthpiece. The mouthpiece went on the small end of the cone and the blow valves went on the body. He then purchased a toilet bowl screw from his new friends at Ace. This part squeezed the round soccer cone into oval. This was important for merchandising, because the round shape took up twice the shelf space as the oval shape. He tested it and it worked.

After completing a prototype, Rich Jr. decided he wanted to sell his invention at Toys"R"Us. A quick phone call to corporate headquarters landed him a conversation with the buyer. I don't think it hurt that he was a kid seeking information. Rich Jr. told the buyer he invented an underwater talking device that would be perfect for his stores. Not only could it be protected by patent, but it could sell at such a price that Toys"R"Us could enjoy a good margin. With a bit of luck and lots of vision from the buyer at Toys"R"Us, Rich Jr. was invited to make a formal presentation.

Three weeks later, Rich Jr. and I were making his first sales call at a Toys"R"Us office in Paramus, New Jersey. I taught Rich Jr. to just tell the buyer the story of how he thought of the idea, and why someone would want to buy it. I also told him that selling is a strategy. For the three weeks leading up to his appointment, we would go over the key selling points, while we were on the way to school. I told him selling is a strategic game. All you have to do is solve four things: price, terms, availability, and delivery. He put the points onto flash cards and we talked about what they meant.

Rich Jr. wore a blue suit and a tie with a paper airplanes print. The anticipation that lead up to the meeting had his legs bouncing nervously as he sat in the waiting room. The buyer, Chuck Miller, invited us into his office. He offered us a soda and we all engaged in a few minutes of small talk. Then Rich Jr. told his story. He set up a fish tank with a Water Talkie so the buyer could hear him talk under water. When Rich Jr. talked about price, he reached into his pocket and pulled out the "price" flash card and laid it on the buyer's desk. Each time Rich presented a strategy point he would do the same. It was really kind of funny—totally suited to a kid doing a sales presentation—and it worked. Soon Rich Jr. gave a demonstration of the Water Talkie in action, underwater. The buyer was absolutely sold at that point.

Rich Jr. then asked for the order underwater. He said, "I would like you to order 50,000 Water Talkies in 90 days and another 25,000 in the following thirty days. I need ten day terms to get this off the ground and I will give you two percent off the price for the terms." The buyer shook his hand and they had a deal (see image page 280).

And That's Not All

Three years later Rich Jr. had a full product line of fun pool toys and sold them nationwide. He went on the *Late Show with David Letterman* and won the prestigious Ernst & Young "Entrepreneur of the Year" award. When he was thirteen, his company was sold to Wild Planet. He has been a Member of the Board for Tim Draper's Biz World, which teaches kids the fundamentals of business. He has been the Chairman of the Board for Made by Kids for Kids, and was a Student Board Member for the Partnership for America's Future. He has met and spent time with Michale Nobel (the nephew of Alfred Nobel) and some famous inventors like Wilson Greatbatch, who invented the pacemaker. Rich Jr. spends much of his time giving back to the community that has been so kind to him. You can read more about him at www.richstachowski.com.

Now you might ask how is a kid able to run a company by himself. The answer is that he did not. I made an arrangement with a man named Robert Miller to work in the capacity of Rich Jr.'s business manager and he was his mentor as well. Robert had the unique skill of being able to understand all aspects of a consumer product business, as well as a passion to make a difference in my son's life. We set it up so Robert was providing advice to Rich Jr. on all the significant decisions he had to make. Their relationship was very special. Robert brought the highest standards of credibility and integrity to his relationship with Rich Jr.; Robert taught my son "life" lessons that he will never forget. Robert was patient, not self-serving, reliable, fun and honest to the core. This is a must if a parent is ever to allow someone to work closely with his or her child. Rich Jr. calls his experience in this relationship the most important aspect of his business and will never forget how much fun he had working with Robert. And as a result Rich Jr. learned one of the most important *Carey Formula* rules: "Surround yourself with people who can do things you can't."

The Eye of a Turtle

By Rich Stachowski Jr.

We were looking at each other eye to eye, with not more than five inches separating us in the clear underwater caves of Maui. At first I was frightened, but awe soon took over. It was a giant sea turtle, a magnificent and beautiful creature. My dad had to see this. I motioned to him frantically to come and look. Although he was only fifteen feet away and I was gesturing wildly, I could not get his attention. I was ten years old. By the time I was thirteen, I had lived through a life-changing experience that began that day, and with that turtle, in 1995.

On the way home from our vacation in Hawaii, I began drawing a diagram hoping to make some sort of makeshift device to talk underwater. When I got home, I made a prototype of my design. My parents really liked it and suggested I call the toy buyer for Toys"R"Us in New Jersey. Me? Little inarticulate Rich Jr.? No way! But Mom said that if I wanted it done, I'd have to do it myself. Quaking in my tennis shoes, I explained over the phone my concept for an underwater talking device to Mr. Chuck Miller, the head buyer for Toys"R"Us. To my utter astonishment he asked me when I could fly to New Jersey and present my product to his company. Knowing opportunity when I saw it, I responded, "Any school day!" Three weeks later (on a Thursday) I was in a brand new suit, shiny black shoes, black belt, and my tie with paper airplanes printed on it, presenting my idea.

Toys"R"Us gave me a purchase order for 50,000 units! They eventually put Water Talkies in all the Toys"R"Us stores throughout the United States.

CNN picked up the story on the five o'clock news, and soon I was bombarded with hundreds of media requests. This formerly inarticulate ten-year-old ended up on forty-six radio and TV talk shows, culminating with a flight to New York to be on the *David Letterman Show*. By age thirteen I had received the Ernst & Young "Entrepreneur of the Year" award. I had also received the Winners' League Foundation "Entrepreneur of the Year" award at the Inventors' Hall of Fame ceremony, where I was the keynote speaker to an audience of more than a thousand people. I am honored to have held a student board of directors position with that organization. By that time, I had invented three more water toys that were being sold in Toys "R" Us, Target, Kmart, and other stores throughout the world. And soon after that, I sold my company to Wild Planet in San Francisco, where I continued in a consulting capacity for one year.

That was a lot to happen to a kid in three years and the varied experiences changed me in profound ways. It is said that the mind is formed by the time a child is seven. Perhaps the foundation is formed early, but it's the build-up of what you put on top of that foundation that can be so life changing. The things I learned from what I call my Water Talkie experience have influenced me in all my choices in life.

The very first and most valuable thing I learned was how important the support of family and friends is in order to achieve personal success. The friends I had when I was ten years old are friends for life. My family and my friends were always there for me during times when, without them, I would have become overwhelmed. They only wanted the best for me and their involvement taught me that there is nothing more important in life than having true, sincere, and caring relationships.

During those years, I had much to juggle. There was the business. (What the heck was a profit and loss statement?) There were school, homework, and term papers. Sports have always been extremely important to me, and during those four years, I played soccer, baseball, basketball and lacrosse, surfed at Santa Cruz, wrestled, snowboarded, competed on a swim team, and started the main sport of my life, football. Sports were a great opportunity for competition, personal challenge, and a chance to be with my friends. But the need to make tough decisions still seemed to be consistently coming at me from all directions. When I was thirteen, I was asked to be on the *Jay Leno Show*, but it was during my basketball championships. Big decision. I decided to turn down the show. That was a choice I have never regretted. I chose commitment to my teammates over the novel experience of appearing on the show and I could tell by how I felt inside that it was the right thing to do. I learned that commitment comes first, right up there with friendship. It helped quite a bit, too, when Mr. Leno announced that I had made the "right" decision.

This last incident brings up another crucial thing I learned from that three-year experience. I learned that life is all about choices, and that these choices pop up on a day-to-day basis. There are little ones and big ones, but they all matter, and in the end the choices you make are the sum total of your life. I had to learn to prioritize during those busy years. I realized I couldn't do it all, so I had to decide which things mattered and to what degree. The only way I could do that was to place each demand into the broader picture and then make the choice. I have mentioned the demands of those three years, but I don't want to forget to mention that I also had a lot of fun during that time. I learned that I must keep a balance in life between work and play. What my Water Talkie experience taught me was that I had to take control of my daily schedule or it would control me and I would be buried. And I mustn't be so busy that I neglect to be involved in the needs of my family and friends, who I care about very deeply. I try to start each day putting each demand in its proper slot. I have at least learned to stop, think, and go through the process of prioritization.

Another lesson I learned during my Water Talkie experience was about failure. I can summarize what I learned in one sentence. Failure is not a defeat, it is an opportunity for change. I have learned that failure is only a dead-end when one doesn't examine it and then go forward in a better way. I have tried to compare myself not with others, but only to the person I was yesterday. I will never forget one of the memories from my young inventing days. I was working on my fourth underwater device and had named it (yes, really) "Bumper-Jumper-Paddle-Pumper."

I envisioned gleefully riding high on this thing in the water while squirting water at friends doing likewise. The trouble was that I made fifty different prototypes over a period of six months and none of them worked. They sank, or they didn't squirt, or they leaked, or they were too cumbersome, or they were too expensive to tool (cost was always crucial in the mass market). I encountered months of devastating and increasing frustration. I seriously considered giving up fifty times, but at the same time I absolutely loved the concept of this product. Again, it was my family and friends who backed me up by encouraging me to not give up on my dream. And on the fifty-first try, it worked! I have rarely felt such elation! I learned that failure had become my greatest ally. Each failure showed me what didn't work so that I could eventually figure out what did work. I learned from this experience that if what you're doing is worthwhile to you, then you must continue the struggle despite all obstacles. Failure showed itself to be my tool for success, and the Bumper-Jumper-Paddle-Pumper turned out to be one of my bestselling products.

By thirteen, the person I was at age ten had learned a lot about character and personal integrity. I was surprised and shocked in those early teens to witness people in supposedly reputable businesses doing unscrupulous things, such as trying to copy and steal my products. It seemed that there were some people who would do anything to reach their goals, which mainly consisted of making as much money as possible by whatever means necessary. I appreciated all my family and friends who were trust-worthy and loyal and who were people I could respect. I made a decision during those years that wherever my life might lead me or wherever I might lead it, my life would be conducted with integrity in all things. I have learned that my relationships must always be a top priority when making choices. I have learned that who you are is the person you face every day upon awakening, and you'd better make sure you can respect that person because you're stuck with him for life.

All this I learned because one day, in 1995, I looked into the eye of a turtle.

Interestingly, one day I was in the office, and a well-dressed elegant woman came into my offices from which Water Talkies was also being run. I recognized her immediately—the woman was Joan Bruzzone, the wife of the wealthy and influential developer who had let me board my horse on his land so many years ago. She peered around a corner and tentatively knocked. I came out to greet her, and she told me that she had seen all of the publicity about Water Talkies and Rich Jr. and wanted to buy some for her grandchildren and meet the young man responsible for them. I had to tell her that Rich Jr. wasn't available because he was in school. I also insisted that she take as many of the products that she needed. I told her that Rich Jr. wouldn't have it any other way, but I didn't go any further to explain my connection to her husband. She graciously accepted my offer. I thought that would be the end of it, but that's a story for another time.

Another example of combining products to create a new item with a unique selling feature is my Bloombra. Not too long ago I was shopping at a mall and I was in one of those gadget stores. I saw that they were selling this super soft pillow that was feather light. The pillow was filled with micro beads. Micro beads are similar to the beads you would find in a beanbag chair but they are very tiny. When I touched this pillow I instantly said to my self, "Omigod, this feels like a woman's breast"! I also had an idea; so I bought one of these pillows and charged down the mall to Victoria's Secret. At Victoria's Secret I purchased a two-ply unpadded bra and proceeded straight to my home. Once there, I cut a tiny hole in both the cups of the bra and filled each cup with four ounces of micro beads that I took from the pillow. I put the bra on and the result was unbelievable— *voila!* It transformed my shape into a most natural and voluptuous new look like I have never seen or felt before. It was weightless and I could not even tell I was wearing extra enhancement the way a padded bra usually feels. The micro beads moved with my body and felt like they were part of my shape. What was most amazing about this new bra was that the micro beads wanted to travel "up" and had a gravity defying effect. I named it Bloombra and four days later I filed a patent application. This was a simple idea that was created by combining the features of two products to create a new item (see image page 282). The Bloombra is also a great product to market under *The Carey Formula* because it is a simple sewing procedure to manufacture and there would be no tooling charges.

Barbara Carey's Simple Secrets of Success:

- Only sell products that can be manufactured with low tooling costs. Not only was the Time-Out Watch highly technical, the entire casing had to be tooled, which is an

expensive endeavor. My Time-Out Watch was dia-
metrically opposed to the keep it simple and have low
start up costs plan I now advocate. It required engineering expenses, design expenses, and circuit design costs,
which added up to $1 million plus. And yet the concept
was so good it almost happened anyway.

- What would I do knowing now what I didn't know then?
  I would have been much more successful had I sourced a
  watch that already had a countdown timer function, had
  it produced in bright colors, and added a booklet that
  taught children the concept of time. There would have
  been no tooling costs associated with the watch, and of
  course the booklet needs no tooling. The added value of
  combining these two products is a sure formula for success because it would have been a unique concept. I
  simply would have asked a manufacturer to make 12
  prototypes. Then I would have mocked up the book and
  the packaging and gone on the road with a startup cost of
  less than $500 instead of practically going bankrupt
  designing and building my own watch.

- This failure taught me to think in simple terms. I call it
  the vanilla ice cream option. A simple, good tasting ice
  cream without the nuts, chocolate, and fruit will always
  sell. You can create a new product from an existing one
  just by changing colors. Now when I see dollar signs in
  a product, I shy away. But I am also a slow learner. I
  made the same mistake again in designing a water toy
  that I will tell you about in a later chapter. Avoiding
  products that have high production costs is one of the
  most important lessons in this book. I cannot tell you
  how many times I have tried to teach this lesson only to
  have budding entrepreneurs ignore it because of their

affection for the product idea that inspired them. I tell them to put their expensive idea on the back burner while they create items they can produce and sell quickly. This way it is inexpensive to create a business. You save your cash reserves while learning the entire process.

- It is much harder to license a product that a manufacturer must produce than it is to create and produce your own product. It is a myth that you *need* a big company's help to market your product. Big companies have always made us feel like we can't succeed unless they are involved in some way. What usually happens is that the big company makes all the money and you make very little. You literally give them your idea for a few bucks. If you are someone whose goal is to achieve great success I recommend that you manufacture your own products. Later in this book I will show you how to find manufacturers and how to get them to produce prototypes of your product with little or no upfront cost. This is a very big part of *The Carey Formula*—sell it before you have it.

- Avoid the NIH syndrome (Not Invented Here). Many times companies get excited when they are presented with a product concept from a passionate entrepreneur. Many times, after a short period, management's interest cools because of what is called the NIH syndrome. This immediately puts your NIH product on the back burner where it dies like the Time-Out Watch did.

- Stand up for yourself and your best interests. While companies have deep pockets and you think you can take advantage of that fact, the truth is some of the money that leaves those deep pockets goes to lawyers. I once licensed a product to a company that made thousands of dollars from it. I got a check for $85. The contract was created in their favor even though it appeared to benefit both sides when I read it. Even if I re-read the contract today it would still look fair to me but tricky wording in the contract basically cut me out of any profit.

- Never give up. One thing you don't have as a new entrepreneur is perspective. When the Time-Out Watch failed I thought I was finished as an entrepreneur because I couldn't see the big picture. In my early years I thought I had failed and wouldn't have another chance. Now I know that business, like life, is cyclical. If you fail, move on to the next idea. You ALWAYS have another chance. I don't dwell on my failures. I certainly don't like them, but I just bounce back and move forward in a positive direction. When I fail, I analyze the product and process until I understand what caused the failure. The lessons I have learned from my failures have made me lots of money later in life. My bout with being emotionally paralyzed by the failure of my first product did nothing to further my goals. Only when I came out and faced the world was I able to rejuvenate my creativity.

- Always be aware of what is going on around you. I don't know if it is a natural instinct with me, but I am always keenly aware of those around me. I am very interested in people's behavior. I am conscious of things people say and actions they take. I try to know which colors are popular with each age group, what design trends are prevalent and what words are trendy as well as what the current cultural and artistic trends are. I look for what makes people laugh, cry, be happy, and be sad. I look for any sign of changes in people's behavior because what I observe helps me create a product that will make enough of a connection with people for me to make a sale. When I saw the Mexican children with their disguises I came alive. I visualized brightly colored masks with a soft tactile feel and the name "Who Am I?" which accentuated the idea of role-playing for the kids. I also saw a highly creative play pattern, something that mothers care a lot about. And most importantly, I knew the disguises would sell at high volume with a high margin. Once this all came together for me, I couldn't wait to get started.

- Always dress for success. The Donna Karan suit enabled me to look my best and gave me the confidence to make an effective presentation. If you don't feel good about yourself it will come across when you meet the buyer. Any hint of a lack of self-confidence on your part could torpedo your sales effort, so always dress for success. If you feel good about yourself you will come off as a passionate, competent entrepreneur who can bring large profits to the buyer's company. Of course you don't have to spend $4,000 to dress tastefully; appropriate style can be bought and creatively put together at a most reasonable price.

- Be prepared to sacrifice. I ate peanut butter sandwiches and slept in my rental car while I set up the manufacturing and product design for the Mexico-inspired masks. But the result was more than $1 million in sales when you add in the reorders for the disguises. Nobody likes sacrifice, but the rewards you get from succeeding after a sacrifice are much more satisfying than success that comes from luxury. In business, that feeling is as good as it gets.

Prison and Perseverance

I want to take you back to my youth and young adulthood. I'd like to share with you some of the most formative experiences of my life and career. In a sense, we'll be returning to the themes of Chapter One: passion, persistence and independence. As you will see, these themes recur throughout the book. As a businessperson, I'm passionate about creating products that will free women from the constraints of time and the many demands made on them economically, socially, and emotionally. My passion to do this for women strikes me as odd in many ways. In most regards I was given a great deal of freedom as a child. I've already told you about how supportive my mother was and though she gave up teaching to raise her children, she was completely fulfilled by that experience. Yet, something compels me to create and market products aimed directly at women. I find motherhood extremely fulfilling, yet have always felt the desire to stretch beyond the boundaries of motherhood to define for myself a new role. Perhaps you feel many of the same impulses.

In raising my brother and me, my mother managed to walk that difficult tightrope between independence and firm guidance. As you read, she had some firm ideas about the proper way to raise children. However, as children age, they spend a greater and greater portion of their day in the care of other adults while attending school. My mother worked hard to exert her influence in the one area of my life in which I felt the most constrained—school.

Odd Birds and Eccentric Redheads

As my mother suggested in the passage she wrote in Chapter One, I was a student of the world. I was constantly seeking out new experiences and new information. I realize that in some ways, it is easy to view me as an odd bird; after all, how many kids find a dead bird and sketch its structures unless forced to by a teacher? I wasn't always engaged in serious endeavors, however. One of my absolute favorite television shows was *I Love Lucy*. The goofy redheaded heroine and her broadly slapstick sensibility appealed to me on a fundamental level, I suppose. I loved to watch her as she struggled with the role of housewife and mother, wanting to be more than just Mrs. Ricky Ricardo. From one zany misadventure to the next, I loved watching her get Ethel involved in one scheme or another. Of course, when I was in elementary school, I didn't have any kind of critical understanding of why I liked the show so much. If someone had asked me for that analysis, I would have thrown my hands up in the air and said simply, "It's funny!"

My mother supported my *I Love Lucy* television watching habit, just as she did nearly everything else I did. Unfortunately, the reruns of *I Love Lucy* came on in our area at eight-thirty every morning and ended at nine. The first bell at school rang at five to nine and we had to be in our classroom and in our seats five minutes later. I was so devoted to the show that my mother (with her status as a former teacher certainly aiding her cause) convinced the school's principal to let me be a few minutes late each day so I could watch *I Love Lucy*. I don't know if my fellow classmates or their parents knew about this little arrangement, but I didn't tell anyone the reason for my daily tardiness. I was hyper-vigilant about being ready to bolt out the door as soon as the show's familiar credits and the heart-shaped logo first began to dim. I watched the show clad in my school clothes, my book bag by my side, so that as soon as the show was over I could dash the couple of blocks to school. Generally, I was no more than a few minutes late, rarely even arriving five minutes after nine. Truth be told, not much happened in those first few minutes of school anyway. The teacher took the roll call, announcements were made about upcoming school programs, and parent permission forms for field trips were passed out or collected. Regardless, I felt privileged to be trusted to get myself there as soon as I could and to be able to indulge my passion for Lucy.

I never abused the privilege, never lorded it over the other students, and never took this gift for granted. My mother going to bat for me made me feel even closer to her. More than that though, I felt trusted and consequently I matured. I realize that school taught me some pretty important things, but when I compare the value of knowing what a murmur diphthong is compared to becoming a more responsible and mature person, phonics seems almost like a waste of time. I will return to this idea of responsibility time and again in this book, because being a responsible and ethical person has aided me greatly in my career and life as an inventor and entrepreneur. We will discuss more on this as we move into other product development stories.

Don't Do—Delegate!

My mother was even more influential in teaching me to be a responsible person. It helped that in certain instances, she treated me almost like a peer and not as a child. I've always loved cars, so one chore that I never minded doing was washing the family cars. Even when I was around six years old, I'd take on this task. My mother assisted me. She would get out the bucket, the washrags, the chamois cloth for drying, and lay out all the supplies in the grass alongside the driveway. She'd help me drag the garden hose from its coiled resting place near the outside spigot. She let me control the spray nozzle, but would help by maneuvering the hose so that it wouldn't kink or get caught under the tires. When I was done wetting down the car, she'd take the hose from me, and when I asked her for the washrag or the sponge, she'd hand it to me. When I got to the next phase in the process, she'd hand me whatever I asked for. The same was true when we baked cookies. Even when I was young enough that I needed a stepstool to stand on to reach the kitchen countertop, she would let me do the work while she acted as the *sous* baker—setting out all the ingredients, marking the page in the cookbook, pre-heating the oven, etc. Whatever I needed, she would bring me; whatever I needed assistance with, she would lend her hands.

My mother made me feel like I could get things done. Mom put me in the position of leadership and let me go. Even though she was there to help me, I was the one in charge. I suppose I grew accustomed to that feeling and wanted to experience it in all facets of my life. That's both a very powerful and in some ways dangerous feeling for a child to have—especially when other institutions like school don't fully support it. For many reasons, school frustrated me. Let me clarify that. In some ways I liked school, I loved learning, but the institution itself thwarted me. I was, I suppose, a child whose needs were very different from most of the students in my classes. While labels and determinations of kids vary so greatly, my needs were expressed primarily through my desire for autonomy. Often I felt school confining with few chances to express one's creativity other than in an occasional art class. I guess I never outgrew the "me do" phase that most kids go through when they are first discovering that they can exert control over their environment. Not only did me want to do, me was able to do—especially at home. I was not a very good passive learner; I much preferred to get my hands dirty and dig in and do something rather than just hear about it. School was a place where passivity seemed to be rewarded, and I was never going to be passive.

Truth and Trepidation: Going Your Own Way

Fortunately, I had a few teachers along the way who recognized my essential nature and independent spirit. I also recognized that there were some real differences between my classmates and me. Mrs. Copeland was my fourth grade teacher, and she had some different ideas about education. She really wanted us to develop socially as well as academically, so she organized little communication sharing sessions with us. In a way, they were like group therapy sessions. She would gather either the entire class or small groups into a circle and ask us to share our feelings about various topics. One session in particular that I have almost total recall of was a large-group session during which she wanted us to talk about our families—particularly our feelings about our parents. I sat in that circle growing increasingly mortified as I heard one student after another talk about how much and why they didn't like either their mother or their father or both.

I was one of the last students to speak, and even though I'd heard nothing but bad things coming out of the mouths of my classmates, I decided I had to tell the truth. I stood up, and looked around the room into the eyes of my classmates. Some of them looked back at me, others let their eyes wander distractedly from the bulletin boards decorated with silhouettes of Abraham Lincoln and George Washington to the Valentine's Day board with Cupid ready to fire his arrow. I said as calmly as I could, "My mother is my best friend. I love my dad and I am his favorite person in the world."

I sat back down to a few snorts and giggles, which Mrs. Copeland quelled in an instant. I stared straight ahead smiling, not wanting to let anyone know that his or her reaction got to me. When I got home from school that day, my mom told me that Mrs. Copeland had called and wanted to see her at school the next day. I was surprised and just a little bit concerned. What had I done to deserve a teacher's call at home? I was confident I hadn't misbehaved or failed a test or skipped an assignment. But still this puzzled me. The next day my mother came in right after the final bell. I sat in my desk until Mrs. Copeland called me up to her desk so that she could say what she had to say to both of us.

"Mrs. Kraft, I just wanted to let you know what 'Barbie' said in class yesterday." She repeated my words in the group sharing session. Then she added, "What 'Barbie' said took a great deal of courage. She didn't cave in to peer pressure, as I'm afraid many of her classmates did. She told the truth. She stood alone."

As an entrepreneur, you are going to be faced with many challenges. The pressure to conform, to go the accepted way is always going to be great. While it is important to recognize a well-trod path to success can be invaluable, you have to keep in mind that there may be an even better way—especially when that direction or choice matches what you feel inside. You have to strike a balance in crafting your business. You need to look at the current trends, but not become so wedded to them that you fail to innovate. Simply modeling another person's methods will work in the short term, especially when things are going well. When you face obstacles, you will need to rely on your inner resourcefulness and the tools you possess in order to overcome them.

On the other hand, if you are too contrarian in your thinking and actions, you risk either being out of touch with your market or alienating those with whom you come in contact. History is filled with forward thinkers whose ideas opposed what was considered the status quo of the time. Galileo and Copernicus in the scientific world, and Steve Jobs and Steve Wozniak (the co-founders of Apple Computer) in the technology and business world are just a couple of examples. You have to find the balance between your stubborn individuality and when that stubbornness serves your best interests, and know when and how to listen to and follow the crowd.

Doing Unto Others…

My mother taught me another valuable lesson that I've been able to put into practice since I've entered the business world. When I was doing those chores like baking cookies (okay, so that wasn't *really* a chore) or washing the car, she let me be the boss while she assisted me. I learned from that how to delegate and how to ask for assistance from others. Because she was first and foremost my mother and not my assistant, I had to treat her with kindness and respect. I continue that practice with my present employees and with any of my other business associates and contacts including vendors. I am a great believer in broadly applying the Golden Rule, and I saw how effective that style of leadership was by watching my parents interact, seeing the high regard my father's employees held him in, and even in my Social Security Card and cookie selling operations.

I've already made the point about not having to do it all yourself, and in those early work sessions with my mother, I learned the importance and value of delegation. The car washing went much faster and proceeded more efficiently if I asked my mother to help dry off the roof, which was difficult for me to reach. Or, if on a particular day, I felt as if I wanted to do the roof because I felt it needed my special attention, I would ask her to help me by retrieving the ladder from the garage. That way, I could continue lower level work like the wheels and tires, while she did the legwork. Remember—independence is a great thing, but having it doesn't mean that you have to do it totally alone. Again, striking that balance between working independently and working in isolation is extremely important. I know my mother's principles in raising children do work. My brother is 10 times more successful than I am, and a leader beyond belief. Plus he is a nice person to be around and has the same sense of integrity that I do. She applied the same principles to him, although we (Scott and I) both know that Mom loves me best!

Un-Edited Commentary

I have known Barb for over forty-five years. We go back to her early days of diapers and bottles. We actually met in the hospital—so I am told—but my memory of those early days is a bit foggy. Barb and I had many firsts over the forty-five years we have known each other. Being thrust together by circumstance not choice, Barb and I have grown up together and developed a special friendship. She has always been there for me and I for her. As we went off to our respective colleges we stayed in touch, sometimes by phone, sometimes getting together for lunch or dinner. I went to her wedding and flew out when her son was born. Barb came to my wedding and has been there for my three children. She not only spoils them but is there to help them day or night.

As Barb and I settled in with our respective families after college, we have stayed in constant touch. We vacation together each year and never miss an opportunity to hook up when our travel paths cross. In fact we own vacation homes adjacent to each other in the hills of the wine country in Northern California.

Although we have enjoyed very successful lives, Barb and I are very different. Barb loves fast cars; I love fast airplanes. Barb is stunningly beautiful and won't leave home without perfect hair and stylish clothes. I have no hair and wear whatever is on top in my dresser drawer. Barb is very serious, loves reading, and is always talking about a new invention or idea. I goof around a lot, like adventurous sports and clubbing.

One of the funniest memories I have of Barb was on a vacation in Las Vegas, Nevada. It was NOT easy to get her to Las Vegas; it just is not her style. As we walked through one of the new major casinos, Barb spotted a game of Roulette. As the players put their bets on the table I explained to her how the game worked. When she saw over $5000 was being wagered it got her attention. As the ball was spun Barb watched as it dropped into a number. There was great excitement at the table as some players had hit their number. But not for Barb. She proceeded to pull out her calculator from her purse to determine the profit and loss for each player at the table. She finally announced that the house had made over $500 on that number, and what a stupid game it was. I was not ready to give up and explained to Barb that she had to place a bet to feel the excitement. So she handed me five dollars and said go ahead. I put her bet on red figuring that she had close to a 50/50 chance to win, and thus I had a 50/50 chance to get her excited about gambling. Red came up and she won! I'm not sure she understood she had won until the dealer gave her $10. She took her winnings and said she was pleased. I asked her if she now wanted to "hit" the black jack tables and continue her winning streak. She said no. She said that gambling was no fun; she needed control of her destiny. I suggested to her that inventing was gambling and she said not the way she does it. She has a point there.

I am writing this with less than two days' notice from Barb as my family and I vacation at over 10,000 feet on the ski slopes of Utah. I'm not surprised by the short notice; it is very typical of Barb since when Barb wants something she wants it now. When Barb and I make requests from each other there is often negotiation and this request was no exception. I said I would make the forty-eight hour deadline, but she could NOT edit what I wrote. She agreed, but shortened the deadline to thirty-six hours. I said okay, but it would be hand written. She said it had to be typed, and extended the deadline to forty hours. I agreed but asked for a free copy of her book. She said half price. We had an agreement.

I actually wrote this in my head as I rode the chair lift with my fourteen-year-old daughter in preparation of a great Utah powder ski run. This was an easy request from Barb. I probably know Barb better than anyone, even her parents ... or should I say our parents. I am her brother and she is the best sister and friend anyone could ever ask for.

P.S. She will probably edit this, and I will probably get a free book ... I'll let you know in the sequel.

Working Smart: Knowing When and How to Adapt Your Methods

A number of times, I've gotten calls from budding inventors who have been stonewalled by a problem in production. They tell me about the number of times they've tried over and over and over and over again to get past a problem and not been able to do so. I remember reading Robert Pirsig's classic book, *Zen and the Art of Motorcycle Maintenance.* He talks about at-home mechanics and how they can fall into certain traps while working and how to avoid them. One of those traps is what he calls the "gumption trap." That is the feeling that if you just work hard enough, apply enough force, or implement persistently the same solution to a sticky problem, eventually you will succeed. If you've ever snapped the head off of a bolt, you know the problems that kind of gummed-up gumption-style thinking can produce. Though he doesn't quite put it this way, Pirsig's remarks remind me of Albert Einstein's definition of insanity as doing the same thing over and over again and expecting different results. Beating your head against the wall may feel normal after a time, but you won't know how much damage you're doing until you stop and assess the situation. Asking for help and seeking out experts is a smart and effective way to overcome problems. I can't say this enough: I really am only very good at one or two elements of the operations I undertake. I let others who are more expert in a particular phase of the project do their thing. Also, as I've said before, one of the main tasks that you as an entrepreneur will engage in is problem solving. Sometimes calling in the cavalry is the best solution; other times, it's simply marching forward.

The "P" Word

Pirsig's concept of "gumption traps" serves as a fine lead into another aspect of the right stuff necessary to be an inventor/ entrepreneur, and that is persistence. Sticking with our theme of finding a balance, it is important to recognize how to work hard and how to work smart. Believe me, I am the living embodiment of the notion that hard work is its own reward. In the business world, though, as in most other practical applications in your life, hard work can't be the only reward. I'm all for achieving a wonderful and fulfilling sense of a job well done, but that feeling is analogous to a well-prepared meal. The hard work should be the appetizer and the financial and personal rewards are the main course. One is a subtle and fleeting sensation that you wouldn't want to pass up, while the others are more deeply satisfying sensations that stay with you longer.

As I mentioned before, I come from a long line of hard workers; it's in my DNA. My father's work ethic set a high standard that I aimed to emulate. Also, as you've seen, in my family, if there was something you wanted, you were expected to work for it. We enjoyed a comfortable lifestyle as I grew up. My father's business was a thriving enterprise, but it was relatively small. The area I grew up in was populated by some very wealthy families and I moved in and around a wide social circle, socio-economically speaking, at school.

Equestrian Dreams

I don't know what initiated my love for animals, but I have always had a real affinity for them. In particular, I adore horses and have ever since I was very young. Among the wealthier families in my neighborhood, owning a horse seemed part and parcel of growing up—especially for the little girls. They would take riding lessons, along with piano and ballet, and engage in other suitable activities. I wanted a horse very badly and I wanted to learn to ride, but I knew that owning and maintaining one was more than I wanted to have my parents subsidize. Unless I could earn the money myself, my need would go unmet. Well, I was so passionate about the idea of getting a horse that I constantly read the classified ads and kept my ear to the ground for any leads on one from my friends and their families. Eventually I learned that a handsome sixteen-hand thoroughbred was available for $750.00. That was all I really needed to know. Once I had a target goal to fixate on, I was set in motion.

I became the Carey Chore Corporation. No job was too demeaning, no fee too small. Every penny would bring me one step closer to my dream of owning a horse. If that meant going over to our neighbors' house to feed, take out, and clean up after the Bennetts' pet dog—an over-indulged Golden Retriever with an insatiable appetite for food and socks, I was willing and able. I was also able to obtain a job at the local veterinarian's office. I would get up at 5:00 A.M. every morning and ride my bike to his office and clean all the dog and cat cages from the previous night. This was an emotionally difficult job, as I would often encounter an animal that was not able to make it through the night, and it was my job to dispose of the lost soul. Besides house and pet sitting and working at the vet, I also made myself a regular fixture at a local boarding stable. There I would muck the manure out of the stalls of the horses boarded there, often the horses my friends' parents had purchased for them, and do any other paying tasks. The stable was close enough that I could ride my bicycle the few miles to get there, and I began my horse-purchasing campaign when I was eight.

What Are The Chances?

My parents fully supported my efforts and told me that as soon as I had enough money, the horse would be mine. Each day I would ask my father what my chances were that day of getting the horse. He would say, "fifty-three percent," or use some other figure to represent how much of the needed funds I'd earned. I suppose some children my age might have lost interest in the endeavor in a few months at the most. Not me. I persisted for years. My daily routine became getting up at five in the morning, eating a hot breakfast, bicycling to the vet, going to the stables and feeding the horses, heading home to bathe and change clothes, watching *Lucy*, and then going to school. After school, I'd head back to the stables and muck out and feed the horses again. After a while, when the nearby stable closed and I could no longer get to the new location as easily, my father took over the morning feeding duties, and I continued the muck-out portion of the work.

Over time, I'd stopped asking my father about my chances of getting the horse. The work became the focus and I knew I was making steady progress. That was enough. One day, shortly after I'd turned thirteen, I arrived at the stable as usual. I went to the tack room and got my mucking boots and a pitchfork. I walked along the row of stalls, greeting each of the boarders, patting a few on the snout and rubbing a few ears along the way. The air was redolent of horse and hay and a barn dog nipped playfully at my heels. All was good in my world. Even though the shady air in the barn was a bit cool, I could see through the doors at the far end of the barn, the rolling countryside, and a corral and pasture, where a big bay mare stood grazing. I didn't recognize her as one of the regulars, so I went outside to investigate. As I got closer to the fence, I noticed a sign hung from the top rail of the split rail enclosure. It said simply, "100%."

Every time I think of this story, tears come to my eyes. My father's simple but eloquent message telling me that this horse was mine was a powerful reminder of the rewards that a 100% effort can bring. Both of my parents showed up at the barn a few minutes later and they told me how proud they were of me. As much as those words meant to me, feeling proud of myself was an even greater reward. My parents could have found a way to give me a horse, but the fact that I earned the privilege after five years of working toward that goal enriched my life immeasurably. Of course, as anyone who has ever owned a dog, let alone a horse, knows, the cost of keeping a pet eventually dwarfs the cost of acquiring the pet. That meant that if I were going to keep my horse I had to continue working.

Sometimes your hard work pays unexpected dividends. The first week after I took possession of The Colonel's Lady, she came down with a bad case of colic. If you think a colicky baby is a handful of trouble, just imagine what that means in a creature the size of a horse. I had to call the vet to come and examine Lady and suggest a course of treatment. I knew Dr. Sharp since he cared for many of the horses at the stable; he knew how hard I worked and what I was working for. Often I would lend him a hand with the horses and, after all, I had experience working for a vet. He was a very caring man who clearly loved his work and the animals he cared for. After giving Lady a quick exam, he came over to me. He must have seen how concerned I was. "She's going to be fine, 'Barbie'," he said. He pulled a pill nearly the size of a bar of soap from his bag. My eyes went wide. I'd only had the horse for a week and now I had a vet bill to pay for the visit and medicine. There were hardly any more hours in the day for me to work. And I simply was not going to ask my parents for help because they were already so kind for allowing me to have this horse.

"Quite the pill isn't it?"

I nodded.

"A lot of times, it's really difficult to get a horse to take these things. I don't know why that is. I wish that they'd sense I was doing something good for them." Even though I had been calculating in my mind how many stalls I'd have to muck out and how many manes I'd have to braid to make up for the cost of a vet visit and the drugs, I didn't say a word about those concerns to Dr. Sharp.

"Listen," he said, "I've heard Lady's a pretty big eater. I don't really believe she'll take this thing. If she does, the visit and the medication are on me. How's that sound? You game for the bet?"

I shook his extended hand and held my breath while he held the pill in his palm beneath Lady's muzzle. The horse snuffled it for a few seconds, then plucked it out of the doctor's hand and with a couple of quick chomps, swallowed it.

"What do you know?" Dr. Sharp smiled and put his hand on my shoulder. "Today's your lucky day."

I thanked him profusely and he simply said, "Keep up the good work," and walked toward his truck. This isn't the only example I can point to in my life, especially later on as an entrepreneur, when I received help from someone—a friend, a family member, another business owner. All our successes are built upon the cooperative efforts of many people.

The Beat Goes On

By the time I was thirteen, I had become a pretty fair equestrian. I was fearless over the jumps. I entered a number of local and regional competitions, but because my funds were limited, my friends usually defeated me for the Best in Show designation by simply being able to enter in more individual events than I could afford. Understanding and dealing with the financial limitations imposed on me was fairly easy; after all, not being able to enter all the events you want to in an equestrian show isn't on a par with not being able to afford new clothes each school year or not being able to pay for the tickets to a school dance like some of my classmates. Still, I have to admit it stung a bit to be denied the opportunity to step to the top of the podium to receive the accolades I felt were my due. I felt that I was a superior rider to most, but had to settle for having my heart and mind—if not my shelves—filled with trophies. Those circumstances certainly kept me humble and fueled my inner drive to succeed.

I was still mucking out the stalls of my friends' horses, but I'd also begun to groom them as well. Braiding a horse's mane is as much art as science, and I gained a reputation as a pretty fair braider. Still, having to take orders in the stalls and barns from adults whom I would later see at their homes served as a constant reminder of the divide between "them" and "us." None of my friends' parents were ever actually cruel or dismissive toward me, but I certainly knew where my place was when I was working for them. Perhaps that is why I so often champion the underdog and do so much in my professional life to support and encourage others who don't have the financial means sometimes necessary to succeed. I always feel the need to help people who are also willing to help themselves.

My dad loves to tell this story about my persistence:

A Horse Story—A Father's Point of View

"When Barbara was in the fourth grade she fell in love with horses. Frankly the news of finding horses brought a sigh of relief to me, for certainly finding horses will put off finding boys for at least a few years. Nevertheless Barbara's interest gained momentum and within three months she was a member of Pony Club and worked to buy her own horse. Pony Club offered the opportunity to take riding/jumping lessons as well as participating in competitive events. The incident that comes to mind happened when she was about fifteen years old. She was competing in a jumping event and was riding the second horse she owned, Venture, a six-teen-three hand thoroughbred. After we arrived at the riding academy where the competition was being held, we took Venture out of the trailer and Barbara proceeded to saddle Venture in preparation to practice before the competition. The saddle cinch came off while taking her first fence; the saddle slipped backwards and down around Venture's hind legs. Venture went absolutely berserk. He started to buck and buck and buck while Barbara was holding on for dear life. A crowd had gathered, all watching this un-scheduled rodeo event. One remark came from the crowd, "Well get her off, she already has broken the time record for staying on a wild buck-ing horse." Finally, after many violent moves right, left, up and down, Venture succeeded in throwing

Barbara and she ended up crashing into the corral fence. Soon after, Venture fought himself free of the saddle belt and calmed down immediately. Barbara, still lying in a heap next to the fence, slowly got up, brushed herself off, retrieved the saddle and walked over to Venture and checked him for injuries. Without a word she saddled Venture, then walked around to the front of Venture and said, "OK, now it's my turn". She got back on the horse, and several hours later won a blue ribbon in the jumping competition."

Another Lesson in Hard Work

Boarding and caring for my horse was an ongoing expense, but earning that money imparted another valuable lesson on me. After a year of keeping my first horse, Lady, at the stable where I worked, it shut down. I had to find a new place to keep her. In our section of Northern California, one family, the Bruzzone family, seemed to dominate the landscape. Russ Bruzzone was the patriarch of a successful land-owning family, and he had ample pastureland and barns on a huge spread just a few miles from my home. One morning, I rode my bike to his ranch hoping to meet this man. I was lucky; he was there. He was inside the barn. I knocked on the door. I shifted my feet nervously on the dirt and waited. A moment later, an imposing figure opened the door. When he saw me his eyes narrowed for a moment and then blazed with a warmth that would soon become very familiar. I explained who I was and that I was hoping I could board my horse on his property. He thought about it for a minute and then said that we'd have to agree on a price before he could commit. He told me that he thought twenty dollars a month was a fair fee.

I didn't think I was in any position to bargain with him, and though twenty dollars a month to a thirteen-year-old girl in 1973 was a lot of money, I agreed. The fee was very reasonable.

Of course, Mr. Bruzzone didn't need the money. He could have easily let me board the horse there for free, but he didn't. I'm eternally grateful to him for not giving me the space in his barn. Just like I had to earn the money to buy the horse, I now had to continue to work to keep her sheltered and fed. Each month, I'd gather together my dollars, quarters, and other change and have my mom or dad drive me to see Mr. Bruzzone. Though he never really said anything to me other than, "thank you so much," and "see you next month," or exchanged a polite "hello" and "how are you," I could tell that Mr. Bruzzone was pleased every time I showed up. I could read the pleasure in his eyes and on his smiling lips. Only much later did I learn how much my visits and prompt payment meant to him. But that's a story for another chapter.

Retail Lessons

Eventually, I was weaned from my horse stall mucking habit and worked while in high school at a Shirtique store in town. We made and sold custom lettered t-shirts. I loved the public contact side of retailing, and learned a lot about customer service and how to develop and nurture those important relationships. I've never felt that any job was beneath me. Every day was an opportunity for me to learn something about other people, myself, or the enterprise I was engaged in. When I left Shirtique for a higher paying job at a nearby drug store, I learned something else about myself. I was more than a little bit shy. I only lasted two days at the drug store, telling the manager that I was mortified because I had to deal with a man who came up to the counter to pay for a box of condoms! I've certainly matured a great deal since then, but at the time I felt scandalized. I beat a hasty retreat to the relative safety of Shirtique where I was grateful to be welcomed back with open arms.

I believe that having retail experience at any level is invaluable to you as a fledgling entrepreneur. If nothing else, working in a store gives you a sense of what the public wants and how retailers organize their merchandise to maximize profits. No work experience is ever a waste as far as I'm concerned.

When I was growing up and saving for my horse, I was largely focused on that single goal. As the years have passed, I've seen how I've drawn time and time again on those lessons I learned about working hard, being responsible, remaining humble, and never being afraid to get in there and muck around. To borrow a phrase: there are no small jobs, just small-minded people. If you work hard, adopt more of a what's-in-it-for-me attitude, and persevere, you will transform what you think is a mind-numbing job into a mind-expanding experience.

See the big picture. It's a lot easier to learn from the ground up than it is to watch and learn as the ground grows larger just before impact.

College and Crisis

One of the major crises in my early life came in 1979 when I was a senior at Miramonte High in Orinda, California. This was the year that my parents became even more fixated on my going to college. Even though I had heard them talk for years about the value of a fine, formal education, I had not given college a thought. I planned to simply go into the world, build my empire of products, and live happily ever after. My parents, however, had always considered me to be in the club: the college-bound club. My family has always placed a high value on education. They've bought into the belief that to be a valuable and contributing member of society, you need to have a formal education; consequently, having me attend college was extremely important to them.

They knew how I felt about the idea of college, and the best reason they could give me for getting a degree was this: "College is for people who want to get a good job someday."

I thought I had made it clear to them that I never wanted a good job. I never wanted a job at all. I wanted to be my own boss. In fact, in high school I opted out of the career testing and counseling program entirely. I didn't need an ASVAB (the Armed Services Vocational Aptitude Battery) to tell me the direction my life should take. I always knew I would be an entrepreneur. I didn't need to "bubble in" a Scantron sheet and have it spit out a career for me like postal clerk or the other things my friends' reports suggested.

After four years in high school, I thought I knew everything I needed to know. And, yes, I was a little bit full of myself, but that's the privilege of youth, isn't it? Anyway, I really felt going to college was a waste of time and would only serve to delay the building of my own business. I was sure college was a totally unnecessary institution for someone like me.

My parents tried to reason with me. They used the power of tradition by letting me know college was a family value and I would be the only one without a college degree if I did not go. They told me about my grandmother who entered the University of California at Berkeley when she was just 14. They took me to fancy private schools to go on amazing tours. Eventually they resorted to recruiting other smart people they knew to come to talk to me to try to influence me because they were getting nowhere. I listened politely, nodded attentively, and thanked them profusely for their time and for sharing their ideas. As soon as they left, I'd look at my parents and say as politely as I could, "Thanks, but no thanks." I flat out refused to go. I told them that I would instead be starting my empire of product ideas.

They asked which one.

I said, "I don't know." I told them I would figure it out and I asked them not to bother me with the details. They wanted a plan. I couldn't or wouldn't give it to them. Then, when I least expected it, my parents found my "sweet" spot. They said, "If you don't go to college we are cutting off your clothing allowance." They knew my clothing allowance was extremely important to me. They knew how I liked to create outfits and design dresses and shoes. Clothing was an art for me. If an idea for a garment came into my head and I could not find it in a store or a sewing pattern book, I made it. With my clothing allowance gone, how could I ever dress for success? Somehow dress for less didn't have the same ring to it. My parents had finally hit the nerve they'd been probing for during the last year.

I agreed to go to college.

School Daze

Truth be told, while I was an extremely bright young woman, I was not into school at all. My high school attendance record was spotty at best. If the subject matter or the teacher didn't hold my interest, I could find many more interesting ideas to investigate outside the four walls of my high school classrooms. I enjoyed the social aspects of high school, and was known for being someone who bridged the great social divide that usually separated the cool kids from the nerds, the preps from the burnouts, the jocks from the brainiacs. I hated those distinctions, but recognized that they were a very real part of high school life. I could find, in nearly everyone I met, a lot to be interested in. Moving fluidly among the groups was like kayaking down a stretch of river. It was particularly exciting and a bit dangerous maneuvering between the hull-piercing, partly submerged rocks of reputations and gossip, jealousy, and ignorance.

The experience exhilarated and eventually exhausted me. There were many nights that rather than paddle furiously through the rapids of high school socializing, I stayed at home and sketched and dreamed, preferring a quiet eddy to the torrents of rushing emotions and hormone-fueled drama.

Fortunately for me, I found, if not a kindred spirit, then at least a sympathetic one, in Nancy Steiner, my high school social studies teacher. She took me aside one day in the late fall of my junior year and told me that I didn't have to come to her class except on those days I wanted to. She knew that I was a different kind of student and a thinker and that the rigid systemized nature of public education wasn't designed for someone like me. At first I was like, "Okay! I am out of here!" But over time, I'd creep back into her class because I found out that her unique approach to me was a reflection of her teaching style in general. Her class was thoughtful and engaging; she invited us to share our ideas and then challenged them in a way that felt less like a threat and more like an opportunity to learn and to think. You had to defend your ideas but not yourself, and I learned so much about myself and how to interact with people that I can neither forget Ms. Steiner nor thank her enough for breaking the rules and not my spirit. Ms. Steiner was also an author and she wrote the book, *The Memory of Sylvia Plath*. Sylvia Plath is famous for writing *The Bell Jar*; she later committed suicide. Ms. Steiner was my super-<u>she</u>ro and I found her writing and her thoughts so fascinating that I wanted to be just like her. I vowed that one day, when I had something to say and when that something would improve people's lives, I too would write a book.

A Plan Takes Shape

The following September I reluctantly went to St. Mary's College in Moraga, California, sporting the best that fall 1979 fashion had to offer. I cried the entire night before my move-in date. My parents helped me move into Mitty Girls' Dormitory and then kissed me goodbye. Almost immediately, I made an emergency call to the counseling office. I needed to see someone right away. I told them I was a new student, and I was in crisis. They said they could see me in the morning. I got up at the crack of dawn to dress for my emergency appointment. I had to present myself in just the right way to get what I wanted. I wore a chestnut brown suit with a tone-on-tone nubuck suede lapel and covered buttons. I accessorized it with a scarf and then finished off the ensemble perfectly by slipping into a buttery pair of chocolate brown leather pumps. It was conservative and fashionable, yet communicated a feeling of confidence and seriousness. I walked into Brother Giles' office and asked if I could close the door. I sat before him, looked at him and said, "Thank you for seeing me on such short notice. I am in big trouble, really BIG trouble."

Brother Giles' eyes widened and concern knitted his brow.

"My dear, what is wrong? Are you pregnant?"

I said, "No, it is much worse than that. You see, my parents are holding me in financial hostage and I am only here for the parties and the cute boys."

He leaned back in his chair, his expression blank. In my mind I saw him shake his head vigorously like a wet retriever. I can only imagine what he thought of me at that point. "Oh I see. And how can I help you?"

"You can help me by getting me out of here in three years instead of four."

St. Mary's College, run by an order of the Christian Brothers, frowns on students being graduated early, but Brother Giles took me seriously. Judging by how bluntly I'd spoken to him, he must have known he was dealing with someone who had the courage of her convictions and a definitive sense of fashion on her side! He knew he could not change my mind. He listened to my dreams and stepped over to my side of the fence. From that day forward he supported me in every way. Three years later he came to my graduation dinner and told this story. Even later he spoke at my wedding to Rich Stachowski Sr.

College: A Review for the Real Test

In looking back at my college experience, it did give me some time to mature and I had a lot of fun. I went to some great parties and met lots of cute boys. I even married one. I also noticed that the rigid distinctions marking your membership in a clique in high school softened quite a bit. Sure there were still some groups you could identify, but it seemed as though many more people would run much more freely among them. Even now, I'm grateful that I went to college, not because it helped me get a dream job, but because it exposed me to so many more people and ideas. If I haven't made it clear by now, let me remind you again of an essential requirement for being an inventor/ entrepreneur: an active and inquisitive mind. That means when you have an opportunity to experience something or speak with someone, you take it. While my parents had to coerce me into attending college—and I still refer to those years as my Prison Years—my fellow inmates taught me a lot. I walked out of St. Mary's an even more keen observer. My absorbency level was even higher. I'd worked summers and taken classes so that I got out a year early, and with a stockpile of furnishings and other accoutrements for the apartment in San Francisco I was dreaming of buying one day.

On the other hand, it was not until Mr. Kolhede's business policy class that I learned anything about business. I still believe that much of business is practical experience. I learned to be an entrepreneur from just doing. I also learned about the parts of business that I absolutely detested, including accounting. Here's what I learned about accounting in college: it is a somewhat complex endeavor best undertaken by someone with an aptitude for and interest in the field. They can easily be found by looking in the Yellow Pages of your phone book or networking with your business associates. I'm serious! This brings us back to the idea of delegation. I don't need to know everything there is to know about accounting. I just need to know how to pay an accountant and to make sure I find one who believes as strongly in integrity as I do. I also need a solid checks and balance system.

Gregarious as I had managed to become socially, speaking professionally in front of a group of people absolutely frightened me. It frightened me to the point of fainting. I am not kidding. I had a number of classes which required me to do in-class oral presentations, and I couldn't do them. The thought of it just freaked me out. I didn't know why, and I really tried hard to find out the source of this fear, but I never did figure out where the fear came from. Only later, after years and years of working at it, did I manage to overcome it, but I never understood it.

As I mentioned earlier, I wasn't thrilled about going to college. I did learn a lot about myself by going, and I did learn some things about business along the way. Mr. Kolhede, my business policy professor, reviewed this chapter on successful entrepreneurs, and offered these insights:

Firms of all sizes use a type of analysis similar to Barbara Carey's ten characteristics of a successful entrepreneur when conceiving, developing, and launching successful new products. This process is called SWOT analysis. It involves diagnosing the internal Strengths and Weaknesses of the entrepreneur's organization (the "S" and W" part of SWOT analysis). Of course no organization exists in a vacuum, so the environment outside the firm must also be thoroughly evaluated in terms of the *opportunities* and *threats* that it presents (the "O" and "T" part of SWOT analysis). By going through this process, a firm can uncover opportunities that result from such external factors as changes in consumer tastes and new technological advancements. At the point when the entrepreneur can identify those opportunities that match up with the resources and overall capabilities of his or her firm, the organization's competitive advantage is discovered and winning products can originate.

However, SWOT analysis shouldn't become a mechanical exercise and can only produce successful results when those with the characteristics Barbara described utilize this tool. For example, the entrepreneur must have the *intrapersonal* attribute of being *observant* of the trends occurring in the market place and tuned into all other dimensions of the firm's environment as well. Also, in order to fully pick up on outside opportunities that a company can convert into winning products, the entrepreneur should examine the firm's environment from multiple perspectives. For example, an entrepreneur whose talents and background lie mostly in the area of accounting and finance might miss new product opportunities that might have been picked up by an individual with a different set of skills. Thus, the interpersonal skills that Barbara Carey speaks of should be brought to bear. In other words, listen to all members of your organization (as well as your current and potential customers), make full use of their talents so that new product opportunities aren't lost when they come your way.

Eric Kolhede, Ph.D.
Chairman, Department of Business Administration
St. Mary's College of Moraga, California

I did take one other course that really excited me. Ironically, it wasn't at St. Mary's but at nearby Cal State Hayward. It was a marketing class and as the semester project, we were to conceive of and then formulate a plan for bringing to market a product. That class and project fully engaged me and seemed like just the preparation I needed to get ready for my next big step—going out on my own as an inventor and entrepreneur. Unfortunately, before I could take that next big step, I had to overcome one more obstacle.

But I Thought You Said All I Had to Do Was...

After my graduation from St. Mary's, my parents again had a plan for me. I was encouraged to start my own business, but only after I had experienced what they called a "real" job. They explained that I had a lifetime to have my own business and in order to be successful at it, I would need real world experience. I would need a more solid foundation than my passionate desire to avoid, at all costs, working for someone else. I asked them how long it would take for this foundation to solidify. They said one year. I was willing to do anything to make sure I was successful at my own business, including waiting to start it. After all, I had graduated one year early from college so this would be a practical experience. According to my folks I was going to learn a lot.

We decided that because I went through school so quickly that it would be reasonable for me to take the summer off following my graduation. I would begin my job search in September 1982. The only company I had any interest in working for was IBM. Back then, IBM was truly "Big Blue". It was the *crème de la crème* of the business world. At the time, IBM was the brass ring that everyone was reaching for, but for me it ended up being the lead handcuffs that weighed me down. To me, IBM cultivated a culture of corporate lemmings, rather than independent thinkers. I know my choice of IBM sounds completely contradictory; if I wanted to avoid the corporate world, why in the world would I want to work for *the* bastion of corporate rigidity? I looked at it this way: if I really wanted real world experience, why not work for the best? I would work for them, but only for a year. After all, I'd mucked stalls for years to get a horse; how difficult could one year in the button-down world at IBM be? I was willing to sacrifice a year because I kept my eye on the larger picture.

Working at IBM would give me the credibility and credentials that I needed to start my own business. Secretly my parents were keeping their fingers crossed that I would find a career in an established corporate environment and stop this silly nonsense about building my empire of products. But I stuck to my plan. I would get my solid foundation and resign 365 days later. Hopefully along the way I would be able to add some value to a company. It would be a win-win situation. What could be better?

An Aquatic Acquaintance

The summer I graduated from St. Mary's College Mom and I went to Hawaii. On our third day there we were basking in the sun. Out of nowhere came a man and woman stepping out of the ocean surreally, just like sea creatures clad with snorkels and masks. They plopped themselves exhaustedly on the sand. I introduced myself and they told me they had just snorkeled for two miles. They looked completely worn out, so I offered to buy them a soft drink when I realized they couldn't have carried any money with them. They accepted. We chatted a bit and I found out, to my surprise, that the man was an IBM executive from San Francisco. I told him I was going to work for IBM in the fall and he asked me what division. I admitted that I didn't actually have the job yet but I was planning to get one there. He chuckled at my naiveté and my unabashed self-confidence, but invited me to call him in September. I am still amazed that the one and only man I worked for literally appeared as if by magic from out of the sea.

Although I was supremely confident that I *would* work for IBM, this chance meeting was really the foot in the door I needed. I called him on September 1st and he set up the first of my five interviews on the 6th. Mom and I shopped for blue dress-for-success IBM power suits, men's style white shirts, and the women's bow ties that were so much a part of the '80s women's look. I pinned my hair up into the most serious looking librarian bun I could, took my serious vitamins, and marched off to battle. After I made it to the next round of interviews, my mother and I went out shopping for another suit. We repeated the process between interviews, until I was offered a sales position. My career at IBM officially started in September 1982. I circled a day on my calendar one year from my start date: September 23, 1983. According to my schedule, that would be the day I walked out of IBM a free woman. If they had let me, during that first day on the job, I would have submitted to the Human Resources Department a dated letter of resignation along with my W-4 form.

IBM Sales Boot Camp

Since my first experience with IBM was so unusual, I daresay very few, if any, of the other employees' first experience with a corporate executive took place on a beach while wearing a bikini, it would have to follow that I didn't tread the usual path once hired. Normally, an account executive worked in the corporate offices for a year before being enrolled in the Corporate Sales Training Program (CSTP). When I think of IBM, I often think in CAPITAL LETTERS, because everything was systematized, programmed, and rigid. Except in my case. For whatever reason, maybe because they had a spot to fill in the upcoming CSTP, I was immediately enrolled. That meant I was in a sales training class with a group of people who'd already been exposed to the Big Blue Way for a year. I don't really know if that was an advantage or a disadvantage, to be honest. All I know is that I stood out a bit just for that fact, and I was already a part of the San Francisco office's corporate mythology. Everyone in the training class knew that I had met the District Manager on a Hawaiian beach, thanks to an insecure rookie girl who found out from the District Manager, then had to blab it to everyone. She conspired with the men in the program, who as far as I was concerned suffered from Big Blue Balls, because they all tried to make life as difficult for me as they could. This turned out not to be so bad. I maintained my composure and my professionalism and never spoke a bad word about or to her. I watched her single-handedly dig herself deep into a hole the size of the Grand Canyon. She not only gossiped about me, but she gossiped about everyone else in the department. She ended up with quite a bad reputation. Why can't people see that when they talk negatively about others, they only make themselves look unfavorable? Chances are that if someone is gossiping to you about someone else, they are also gossiping about you to others. Don't trust this person.

I tried my best to stay above the fray and just went about doing my best. I have found that no matter the situation, quality will always win out eventually. Even though my fear of public speaking still plagued me, I made it through the program and became a rookie salesperson. I was given Idaho as my territory and in just one month I made my entire year's sales quota.

One of my most vivid memories of my time at IBM has nothing to do with sales. The training program was held in New Jersey, and one day they gave us the afternoon off and a group of us headed into Manhattan to do some shopping and to dine out. We were down in SoHo, a trendy shopping area, and I was standing at the corner of Spring and West Broadway when a pair of mounted policemen and their beautiful horses trotted by. I thought, "How great is that? Those guys are doing something really worthwhile with their lives. They're performing a valuable service and doing something that they clearly must love. That's how life should be."

The light changed and we crossed the street. A few minutes later we were sitting in a restaurant and the conversation revolved around quotas and toner cartridges. It all melded into a drone of noise. I sat looking out the window at the lively scene playing out in the streets. A woman clutched the hem of her wind-swept skirt with one hand while she hailed a cab with the other. A young couple walked hand in hand and then raised them like a tollgate as an older man pulling a shopping cart sped between them. They turned and laughed, bowing and waving to him while the flow of pedestrian traffic split and merged around them. I was going to trade my moment of Manhattan idyll for my own private Idaho in a few weeks. How would I get through this?

In September of 1983, I put my notice in and left the company two weeks later. IBM had treated me wonderfully and I learned a lot while working for them. *I* was the one who did not fit their mold. I learned I hated working to fulfill someone else's vision. I just couldn't find any passion or excitement at IBM. It was the most boring time of my life. I was a clock-watcher and the first out the door at the end of each day. I had a calendar on my wall and crossed off every day. I highlighted one special day in September 1983, because that would be the day I would be free.

Barbara Carey's Points to Remember:

- Persistence and patience are two important traits that any entrepreneur needs. I'm a pretty determined individual and I've worked hard to get where I want to be. I've also overcome a number of obstacles along the way. The great thing about challenges is how much you learn from them—especially about yourself. Maybe high school and college weren't obstacles for you, but they were for me. I was able to get through my Prison Years by keeping my eyes on the prize and being persistent and patient.

- School was never that important to me because it always seemed to focus on getting a good job. That was never what I wanted to do. I didn't want a job. I wanted to be an entrepreneur. It was only when one of our assignments was to conceptually bring a product to market, and I was able to takes bits and pieces of information from other classes to do this project, that I realized the value of general knowledge. I constantly gather information now, knowing that I may be able to put it to use in service of what I really want to do later.

- Today, I am a voracious reader and prolific writer. I read to become a multifaceted person who understands other people and other cultures. I write to express myself and to challenge my mind. Despite my success, I still thirst for knowledge. My hobby is research because I've figured out that the more I know, the more complete a person I can be. The more I understand about other people, the more compassionate I can be toward others. I use Google's search engine every day to check out new ideas, new concepts, new anything. I still don't believe you must have a formal college education to succeed, but you must have knowledge. Knowledge is power.

- Surround yourself with people who believe in you. Brother Giles, who was my counselor throughout my college years, was also my art teacher. One class I took from him was decorating Ukranian Easter eggs (my parents actually paid good money for that class). This may seem like a frivolous class but I loved art and Brother Giles and I had a tremendous connection. As I mentioned earlier, he knew that I felt college was a prison and that my goal was to finish in three years. He was totally supportive of that goal. My association with Brother Giles reinforced this valuable lesson, which is worth repeating: surround yourself with people who believe in you. But don't just use them; don't just take. Give back to these people. I used to make brownies for Brother Giles, and I spent time visiting with him because not only did I enjoy his company, but I felt he enjoyed mine as well. Today I never turn down a budding entrepreneur who asks for my advice. I am willing to learn from anyone who has had success or failure if they are willing to share it. The lesson here is to build a circle of supporters, and to treat them with support and respect as well.

- At IBM I learned there were a lot of people who thought like I did but were afraid to break away from the perceived security of a big company. Unfortunately, many of these individuals were miserable. Some had been there 20 years and were simply clones in blue suits and white shirts. When I struggled through IBM sales school, my instructor said that maybe IBM wasn't the correct career choice for me. I thought, "no kidding." I clearly wasn't that type of person. I just had to survive for one year. While some people thought they were part of a privileged group at IBM, I just felt like a robot who could not speak her mind. My experience there confirmed every negative thought that I'd had since the beginning about working for a big company. At the same time I learned a lot from the people there. I talked to them about their goals and aspirations and learned that excuses for not leaving the company were all about fear. Many of them told me to get out while I could. I am sure working for IBM or other large corporations is grand for some people, but it is not for everyone.

- One thing everyone needs to learn is to listen to the advice of others, seriously considering the knowledge and experience they can bring to the table. You don't have to take anyone's advice and certainly not in its totality. However, by being a good listener, you can meld ideas from others to form your own unique thought process and actions. Being able to network and learn from others is an extremely valuable business tool.

- I have made a point of talking with anyone who wishes to share anything—people on airplanes, in taxis, on buses. And I learn something from all of them. What you need to remember is that you really can do what you want to do. You can become a successful entrepreneur if you really want to. I have always looked for reasons why I can do something, not reasons why I can't. I have a plethora of reasons to value this approach.

The Apple Doesn't Fall Very Far From the Tree—Even When It's Pushed

Just as I carefully planned my career, I also had a straightforward plan for my personal life. I would marry the love of my life and have six children—a boy first, followed by five little girls. I love children and among my grandparents' grandchildren I believed I was the one destined to have a litter of kids. My plan started well when my son Rich Jr. was born in 1985, but it was a most complicated C-section birth and Rich Jr. would be the only child I would ever have.

The next day after the C-section, the doctors placed our baby in my arms and said, "It's a boy." I fell in love with him instantly. I instinctively knew I needed to be the one to nurture him. I did not want my child growing up in daycare and having strangers care for him. I did not want him coming home to an empty house because I was working. I vowed to be there for him.

When Rich Jr. was three weeks old I was ready to throw a party because I had kept him alive that long! This mother thing was much harder than I expected. No one told me babies don't talk to you and I felt as if my brain was turning to mush. I had a conflict. I loved being a mom but I was in desperate need of mental stimulation. I could not leave my baby, but I was craving the adrenaline rush I got from selling my own ideas. So I resolved my conflict by packing up my son, his car seat, my breast pump, and my presentation materials and heading for Bentonville, Arkansas, to visit with a Wal-Mart buyer. We flew in a small plane. If you think it is tricky traveling with sales samples and presentation materials, imagine how much fun it is when you include a baby and his necessities. I would like to see a man try that!

So I suppose it's no wonder that in many ways he followed in my business footsteps. Ironically, I followed in my parents' footsteps by making sure that my son pursued a college education. Like me, he wasn't interested in college per se, but fortunately his agenda included playing college football, so I didn't have to resort to anything like the means my parents did to convince me.

I knew that Rich wanted to be a man who works with his hands and follows his own path, but I realized that I was fortunate to have a college degree and a year of work experience when I tried to find people to help finance my Time-Out Watch. Though it didn't matter to me that I'd graduated and had gone on to work for Big Blue, it did impress the investors. If nothing else, it signaled to them that I was a serious and responsible person who could follow through on and complete tasks.

It shouldn't have come as a surprise to me that my son Rich Jr. came to me recently and said that he was really tired of college. He wanted to enroll at a specialty school so he could get the training he needed to fulfill one of his dreams—he wants to design and build race cars. Being an automotive enthusiast myself, I could hardly stand in his way. He's going to get an education, just one that is more specifically suited to his needs. I'll make sure that together we round out the general knowledge part.

Barbara Carey's Characteristics of a Successful Entrepreneur

Now that you've heard about my development as a person and as a professional, I want to take a few moments to summarize the important elements of these opening chapters. Obviously, I think it is important to do a thorough inventory of your skills, aptitudes, and desires. I think this is important no matter if you are interested in being an entrepreneur or not. Once we leave school, we stop getting report cards, but that doesn't mean that a periodic assessment isn't necessary. During my twenty years as a successful entrepreneur, I have studied my own actions as well as those of others to determine what has led to my success. In this chapter, we're going to examine the characteristics that I believe have helped me succeed. I was born with some of them, others I have had to work very hard to develop, but all of them have required a conscious effort on my part to refine and to hone. After each project I have gone back through my actions to determine which moves made me succeed or fail. It is my opinion that developing all of these characteristics can dramatically improve your success rate as an entrepreneur. Read through them carefully and determine which of them are your strong points and which of them you need to develop.

Start With Yourself

I strongly believe that unless you have a desire for self-improvement, you will have a difficult time leading the kind of life and business that this book proposes as its model. In the course of my varied experiences, I've met a lot of people who were successful, but not nearly as many who were fulfilled. We always seem to be circling around this idea of how to define success. Can you put a dollar amount on it? A number of units shipped? Cars and houses owned?

Perhaps you can and many people do. But *The Carey Formula* is designed to do more than just increase your financial net worth. It is my fervent hope that you can also employ these steps to increase your personal worth and, by extension, make a difference in the lives of your friends, family, and community. When I look at someone like Bill Gates, I'm impressed by the incredibly successful business he created, amazed how his and his company's innovations have transformed our lives, and in awe of the fortune he has amassed. But I'm equally in awe of what he and his wife, Melinda, have done with their foundation and their commitment to making the world a better place. A cynic may say that they can afford to be generous given how much of a personal fortune they have, but there are many other wealthy individuals who have not contributed as generously as the Gates have.

Bill Gates is just one contemporary example of a wealthy person whose philanthropic efforts should be recognized. Historically, we can point to individuals and families like the Fords who transformed an industry and a nation, and whose charitable works continue to transform and better our society. Whether it's Andrew Carnegie creating public libraries around the country or endowing a world-class symphony hall, or the many, many contributions of the Rockefeller family, our business leaders have set the bar high for our charitable works.

One Family's Story of Giving

Why am I talking about this issue at all? Well, there is one family, more specifically one individual, who is probably less well known than those previously mentioned, but whose foundation has had far-reaching impact that you should know about. By some accounts, John D. MacArthur was a cantankerous and notoriously miserable man. The son of a firebrand preacher who traveled the country evangelizing, he kept his family on the brink of financial ruin. His youngest son dropped out of school at age eight; he himself couldn't cut it as a reporter, pilot in the Canadian Royal Air Force, or businessman (three of his ventures failed) and was, according to his biographer, a miserable father who engaged in a long-lived and bitter feud with his only son. He was a man who once claimed to have 3,500 lawyers on his staff to pursue lawsuits against others and to defend him from the suits others brought. Even after amassing an enormous fortune that began in the dark days of the Depression, when he hit on the idea of selling one-dollar-a-month insurance policies, he still flew coach. He was also reported to whisk away half-eaten sandwiches from empty tables in restaurants so he could eat them later, and, for a man who at this death in 1978 was the second wealthiest man in the country, lived modestly with his wife in a small apartment.

Fortunately, by the time he died, he hadn't done much with his fortune. He claimed that he was good at making money but not so good at giving it away. To avoid a huge tax penalty upon his death, he had established a foundation using the majority of his two and a half billion-dollar empire. Like me, he believed that if you were good at something, hire people to do the other things. And that's exactly what he did with the foundation. He hired people who could find a way to use his fortune for the betterment of society. He left no instructions on how it should be spent. The board of the MacArthur Foundation decided that one of its actions would be to award a prize named after the foundation's benefactor. Each year, about nine million dollars are awarded to various recipients in a wide variety of fields.

The number of recipients and the amounts awarded to them vary each year, but the total number of dollars awarded is but a fraction of the other monies disbursed. The awards have gone to writers, scientists, business people, musicians, filmmakers, carpenters, and anthropologists, to name just a few. The selection committee has few hard and fast criteria other than that the recipient be a US citizen and not hold political office at the time of the grant. Essentially, a nomination committee scours the country looking for creative people in all areas. Each year, often twice a year, at no regular intervals, those nominated go through a review process (they aren't aware they've been nominated, and no, you can't nominate yourself or anyone else you know), after which the winners are notified. The money is to help them do what they do best better by freeing them from other obligations, which might distract them from their work. Imagine how much faster your idea might be put in motion if you could devote yourself to its pursuit full-time and not have to worry about feeding your family.

The Genius of Creativity

Nice story, but what the heck does this have to do with the qualities of entrepreneurs? Good question. Over time, the MacArthur Prize (sometimes known as a MacArthur Grant or MacArthur Award or a MacArthur Foundation Fellowship) has come to be known popularly as a "genius" award. I'm not going to spend any time debating with you what exactly the word "genius" means and whether every one of its recipients is or isn't a true genius. That's not the point here. What I want to talk about is a wonderful little book I came across a few years ago called, *Uncommon Genius: How Great Ideas Are Born* by Denise Shekerjian. In her book, Ms. Shekerjian interviews forty winners of the MacArthur Prize and asks them to talk about creativity. The book's cover announces her intent of "tracing the creative impulse."

I find the stories and the insights of these winners to be absolutely fascinating. Ms. Shekerjian's work in identifying the source of these so-called geniuses' ideas and the methods they employ to foster their own ideas and creative development makes for invaluable reading. I feel there is a very clear distinction between an inventor and an entrepreneur. It is the nature of the inventor to be creative. Entrepreneurs may think creatively, but they often don't conceive a product or a process.

As you work your way through this chapter, I believe that the difference between the two will become much clearer. My job wouldn't be complete if I didn't do something else besides identify the key characteristics of each. I will also offer suggestions on how you can develop the qualities I find to be most evident in entrepreneurs/inventors. Keep in mind that this list is not definitive, but is based on my experiences and on the reading I have done in the fields of creativity and creative problem solving, as well as intelligence.

Multiple Intelligences

Ironically, one of the people Ms. Shekerjian interviewed in her book is a man by the name of Howard Gardener. Dr. Gardener was, at the time of his writing, a researcher at Harvard University. One of his claims to fame is his work in the study of intelligence. In particular, he popularized the notion that we should think of intelligence not as a single quality, but as a set of what he called "Multiple Intelligences." Essentially, Dr. Gardener quantified and formalized a concept we all understand. For example, it's likely that at some point in your life you've heard someone say, "I'm not so book smart, but I'm people smart." Dr. Gardener calls that "people smart" form of brainpower intrapersonal intelligence. The six intelligences that Dr. Gardener identified are: linguistic, logical-mathematical, spatial, musical, kinesthetic, and intrapersonal. As I've said before, I'm really only good at a very few things, or stated another way, I have a more highly refined intelligence in a few areas, while I struggle with others.

One of the things I love about Dr. Gardener's work is that, as he says, he has taken the age-old question, "How smart is he?" and turned it into a more meaningful and inspiring question, "How is he smart?" Some of you reading this book may not be fully convinced that you have what it takes to make it as an entrepreneur/inventor. Well, in the old days when we looked at intelligence, we measured it as a single dimension like IQ. Gardener's work has opened up intelligence to reveal its multiple dimensions to show us all the many ways we can be smart and creative. Instead of focusing on what you may be lacking, I urge you to focus on what you have and what you can do with what you have.

What I've been stressing all along in this book is that it is important to have a great deal of self-knowledge or intrapersonal intelligence. As I told you before, I'm a fairly introspective person, but I'm not one of those navel gazers who fixate on myself simply for the sake of being self-involved. Instead, I'm constantly assessing myself in terms of my skills, interests, and strengths and weaknesses as they apply to my work. I encourage you to do the same kind of inventory. You may want to use Dr. Gardener's scheme as a framework for this self-assessment. To help you, I've taken these somewhat technical terms and explained them in the next section.

Know Yourself

Linguistic	Your linguistic intelligence reflects your verbal skills. In school, you may have been tested for reading speed and reading comprehension. In addition, when you talk about linguistic intelligence you are referring to someone's ability to express himself in words—either written or spoken. An important component of being an entrepreneur is being able to articulate your ideas clearly and succinctly in presentations to buyers. Marketers are masters of manipulating words to not just convey information, but to elicit emotional reactions. Your facility with language can often make the difference between success and failure.
Logical-Mathematical	As I told you earlier, I could not get my head around accounting. As good as I am with words, that's how bad I am when it comes to numbers. However, I understood early on that I needed to have a grasp of basic concepts in order to determine the financial viability of a proposed idea. Today, I know my way around a profit and loss spreadsheet like I do the alphabet and can shake

down a balance sheet in seconds. Numbers have become second nature to me. Designing strategic business plans and cash flow scenarios has become my hobby and I am almost addicted to this. This was one skill area that I knew needed improvement in my early years. I've gotten myself up to par for many of my needs. The rest I turn over to experts. What I find interesting is that math and logic often go hand in hand. Though I'm not a numbers person, I do consider myself to be logical. In other words, I feel as though I am proficient in using a systematic and rational thought process to arrive at a conclusion that is soundly based on objective facts.

When it comes to numbers, most of the numbers we are concerned with have a dollar sign in front of them. For that reason, I also have been doing some reading recently in the emerging field of behavioral economics. This field of study has some interesting things to say about the thought processes we engage in while we make financial decisions. Generally, what behavioral economics tells us is that each of us thinks we are smarter and more logical than our choices prove us to be. It is also interesting to see how what seems logical to one person seems completely illogical to another. For an interesting look at how this plays out in business and personal finance, I highly recommend Gary Belsky and Thomas Gilovich's book *Why Smart People Make Big Money Mistakes and How to Correct Them*. Not only can you learn to avoid making those mistakes, but you will also learn a great deal about consumers' habits—

valuable information when you are doing your market analysis, pricing analysis, negotiating with buyers, etc. As important as it is to know yourself, it is equally important to understand others.

Spatial

I have a friend who I consider to be a very smart person, but he is clearly lacking in this area. The other day, he bought a circular saw that came with a plastic carrying case. The saw came packaged in the case, and the case fits in a Styrofoam block the same outside dimension as the inside of the box. Well, after taking the saw out of the case, it came time to put it back in. He had a devil of a time orienting the power tool so that it could fit snugly inside the molded outline of the saw. He sat and muttered and turned the saw over, flipped it end for end and could not get the saw oriented properly to fit in the space. He's not alone. I know many other people who are not very proficient at manipulating objects in their heads. Remember those IQ tests that showed you a line drawing and asked you to identify which of the other four choices represented the same figure turned ninety degrees? Well, those questions were designed to test your spatial intelligence. Why is it important to have a good spatial intelligence as an inventor?

For one thing, I can't imagine any design idea that doesn't require you to be able to visualize and manipulate an object in space. In addition, creating the right packaging requires similar thinking. One issue that you may not have even considered is how many units will fit in a box.

What size shipping boxes are most cost-effective? Again, all of these considerations go into design and it's your spatial intelligence that you will draw on to help you solve those problems.

Musical Of the seven intelligences that Gardener identifies, this one is probably the least important when it comes to implementing *The Carey Formula*. However, if this happens to be one of your interests or strengths, you should consider creating a product that would be useful in this area. The same is true for the other intelligences as well. Chances are if you have strength in a particular area, you will find enjoyment in doing an activity that relies on the application of that skill. Remember: individuals have made millions by focusing on a hobby or interest and inventing a product that meets a particular need in that area.

Kinesthetic The easiest way to remember what this type of intelligence is, is to have an image in your mind of a modern dancer running and leaping across the stage or a basketball player driving to the basket, jumping, twisting underneath the rim, and then reversing their position in the air before slamming the ball home. We admire these people for their skill but probably don't attribute it to any kind of intelligence. Yet, if you've ever watched a diving competition or a gymnastics event, you've probably marveled at the participants' skill at controlling their bodies. How do they know when they've completed two full revolutions and one and a half twists? Well, their brains are keeping track of their position in the air. They are keenly aware of their surroundings as well as what each muscle group is doing. Now, you don't have to be a world-class athlete in order to have kinesthetic intelligence. If you are some-one who is keenly aware of what is going on in your body, learn best by doing rather than read-ing a book or following a set of instructions, or are a very tactile person whose sense of touch is finely honed, you have a kinesthetic intellect that is highly developed and of great value to an inventor. One of the things I like about my job is how I've transferred my passion for fashion (which has a strong tactile component—have you ever seen how women shop by touch?) to my inven-tions. I get to work with my hands, which is one of the reasons why I love gardening so much. As a result, I am hyper-aware not just of what my prod-ucts look like, but how they feel. Again, I garden as much for the visual pleasure I take in seeing the plants and flowers as I do in the tactile sensation of feeling the earth in my hands or the taut skin of a succulent brushing against my knuckle.

The whole field of ergonomics, studying how a product fits with and harmonizes with the human form, is a kinesthetic playground. Think of the Good Grips line of kitchen products. A manual can opener is a manual can opener, but the Good Grips can openers, spatulas, etc., all feel particularly comfortable in your hand. Remember: you don't have to invent a new way to open cans or turn over eggs; sometimes all you have to do is refine an existing concept. Don't discount your kinesthetic sense!

Intrapersonal People who are "people" people are the luckiest people in the world (sorry, I couldn't resist testing your musical recall) because of avenues opened to them through their social skills. What can I say about this kind of intelligence that you don't already know? We all have come across someone at one point or another in our lives who is a brilliant person but a cold fish in social situations. Your entrepreneurial business ventures are as much about communicating and interacting as they are about innovating and creating new products. I've told you already that I consider my skills as a salesperson to be my major strength, but selling someone is only one color in the intrapersonal spectrum. I get many of my ideas for products simply from talking to and listening to people. I also refine my concepts, even after they've gone to market, by eliciting feedback from others.

I Knew Her Way Back When...

"Barbie" is one of my oldest friends. Not by age, but length of time I have known her. Some words that come to mind when I think of "Barbie" are: risk-taker, adventurous, fun-loving, full of life, spontaneous, spirited, and the first one to try something. One could never have a truer friend in life. Though I live on the East coast now, and "Barbie" on the West coast, e-mail has made it easier to keep in touch.

It all started in Mrs. Hoisington's first grade class. We were inseparable and often spent the night at each other's house. We shared everything, including our families. I had an older brother who used to take us "cruisin' the main" in his souped-up GTO. We giggled and laughed and thought we were the coolest things to hit the streets.

At fifth grade camp in the summer of 1972, a group of us decided to try fishing. Just as we finally figured out how to bait the hook, "Barbie" got stung by a bee and was rushed off to the hospital. ("Barbie" is highly allergic to bee stings.) You would think that she would stay away from bees, but at my house we had rosemary bushes that were covered with bees. "Barbie" devised a game called "Bug-a-bee" where we would tickle the bee with the garden hose and then run away.

"Barbie's" family had a place on the Russian River, and the two of us spent countless hours mooning over a cute boy named Steve. We had our own secret language called gibberish, so no one would know what we were talking about. One year, "Barbie's" mom took us to the Russian River early while the river was still in flood. I very carefully walked to what I thought was the edge of the dock and dove straight into the swollen river. It turned out that a second dock came out, and I dove head first into cement. I came back up with the entire front of me scratched and bleeding, and my teeth smashed in. "Barbie" held my hand the whole way home. Her mom took me straight to our orthodontist's home, where he pulled my teeth back out and wired them together. It was the most painful experience, but "Barbie" was by my side the entire time, holding my hand.

"Barbie" was friendly with everyone she met. Whenever we drove somewhere in the car and there was a car next to us with out-of-state plates, "Barbie" would roll down her window, and with a big grin yell, "Welcome to California!"

There are a lot of firsts in "Barbie's" life too. She got her ears pierced first and we decided that I should have mine pierced, too, though my mother said no. That didn't stop "Barbie". She got an ice cube and a needle, and we went into her bedroom, and she poked that needle through my ear, and we put in a pair of her earrings. Ouch! She was the first one to kiss a boy, and we talked and laughed about it all night. "Barbie" was impatient to get on with life, so she quickly went through high school and graduated from college in only three years. At our fifth year high school reunion, "Barbie" was the first one to be married.

In business, "Barbie" worked as a "think tank" trying to always come up with new ideas or inventions. As you will read, some of them worked and some of them didn't. My nine-year-old daughter is a huge fan of Hairagami®; she also asked me if my friend, "Barbie", still had any of that doggie nail polish left, so she can paint our dog's nails.

I still can't help but be impressed whenever I go to the toy store and pick up any of the Water Talkie series from Wild Planet Toys because "Barbie" has passed on the entrepreneurial gene to her son, and he invented those toys. Both "Barbie" and her son, Rich Jr., have been featured in several leading publications, and I love to read about them and think I knew her way back when...

Kathryn P. Bowler Mitchell
Domestic Engineer/Home Manager ☺

I started this section by mentioning the importance of knowing yourself. This is important in terms of assessing your skills, evaluating your strengths and weaknesses, and deciding on a direction to take your product development initiatives. I don't know about you, but I have a hard time dealing with people who don't seem to have a firm grasp on who they are or how others perceive them. I'm talking here about simple things like people who don't recognize how harshly they speak or who have distracting vocal or body habits when they do presentations. I'm also thinking of people who aren't aware of how they tend to finger point or get overly defensive when you challenge their ideas or statements, or people who are inconsistent with their statements and thoughts and contradict themselves, revealing their insecurities. I'm sure an entire cast of characters is parading their annoying faults and blind spots in front of you as you read this. Why can't they see what they are doing? They don't seem to feel a sense of others' reaction to their actions.

Well, not everyone has a fully developed intrapersonal intelligence. Much of those people's problem can be attributed to their not being as observant as they need to be. Being observant is the first necessary attribute for success that we'll turn our attention to in the next section.

Being Observant

I love the old joke that goes, "When I was a kid we were so poor, I couldn't even pay attention." Well, neither being observant nor paying attention costs you anything at all except your energy. Having an open and active mind doesn't depend on your bank account's total. However, developing your powers of observation can pay huge dividends. I can't stress enough how important it is to always stay aware of what is going on both in the marketplace and in the world around you. It is far too easy to go through life as a passive observer. You are bombarded daily with so much sensory stimulation that it is easy to get overloaded and choose to tune out completely. You can't do that. I know that it will take focus and effort, but if there is one skill that will really aid you the most, it is being observant.

Sometimes being observant will necessitate that you slow down, stay still, and stay quiet. For many people doing any of those three things feels like an impossibility. The fact that we live our lives at hyperspeed doesn't help. One of the things that I've found most useful in developing the skills of observation and slowing down is to record my observations on paper. I highly recommend that you carry a notebook with you wherever you go. A small stenographer's or reporter's notepad can easily fit in your handbag or pocket. Any time an observation or thought comes to you, jot it down. Whether it is a spiral-bound notebook or a three-ring binder doesn't matter, just so long as it is a notebook that is solely devoted to your observations and ideas.

As far as finding quiet time to reflect, all I can say is that it's necessary. Even fifteen minutes alone in your room without the television, your spouse, your children—or anyone else—to distract you will not only relax you, but put you in a better place to receive inspiration. I know that some of my best ideas have come to me in the bathtub. I've always wanted someone to invent a watertight container for my notebook or PDA so I could enter those ideas before they get lost. Anyone?

Book of Knowledge: Recording Your Thoughts

Ever since I left college, I have been keeping my thoughts on paper in a series of leather-bound notebooks I call my Book of Knowledge. I now have forty-two of these notebooks, and I'm working on another as I write this. I take the notebook with me wherever I go. In addition to the usual to-do lists, I include lists of goals, future products, and impressions and observations in my Book of Knowledge. Why bother to write these things down? Well, if you're anything like I am, the pace of your life is so hectic and the rate of your thoughts is so fast, that unless you write it down you may lose it. I also think that writing things down represents a commitment of time and energy. By putting something in your notebook, you are saying, "This is important enough that I want to take the time to preserve it." Mentally, this is an important process. It's important also to treat your notebook as a non-judgmental friend to whom you can share anything and everything. This is not the time to listen to your internal editor telling you what's good and what's bad, what belongs in it and what doesn't. It is simply a recording device and neat handwriting isn't necessary!

How can your notebook help you develop the skill of observation? By calling it your Book of Knowledge, the title helps to reinforce that it is a record of what you've thought about and noticed during the day. I don't like the idea of it being a journal or a blow-by-blow account of everything that went on during your day. This Book of Knowledge has a more specific purpose than that. I suggest that you divide your Book of Knowledge into various sections: Observations, Thoughts, Goals, Dreams and Questions. To start with, make a decision that each week, you are going to record entries in each of those sections. In other words, record things you observed/ noticed, five things you thought about, things you heard/overheard, goals/to-dos you have for that week (related to your main goal of becoming an entrepreneur), and things you wondered about.

The main objectives here are to train your mind to be on the lookout for input from your environment, to become more aware of trends in your own thinking (which is something experts refer to as "meta-cognition" or thinking about thinking), to reinforce the commitment you've made to being a creative person, and to have a record you can refer back to when you have one of those, "It's on the tip of my tongue/ brain" moments of failed recall. For example, have you noticed how Campbell's Soup cans are now stacked in new plastic rollout shelf units instead of being stacked right-side-up in rows? I wonder how much Campbell's charges the stores for those units? Or do they have to pay the stores a fee for the privilege of this type of merchandising? Do the stock boys like this kind of shelving better? Does the soup being on its side have an effect on settling of ingredients? Is that the most space efficient type of packaging for that product?

While some of those questions may not seem earth shattering, they aren't Jack Handey's *Deep Thoughts*, either. They are useful questions that you may choose to pursue the answers to or not. Most important, they are training your mind to think in a new and more focused direction. To be an entrepreneur you have to think like one. Being a more skilled observer and recorder of your impressions is one step in that direction.

Being Empathetic

Having an understanding of what people want and need will always serve you well as an entrepreneur. Remember when I talked about shifting your focus from inner world (yourself) to outer world (others)? Well, here is where you tune your antennae to focus on the external world of other people, trends, and movements. I always think of creating products that can make the average person's life easier. When something in everyday life frustrates me, I am aware of it. I begin to think of ways to eliminate that frustration though a product. I talk to my friends and people I meet. They tell me what they'd like to see in the product arena. We all want things to be easier or at least more efficient so developing a mass-market product that does that has the potential for great success. I also look for products that are fun.

Being Knowledgeable

Developing an understanding of the marketplace and the competition will go a long way toward success as an inventor and entrepreneur and save you countless hours of fruitless effort. If there is a perfect product that exists (if there really is such a thing as "perfect"), why expend hours and dollars to compete against it unless you can come up with a hook that compels change? Even though my Dittie™ tampon product (See Chapter 8) faces long-term established competition from several fronts, I chose to challenge that competition with a different tactic. When you walk up to a store counter with a Dittie™ box (see image page 283), my breakthrough package design doesn't yell to all those in the store that, "She is buying feminine protection." The bag boy doesn't become awkward because he doesn't automatically know what he is putting in the bag. The established competition's packaging shouts it out. Also, I don't need to be number one in such a huge category, because a fortune can be made with just a small share of such a large market.

I also thoroughly scan the retail aisles looking for products that, like tampons, need to be updated or refreshed—whether it's the product itself or the packaging/marketing. In addition, you need to pay attention to the prices of the products in your category, what their packaging consists of, etc. We will go into this in much more detail later on, but suffice it to say you can't live in a vacuum because your products certainly don't.

Being a Visionary

By this I don't mean that you hallucinate, rather that you have the desire to create a dream, the perseverance to follow it, and the intelligence to orchestrate it. As you saw in Chapter Two, I got my business off the ground with my "Who Am I?"

Halloween disguise product, despite a lack of funds and a pressing deadline. I used my perseverance to make it happen. If I have an idea and I know it will work I just don't give up until I take it as far as it will go. I have overcome obstacles as challenging as the lack of funds by selling my product first. It is amazing how everyone suddenly wants to do business with you when you have orders. It is also amazing how many times I tell budding entrepreneurs this rule but they don't follow it. In fact, I have seen dozens of people close their businesses because they did not follow this rule. After settling on a product I know will sell, I try not to think about any of the obstacles I may face. I simply focus on my to-do list. Instead of spending time worrying, I spend my time making sales appointments and building relationships. Again, something magical happens once you get the order— everybody wants to do business with you and all the pieces seem to come together. When I go to manufacturers with orders in hand, they want to do business with me. The same is true with designers, bankers, and other vendors. Orders are powerful. Orders are the real deal. That is why selling your product first is the cornerstone of *The Carey Formula*.

That also means that you have to keep your eyes on the prize at all times. You have to develop a vision that encompasses both the big picture and the day-to-day little picture. In a sense, you have to be like a sophisticated camera lens that serves as both a telescope, so you can see long range, and a microscope, so you can examine every detail.

Why I Write in Longhand

Some people don't like to write and may want to record their immediate impressions on a portable tape recorder. That's fine for your immediate impressions. You can even call your home phone number from your cell phone and leave a voice mail message for yourself. However, when it comes to making a more permanent record of your thoughts, I really do urge you to write these things out longhand. Typing may be faster and produce a neater document, but we're really interested here in SLOWING DOWN rather than speeding up. Why? There is something called the Thought Rate/Speaking Rate disparity that you need to be aware of. Human beings can speak at roughly 200 words per minute. They can think at a rate of 2,000 words a minute. That's why it is sometimes so hard to pay attention when someone is giving a speech or presentation. Our minds are so much faster than our mouths, that we're listening but also thinking about our dry cleaning, why Melissa said that thing about Dan's recent negativity, why my shoulder muscles are so tight this morning, and whether I want a tuna fish sandwich or a salad for lunch.

There's a kind of inverse corollary to that. A good typist can type about 70 to 100 words per minute. If you're typing up your notes at that rate, you'll get through your thoughts that much faster than you will if you're writing them down longhand at a rate of about 40 words per minute. It also takes a lot more concentration to write things down compared to typing, which for most typists is a kind of automatic response. In those extra moments while handwriting, and with that added bit of concentration, you'll be surprised to find that more focused thoughts come to you about the subject. I don't have absolute scientific evidence to support this, but in my experience, when I write longhand, I find my thinking is sharper and more focused.

That said, depending upon the task, don't be afraid to let your mind wander. Sometimes the tangents you go off on can yield the gems. When you are mining your mind, don't always keep the drill perpendicular to the surface of your thoughts. Let it follow another vein if it seems to want to go in that direction.

Being Passionately Independent

When you are possessed with a passion for creation spurred by the feeling that creativity is diminished or restrained by working for others, you are well on your way to being an entrepreneur. My year at IBM (see Chapter Three) confirmed what I believed all along. I just couldn't work for somebody else because my commitment to my ideas was so much stronger than any commitment to selling somebody else's product. I believe a real entrepreneur is miserable working for somebody else and, while doing so, would tend to just go through the motions rather than aggressively pursue every opportunity possible. Not until your heart and mind are aligned will it all come together. And when it does, there is nothing quite like it.

Being Self-Confident

I always give my ideas my full effort from conception to the conclusion of the project. Early on, even though I unrealistically didn't expect them, there were failures. But in the past few years, almost every product idea has yielded success because my experience enables me to think out every project fully before I embark upon it. One of my secrets to creating this strong belief is building a network of friends and family who believe in and support you. If they believe in you it is much easier to believe in yourself.

Being Persistent

You have to have the persistence to bring any worthwhile project to market, no matter what the obstacles. Once I determine that a project is viable, I use every resource at my disposal to make it happen. Early in the development of my company I made some mistakes, but since *The Carey Formula* matured, those mistakes have been few and far between. Still, I am on the alert for indicators that a well thought out project either won't work or won't yield profit margins that make the effort to develop the product worthwhile.

Being Realistic

You have to develop an instinct for knowing when it is time to cut your losses and get out or when to stay the course. These instincts were more important in the early formation of my company. Now, thanks to *The Carey Formula,* there are few losses to cut. But a savvy entrepreneur needs to know when the challenges are too big, too risky, and too costly to continue. After all, you can only swim upstream for so long before your arms give out.

The life of an entrepreneur is a marathon, not a sprint. I have a friend, Lisa, who runs several marathons a year. No matter how bad she is feeling, she finishes. She was surprised to learn that many world-class runners will drop out of a race when they know they don't have the legs that particular day to win or finish near the top. They've learned that its better to save their legs for another day than it is to plow on and risk injury.

When I was developing children's toys I met an amazing woman by the name of Margo Plummer. Margo's background is in product development and she worked on dozens of hot items. She is so incredibly creative and a fun-loving person, as well. When we met a decade ago we instantly became life-long friends. I can bounce ideas off Margo. She always tells me honestly if I should pursue something or go back to the drawing board. She is honest, smart and objective. Find people who can take the role that Margo has for me. Give back to them too. Here are some thoughts from Margo.

A Friend and Colleague Responds

"I have known Barbara Carey for over fifteen years. We go back to her early days in the toy business. Barbara thrives on something that makes great sense, but doesn't fit a mold. In other words, something the industry won't embrace because it simply hasn't happened yet. Barbara has taken ideas from a grain of salt and embraced them herself and shaped them into a mold of their own— products that the industry has to accept because of the sheer force and will that Barbara gives to them.

"Her belief in her ideas and the grace she uses in interpreting her ideas is what makes her unbeatable. She believes in something and doesn't let conventional thought processes stop her from moving forward. She is phenomenal at getting everyone around her to believe in her ideas and to make them want to succeed.

"Barbara and I have spent many hours discussing the merits of one idea over another. We have also spent many hours discussing the merits of one color or package design over another. Barbara takes every facet of her product development process into account. She works with many different people and asks for suggestions and comments about everything. She very quickly processes a lot of information and makes decisions and moves ahead—come hell or high water. She knows what she wants and she goes after it—after she has collected all of the necessary data to make a smart decision.

"This is, to me, what separates Barbara from other product development entrepreneurs:

- She is not afraid to go after the "out of the ordinary" idea.

- She is an expert at getting people on board with her unusual ideas.

- She has a great arsenal of experts in many fields to turn to for help in developing her ideas and she shares information with everyone.

- She isn't afraid to ask for help.

- And, finally, once she gathers all of the necessary information and decides the product has merit, she goes for it.

"She is refreshing in her ability to see beyond the ordinary and make something extraordinary. She constantly amazes me with her "what if we…" and "maybe we could do…", or "what do you think of…" comments that just pop out of her head and become the start of the next big idea."

Being in the Moment

You have to be able to learn from your mistakes *and* move on from them. This is one of the key ingredients in my success. My first big failure taught me never to depend on anyone else for manufacturing and I never made that mistake again. Following *The Carey Formula* simply eliminates mistakes, even those of judgment. Sometimes when a project is not working, it may not have to do with product or the marketing, or it may have to do with the distribution channels you are using. Some products sell on TV; others do better in retail. As I have said before, learning from your mistakes will make you a boatload of money in the future.

Thinking Globally, Acting Locally

Once you understand that wealth is simply a by-product of success and not a goal within itself (win the marketing game and the rewards will take care of themselves), your life as an entrepreneur will proceed much more smoothly. I have never focused on how much money I could make on a specific project, just on how to make a product that will sell and be of value for a long time, if not indefinitely. If you reach the mass market with a solid marketing plan you will automatically gain wealth through volume sales. I have found it extremely rewarding to take a product from idea to reality. I get more joy out of seeing one of my inventions on the shelf of a local store or being sold through a national TV commercial than I do from looking at my bank account. I value wealth but I am not obsessed with it. Freedom to be creative on my own terms is why I became an entrepreneur. Wealth is a by-product of my creativity.

Some Final Thoughts on the Creative Process and Entrepreneurship

In *Uncommon Genius*, Denise Shekerjian came to several conclusions, among which one stands out. If creative people seem to agree on one thing, it is this: most people are blessed with one thing that they do extremely well. Successful people do the one thing they do well over and over again for years and years. What separates the successful creative person from the less successful creative person is a measure of output. Did you know that Johann Sebastian Bach, who by the way wasn't considered a very talented composer in his day, wrote a cantata every week? Week in, week out, no matter how great or poor he felt, or what else was going on in his life, he sat down and composed a piece. Not all of them were good, but the fact to remember is this: he was working at it all the time. Another aspect of creativity that the eminent paleo-anthropologist Steven Jay Gould (who was known for his wonderful writing on science and who unfortunately passed away recently) pointed out is that we all too often dismiss the one thing that we are good at as something ordinary. (Sound familiar?) We assume that because it is a skill we have had for a long time and were seemingly born with, everyone else must have that skill too. It is only when we recognize that it is our specialty and treat it as such that we really unleash our full potential. To us, just messing around with X may not seem to amount to much, but to the outside world it could be a remarkable accomplishment.

Keep that in mind, cultivate those taken-for-granted skills, and utilize them for the full distance.

What going the full distance means in practical terms is that creative people have the ability to sustain their level of concentration and drive longer than most other people. We all know bands or singers who became known as "one-hit wonders". That term can be applied in just about any field. I don't know about you, but I don't want to end up the question to an answer in that category on *Jeopardy!* I'd rather be known for a long series of successes spanning decades. So how do we do that? How do we stay in it for the long haul? Certainly, as I've mentioned previously, loving what you do and being passionate about your pursuits is going to make that long haul task easier.

The Role of Luck

Interestingly, one of the other elements of creativity that several of the MacArthur winners pointed out is luck. They stated that a certain amount of luck is involved in nearly every creative endeavor. What makes you "talented and creative" and not merely "fortunate or lucky" is the ability to produce winning results time and time again. In other words, the repeatability of the end product could determine whether you've been fortunate or efficient. But can't you be lucky more than just once? Is it really luck if you are able to repeat the positive results time and again? There is definitely something to be said for preparing to be lucky. What do I mean by that?

We all know someone who seems to always be just a step behind and who bemoans their fate of being the a-day-late-and-a-dollar-short sort of guy. We all also know someone who seems to have a knack for being in the right place at the right time. Is it really the stars, their biorhythms, or fate that determines the results each one enjoys or endures? No. What separates them over the long haul is that Mr. Lucky puts himself in a position to be successful through thorough preparation. While he or she may appear lucky, chances are that person is simply well prepared. Luck, by itself, is not part of *The Carey Formula*.

Seeing Change

Successful creative people also adapt well to change and often seek it out. We all know that change is inevitable. So why do some people act as agents of change and why do some people merely respond to it? A lot has to do with preparation and attitude. One thing I know for certain is that successful entrepreneurs are also able to see things from multiple perspectives simultaneously. Here's where empathy plays a part. When you are able to better identify with other people and put yourself in their shoes, you are going to be a more flexible thinker and problem solver. You will also become a more interesting person to others.

Finally, I think it is important to remind you of the fact that most creative people learn by doing. While it is possible to take classes about how to run a business, I'd choose, every time, the person who tried and failed to the person who studied and passed. One of the things that book learning encourages is taking a linear approach to solving problems or accomplishing any task. Makes sense, doesn't it? After all, in order to read english, you have to proceed from top to bottom, go from left to right, letter by letter until you get to the end. Well, in real life, we seldom proceed in that orderly of a fashion. Process is often just another word for a mess. Creative people understand that leaps and bounds of intuition and insight, reversals of field, and false starts and head starts are all a part of the task. What they're able to do is to put themselves in a situation where they can best put in place the chaotic-looking process they've developed through trial and error and success.

I hope that by now you are starting to think about doing a thorough examination of your own skills and attitudes. Write them down in your new Book of Knowledge. We've still got a lot of work ahead of us, but I'm confident that with the groundwork now laid, we'll be able to build the model for successful entrepreneurship more quickly

Creating Successful Products—
How Two Rusty Pieces
of Steel Made Millions

With the groundwork established for successful entrepreneurship, it's time we take a look more specifically at how I go about creating a product that will sell. In this chapter, we'll take a look at the formative stages (Idea + Creation = Ideation), research and development, creation of prototypes, and the basics of sales and marketing. As a case study, we're going to use one of my most successful products ever, Hairagami®.

IDEATION: Inspiration and Early Trials

As you know, my process for finding a new product begins with some basic questions. Is it something that many people need or would want? Is it something simple that does not require expensive tooling in the manufacturing process? Is it a one-shot product or one that could be built into a company through continuous long-term sales of spin-offs or combined products? Of course these questions may seem extremely basic, but I believe their answers are the heart of a successfully launched new product and company.

Hairagami®, my most successful product to date, with more than $80 million in retail sales worldwide, is a perfect example of product selection because it has all the components of a dream product. It has an extremely low unit cost, high sales margins, virtually no tooling costs, and a much higher perceived value than a hair clip because it styles the hair. Additionally, it saves money and time by reducing or eliminating trips to the hair salon. But, most importantly, Hairagami® has the magic of demonstration needed to inspire sales. I still am amazed when I see Hairagami® make a person's hair go "poof" into the perfect hairstyle (see image page 276).

Hairagami® is a great example of necessity being the mother of invention. The inspiration for Hairagami® came directly from my own frustration and impatience. All my life I had spent the better part of an hour each morning curling and styling my hair for the day. I just knew there had to be a better way. I remembered that in the 1980's I'd seen a product called a slap bracelet that used spring steel to sort of snap onto your wrist. They were inexpensive costume jewelry made from little strips of metal about one inch wide and eight inches longs. I bought a dozen of them at a party supply store with the idea that there would be a way for them to spring my hair into curls. After all, the principle behind hair curlers is that you must attach them somehow. Anything had to be better than bobby pins and roll-up curlers.

One day in early November of 1998, my son and I were working in our shared office and I pulled out the slap bracelets. I told Rich Jr. that I wanted to curl my hair. I placed the bracelets in my hair vertically and attached my hair to them with a rubber band, but when I bent them to make them spring they just fizzled out. They wouldn't spring shut like I wanted them to and they just fell out on the floor. I picked them up and hurled them across the room, and I heard the "swoosh" as they landed in the garbage. And I said to my son, "See, Rich Jr., this is an example of my 1001st idea that DOESN'T work."

My son looked up at me and then went to the garbage can to rescue my next big success. He took the bracelets in his hand, walked over to me and said, "Mom you need to work with this. After all, you don't let me give up that quick!" He was right and just to be a good mom, I agreed to work with it a bit more. I took my blinders off and this time I placed the slap bracelets in my hair horizontally. When I rolled them up, then bent them, they did spring shut. But soon they, too, fell out. It was obvious I needed stronger steel. The next day I researched steel suppliers and ordered steel samples of various thicknesses with the same curve of a slap bracelet. What I ordered was called sheet and strip steel, a flat, rolled steel usually less than three millimeters thick. In total, I believe I spent less than one hundred dollars on samples, and this expense was for shipping charges.

Inexpensive Research and Development

One of the great things about manufacturers and suppliers is that they want your business. In order to get your business, most suppliers will provide you with free samples of their products—all you have to do is pay the shipping costs. Just as I had done when researching suppliers for the Halloween masks, I went to the incredibly handy Thomas Register and looked up various steel suppliers in the United States. I called them up, told them the type of steel samples I needed, and they sent them out.

Obviously, someone could order samples from many different manufacturers and then use those free materials in a production run. That would be unethical and unprofitable. When you factor in all the shipping costs for those samples, plus the variations in product from supplier to supplier, you're creating a headache for yourself that may never go away.

I've never paid for a sample in my entire career and if you purchase *The Carey Formula CD Library*, you'll find that I've provided you with contact information and links to thousands of manufacturers worldwide in most all categories. A word of caution: I know you'll be tempted by the many offerings available to you. For example, you could order a sample coffee maker from a Chinese manufacturer for $3.50. Tempting, right? Well, the shipping costs, particularly because you are ordering a single item that is considered LCL (Less than Container Load) would bring the cost of that coffee maker to nearly $300. Not such a good deal, now, right?

Remember, one of the key qualities of a successful entrepreneur is integrity. If you expect to be treated with respect and honesty, then treat the other businesses you do business with in kind.

Forget R&R; I'm Doing R&D

Two weeks later my samples arrived. I was pretty excited to see what I could do with them. I opened the boxes, used a pair of tin snips to cut the steel to size, and proceeded to roll the strips in my hair. This time they did not spring at all. I thought, "What's going on here?" I didn't get it. I was totally perplexed as to why the steel was not springing like the slap bracelet's steel had. This was another challenge I had to take on. I love solving problems and in this case I had family on my side.

My grandfather, the late Admiral Dawson, had been a metallurgist and kept books on the subject in storage above my mother's garage. There were so many books, and I was uncertain of which ones would prove helpful, that I couldn't see lugging them down a ladder. I spent the next two weeks in Mom's garage attic with my flashlight reading everything about steel and its properties. I got to know more about luster, malleability, ductility, tensile strength, conductivity, alloying, and coating than I ever imagined I would. It was fascinating to me. Soon I learned that the spring in the steel had to do with heating the steel (annealing) and applying pressure at a certain point. I ended my attic antics just in time to enjoy Thanksgiving with my family—but my research wasn't over yet. I went to the library at the University of California to get the latest research information available. Later I would be granted a patent for the intrinsic value of potential energy that I captured in the steel of the Hairagami® product.

For Christmas I asked my family for yellow industrial safety coveralls, steel-tipped boots, an acetylene torch, and protective eye gear. I'm a bit of a workshop and tool junkie anyway, so the fact that I was more excited to order from the Snap-on tool catalog than from the Victoria's Secret catalog came as no surprise to anyone in my family. I had to experiment with my new knowledge of the properties of steel. I got for Christmas precisely what I asked for. The day after Christmas, I went to work in my garage. I tested the steel at all the temperature levels, pressure levels, and combinations thereof. I used my new torch to heat the steel up and then, using the engine-pulling hoist we already had in the garage, applied weight to the steel to shape it. I was having difficulty bending the steel to match the proper curve profile I wanted, so I contacted a local steel shop and they let me use their four-slide machine to bend my sample strips to the proper shape. I went back and forth between home and the shop, trying different combinations of temperatures, pressures, and thicknesses.

Seventy-eight hours later I emerged exhausted from my little two-car garage with two beat-up pieces of rusty, ugly steel that you wouldn't want to touch to your hair. But I was confident they would work. I developed a system for heating the metal that made it stronger and yet more flexible. I ran into the house, went into the restroom and tried them in my own hair.

What I saw in the mirror frightened and exhilarated me. I saw a woman—with sooty raccoon-eyes from her goggles—have her hat-head hair transformed instantly into a perfect bun. I'd done it!

What I was holding in my hand was a "works-like" prototype. It was ugly and only faintly resembled the finished look of the product, but it worked like it should and like the final product would. Based on my years of experience, I knew that a works-like prototype would function for me in my need to offer a persuasive case to a buyer. The other option was to produce a "looks-like" prototype. In that case, I would have made something that looked like the hair clip with a lovely fabric or plastic cover, but it wouldn't have worked like the product should. The key to the success of this product was getting buyers to see how it transformed my hair—regardless of how the product itself looked, my hair had to look fabulous.

Depending on Patents

I mentioned earlier in my discussion of combining products that I always look for products that can be easily patented. The issue of intellectual property rights and patents is so complex that book after book after book has been written about the subject. It is important that you protect your ideas and don't violate the copyright/patents of others. Remember the enormous spring 2006 settlement the maker of the Blackberry hand-held device had to engage in when faced with an infringement suit? I'm no lawyer, and can only offer you some guidance about the process I engage in, so in no way should you take what I do as the be-all and end-all of intellectual property protection.

Since this book is all about keeping up-front costs low, it should come as no surprise that I believe in a do-it-myself patent application process. I recommend you consult the book, *Patent It Yourself*, by David Pressman. It is a wonderful resource to guide you through the process. Keep in mind that depending upon the type of product you are bringing to the market, you will have to employ a different kind of patent strategy—there is no one size fits all strategy to employ. I often don't apply for a patent until I have an order in for the product. Why go through the time and expense of getting a patent if the product won't ever get to market? Because I bring out simple ideas I can get from the idea stage to the production stage very quickly. You have a certain window in which to file your application, and I usually can get orders well within that timeframe. If I get orders for my product, then I patent it. I do protect my ideas in other ways before I go out and pitch them. Again, you can find detailed information about how to protect your product in the above book. For those of you who would like some assistance with the patent process there is a state-by-state list of patent attorneys in *The Carey Formula CD Library.*

I walked out of my restroom and up into my office. Along the way, I re-formulated a plan I'd been developing in my mind during the weeks of research and development. I was going to the top immediately. I sensed something special had just taken place, and I was going to hop on that intuition and ride it over every jump without a fault. I was going on TV, you know, to one of those home shopping channels, with my new invention! I picked up the phone and called the president's office at QVC. As soon as his assistant said "hello" I was galloping off on my planned, but still improvised, pitch. When I finally slowed to an easy canter and then came to a stop, I heard nothing but silence on the end of the line. For a second all I heard was my heart pulsing through my temples.

"Omigod! That sounds amazing! Tell me again what it can do!"

I'd found a kindred and enthusiastic spirit on the other end of the line in West Chester, Pennsylvania. I'm sure my enthusiasm was contagious as I told her what my product could do. All I wanted was a chance to show QVC my new invention. I now had a crusader on my side, and she was going to help me get to the Holy Grail—my own selling spot on QVC. She told me to hang on; she was going to talk to some people and get back to me.

Later that day I received a call from Carolyn Hendrickson. At the direction of the QVC president, she was inviting me to come present my idea. Not only did she set up our meeting, but she booked five or six additional sessions with various departments, including their Direct Response Commercial department. She also booked me for a tour of their facilities. I was amazed at the fast, positive response. No wonder QVC is so successful.

The following week I flew to West Chester, Pennsylvania, for my presentation. My first meeting was with Karen Hahn, a buyer of fashion accessories for the network. She was a lovely woman, with big kind eyes and a happy smile. Uncharacteristically, my voice quivered a bit when I introduced myself, and my hands shook. Karen looked me square in the eye and welcomed me. She had such a soothing, pleasant voice, I thought I was listening to her on the radio. In just a few sentences as we exchange pleasantries, I felt immediately relaxed. Just a few minutes of small talk with her and I felt I was talking to a sister—her dancing eyes and vibrant smile were like a comforting hug. She listened patiently as I told her about my product. Then I pulled out these two ugly beat up pieces of battered steel and rolled my hair up. When I got them to the top I bent the metal and my hair went "poof" into a perfect secure bun that was going to stay that way all day long. It was a magical transformation. Karen's eyes went wide with surprise and delight. I have to admit, so did mine. She leaned back in her chair and shook her head. Then she leaned forward and looked at me with a steady gaze. I watched her right eyebrow rise like a just awakened cat arching its back to stretch, and then she asked, "How many of these can you make?"

Without blinking, I said, "As many as you need."

The rest of the meetings went equally well. With Karen endorsing the product, my confidence soared. Everyone at QVC was enthusiastic and kind. They all seemed to be genuinely interested in hearing about the product's genesis and it was a story I was happy to tell.

All she wanted me to do was cover the ugly steel with stretch velveteen fabric, for cosmetic purposes and then we could do the deal. As soon as I got out of the last meeting, I gave Zephyr Manufacturing a call to tell them what I needed. I had worked with the company before, so I sent them my battered pieces of steel that were covered with velveteen, along with the secret specifications for making the steel strong and springy enough to work. They duplicated my design and fourteen days later I had 100 samples that worked perfectly and looked great. I now had works like/looks like prototypes to send to the folks at QVC. Since I'd worked with Zephyr before, I got thirty-day terms to pay for the prototypes, and I was confident that I would pass the QVC quality check and be able to pay Zephyr from the proceeds of my soon-to-be-finalized deal with the premiere home shopping channel. The next thing I did was shoot a "how-to" video, prepare a thirty-two-page Glamour Guide insert, and package it with three Hairagami® devices. I sent the package to QVC for the quality check and my Hairagami® package was approved. They faxed me the order.

The price was $19.99 for this exclusive TV offer. I had taken a look at what it cost to visit a beauty salon for a wash and set or similar styling service, and then undercut that price by about fifty percent, depending on the region of the country surveyed. That price was the perceived value of the product—the DIY (Do It Yourself) product had to be a better value to the consumer than the professional service. Simple enough. But since this was a DIY product, I had to provide QVC's viewers with a visual demonstration of the product's ease of use and effectiveness. I knew that I was the one person who could do that—after all, I was the one who developed the product, had worked with it the most, and as professional as the models can be on infomercials and broadcasts such as those on QVC, I didn't want to risk having anyone fumble around with the product and make it look less than easy.

I told Karen I really wanted to personally go on the air to show how to use Hairagami® and she agreed I would be the spokesperson for the product. What had I gotten myself into? I hated speaking in front of groups, but now I was going to go on television in front of millions. I'd gotten better about speaking engagements, but this was a whole new ballgame filled with its own set of complications and adjustments. Before I could worry about that, using its own proprietary formula, QVC computed how many sales I would have to make to justify being on the air. I can't tell you the formula they used to compute the gross sales amount because they never told me (understandably), but they did tell me I needed $3,000 in sales per minute, or roughly 900 3-piece Hairagami® kits with video, for it to be a viable product for them with my six minutes on air. In my first show I made the targeted projection. By the third show I had tripled that amount. I was ecstatic, and the people at QVC were quite pleased.

China and the "Hubba Hubba" Program

All of the manufacturing for Hairagami®, with the exception of the first 100 pieces, was done in China. I would have loved to have found an American company who could have matched or even come close to my Chinese manufacturer's bid. I've found that the Chinese are incredibly serious about doing business— they can get you a good price, excellent turn around time, and fine quality. I don't think you have to always turn to China. Here's a list of points to consider when evaluating any manufacturer:

- Do they communicate clearly and quickly?

- Are they detail oriented and do they ask the right questions of you?

- Are they good problem solvers and offer multiple solutions and not just excuses?

- Do they ask enough questions of you?

- Do they keep you in the loop?

In the process of getting Hairagami® to market, I encountered one very bad manufacturer. If I were to answer the questions above in regards to them, I would have to answer "no" to every one of them. The manufacturer flat-out lied and told me that a supply of the clips was getting put on a boat in a day or two; I later learned that they hadn't even purchased the steel to make them at that point. I had to convince my buyer to give me a sixty-day extension. She agreed, reluctantly, and I had to, gladly, find a new manufacturer I could trust. Zephyr was my second manufacturer and they helped me recover from the experience with the bad manufacturer. When talking to a manufacturer about the status of an order, I don't want to hear, "Everything's fine." I want to hear specific details about the phase the operation is in currently. I remember a writing teacher telling me that the "specific is terrific". The same is true of the information you get from reliable manufacturers.

Remember what I said before about exclusivity? Well, even though the product was working well on QVC, that wasn't the only front on which I was going to work. Simultaneously to first developing the idea for Hairagami®, I had targeted CVS drug stores (a chain of approximately 3,000 stores at the time) to sell Hairagami® at their locations. Eventually, it would be available at QVC and CVS at the same time. But I had a lot of groundwork to lay before I got there.

I found out who the hair accessory buyer was at CVS, and gave Mr. Gary Marcott a call.

"Hi, Gary, this is Barbara and you and I need to know each other."

I heard a soft chuckle. "Okay, why's that?"

"Because I have the next latest, greatest item for hair. But I don't want to sell you on anything just yet. I only want to let you know that I'm designing a product that will automatically snap a woman's hair up into a bun and I'd like to come see you in a few months when I have all the details of manufacturing and packaging worked out, so I can present to you a meaningful program that makes sense."

He told me that sounded good. My relationship with Gary Marcott was off to a good start. I worked very closely with CVS for nearly eight months as the product idea came to fruition. Gary was a marketing and merchandising genius and we worked incredibly well together. He was one reason why I decided to give CVS retail exclusivity for four months—120 days on the shelf.

So, okay Barbara, if exclusivity is a bad thing, why'd you do this? Because the terms of the deal I worked out with CVS, based on giving them exclusivity, were extremely favorable. Here's the key point: I gave them limited-time exclusivity, and my terms with them were final. I wouldn't be obligated to extend our agreement beyond that or give them right of first refusal on any subsequent terms. Don't be afraid to lose a battle if losing will actually help you win the war.

I thought that having two different distribution channels was the ideal situation. I had a targeted core audience at QVC who were predominantly female who were clearly predisposed to buy from television. The demographics showed that QVC's prime audience was women. Who better to sell a convenient and cost saving product to? At CVS, I sold a single unit under the brand name Flip Clip for $3.99. (Since CVS was a different distribution channel and in order to differentiate the brands I decided to name the CVS product Flip Clip instead of Hairagami®.) So, now I had my product in two different distribution channels and at two different price points and branded with two different names. I was experimenting, seeing which worked better and why.

Well, if you want a case study of success in a mass-market retailer, you better look elsewhere than the Flip Clip. Seems that women couldn't have given a flip for the product. The reason? Simple. I went to QVC because I knew that the product needed to have its effectiveness and ease demonstrated clearly to the consumer. The small package of a single clip didn't allow for much explanation of its use. Success can be measured in a lot of different ways. Even though the product didn't sell well, my initial order from CVS earned me a handsome profit, even after markdown monies.

Between the first orders from QVC and CVS, I earned over $500,000 but still had that nagging slow sell problem at the retail level. The buyer and I worked together on this to get the product to where it needed to be. Gary did not give up on my product, but gave me suggestions on how to reposition the promise and value to the customer. The product was a big success when seen on television, so clearly what I needed to do was to go back to one branded item and get it on the airwaves via a national TV commercial.

I did a two-minute television commercial as a national campaign. The goal here again was to maximize the television exposure via two distribution channels. The commercial would build awareness so that it would sell at retail later when Hairagami® would re-enter that channel. When Hairagami® re-entered the market we would only go by one brand name, Hairagami®—no more Flip Clip. Meanwhile, until then, consumers could buy it directly from me. Previously, the people at QVC had me meet with their direct response people in a division called QDirect. This is where they take top-selling items from their network and create a commercial to go on other stations. (Direct response means going to the consumer directly to get orders. This can be done through print and radio campaigns and through television spots and shows.) QDirect wanted to produce a commercial for me and then handle the orders and eventual filling of those orders. As tempting as it was (in reality, it wasn't all that tempting) to turn over the burden of producing a commercial, etc., I declined going with them, and decided instead to create my own direct response campaign. No matter how good and how experienced the partner you bring in, you are still going to show a lower return on your investment because you are sharing profits or only getting a royalty. In this case, I'm certain that even if QDirect had nailed the commercial out of the gate, I still made more money doing this all myself and hiring the appropriate vendors that I wanted to work with.

Beam Me Up, Scottie—Electronic vs. Print Direct Response

Most of you have probably been exposed to a direct response campaign. These often involve creating a postcard or flier that goes directly to consumers with a

special offer, bundled in a single envelope along with
other similar offers. The consumer can either respond
to the offer via the card or an 800 number. The
number of services you can get from a direct response
company varies widely. You could opt to have them
design and mail your piece, have their phone center
handle the order calls, utilize their fulfillment department to send out the purchased products, and handle
all your billing. Generally speaking, a one to two percent redemption rate on direct mail campaigns is
considered a success. I did some initial investigation,
but opted not to pursue it. I wanted to stick with electronic media, figuring that while the cost of buying
TV media time was incrementally higher than print,
so was the response (sales) rate—as much as forty to
fifty percent higher.

I needed that kind of response rate to fund my media
campaign. Again, the same principle applies here as it
does to the production phase—use the money you are
garnering through sales to fund the marketing. Eventually, I would spend $5.4 million in marketing and
advertising Hairagami®, and all of those funds came
from the sales of the product. All of it was easily
earned back, thanks to the power of the electronic
media to reach millions in their homes comfortably
and with few barriers. How many times have you
gotten a direct mail piece and simply pitched it without opening it, or not felt like filling out a form or
putting something in the mail?

What a Concept

I hired Concepts TV to produce my piece. After a long process of interviewing all the "As Seen on TV" producers, they were clearly the best. I hired them to produce the two-minute spot for Hairagami® because they had a proven history of producing not only the top hair accessory spots on TV, but many of the top spots in all categories. According to the folks at Concepts TV, I had to have an offer that "blew people away." We needed to develop a heartbeat in the commercial—it needed a certain speed, a certain sound, and a certain pace to capture viewers' attention. I spent $23,000 to do the "perfect" commercial. I was exhilarated when it aired the first time. I was waiting for the phone to ring. It almost never did. My first attempt yielded the worst selling commercial spot in U.S. history at that time. I did the calculations and determined that it was costing me $173 in media for each Hairagami® package that sold at $19.99.

Obviously, since revenue must exceed cost in any business, you can't sell this few products and survive. I was totally frustrated and disappointed, so I decided to take matters into my own hands. I began talking personally to those who called about the product. I talked to over 1,000 people who had phoned the call center but hadn't purchased. I quickly learned that I had only used long-haired models in my commercial. People with shorter hair felt Hairagami® wasn't meant for them. I kept hearing, " My hair only goes to the middle of my back and it is not long enough for Hairagami®."

As a result of this personal feedback, we re-edited the commercial to say, "Hairagami®: for shoulder length hair or longer." Then I bought more media and the subsequent sales made the price of the media drop to $40 per order. Better but still not low enough. I kept talking with my customers and finding areas for improvement. Five edits later, I had one of the top performing commercials in the country, according to Jordan-Whitney Reports, a media reporting and analysis company.

Collette Liantonio at Concepts TV was wonderfully tenacious in sticking with this project. She listened to my results and suggestions and together we revised the commercial five times to get it just right. Concepts TV spent countless hours and had a dedication to succeed much like mine. I then worked with Diray TV, a media buyer, to carefully select the channels and time slots that were best suited to sell Hairagami®, which brought the cost down even further. I changed the offering to $14.99 instead of $19.99 and it more than doubled the number of phone calls. We eventually got the TV media cost down to $8 per order and the revenue was $29.42 per order. Soon I had more than thirty-two pre-sold cargo containers of Hairagami® coming from China.

Hairagami® was completely self-funded with the revenue from the merchant account (credit card sales). Once I got the commercial right, I rolled it out on select stations across the country. I used proceeds from the previous week's sales to pay for media the next week. The media campaign was so successful that, not only individuals, but also retailers were calling to buy Hairagami®. But I wouldn't sell it to them until I offered CVS a second chance to be first. Gary jumped on the opportunity and it became one of their best selling items ever. After giving CVS another exclusive period of thirty days with the item, I put a sales plan together and went out on the road for 120 days, commuting daily to the East Coast and back. (I did not stay in the East because I wanted to be home with my family. Life on the road can't mean your family life stops.) I met with retailers and catalog accounts. I met with buyers who bought for "As Seen On TV" items, as well as buyers who bought the hair accessory category. It took only forty-five days for me to get Hairagami® into 23,000 retail locations. I encountered little difficulty selling buyers on the product because I had a media plan, and because the commercial we had collaborated on was named in the top 10 direct response spots on TV. There was no mistaking that Hairagami® was supported by a major and impressive marketing plan. Those two things carried a lot of weight with buyers. They were accustomed to seeing media plans and direct response spots from major and mid-sized companies. Seeing these things from an individual entrepreneur impressed them. They knew I was someone who was determined and who had a plan, a real plan. When we shipped to Target, the first week after an ad, we sold more than 25,000 units in just two days, producing more profit for Target than the entire department normally made in that same period. Two years later we had sold more than five million Hairagami®s worldwide.

Switching Channels:
Claire's Boutique and the Price Point

After months of strong sales, I had a decision to make. I wanted to sell Hairagami® to a mall-based teen destination store called Claire's Boutique. But at that point they did not sell too many hair accessory items at the $14.99 price point. The buyer suggested that I sell to them the single Hairagami® units rather than my three-piece Hairagami® kit with video. I did not want to do it. I was worried about having a lower price at Claire's that would cannibalize the sales at my other retailers. The buyer, Michael Rosa, was a really smart man. He explained to me that Claire's was a different distribution channel, and that I would still be protecting my other retailers. He explained it to me this way: if I multiplied the price for a single unit by three (since that's how many were in the three-piece Hairagami® kit with video), the kit represented a different value for the customer. Claire's needed to have an item at a certain price point, and I'd had some experience (not particularly good) at CVS at a low price point. But this was before I'd refined all of my sales and marketing strategies and this was before my TV campaign. I decided to do a test to see if there were any hidden ramifications at this low price point. I did and there were none. We rolled out the Hairagami® single unit nationwide at Claire's and it was easily their number one hair item for a long period of time. I will never forget this buyer working with me to grow the business. He was smart and together we have made a lot of money. I learned much about merchandising from Michael. I made over $5 million from the Hairagami® line at the Claire's group of stores worldwide. Going into Claire's was a good move.

Meanwhile, Hairagami® became the number one spot on TV. David Letterman brought it on his show twelve times. Each time he did, my fax machine, my home phone, and my business phone all broke down due to call volume. I did more than $1 million in orders that week. Hairagami® can be found in countless marketing articles and college textbooks. *Sports Illustrated* magazine referred to it as an American phenomenon. Today I still own the Hairagami® Company. It has nineteen products in the line, which you can see at www.hairagami.com. Hairagami® is now sold all around the world, with success in countries outside the US including Slovakia, Russia, Kazakhstan, Romania, Czech Republic, Slovenia, UK, Belgium, France, Germany, Austria, Switzerland, Turkey, Hungary, Spain, Denmark, Australia, New Zealand, Japan, Korea, Canada, Mexico, India, Sri Lanka, Argentina, Russia, Uzbekistan, Georgia, Poland, Azerbaijan, and Turkey. By the time this book comes out I hope to have Hairagami® in the Philippines as well. I am not the one who travels to these countries; I use reps and agents that we have built relationships with to establish international business. You can find all the contacts of these reps and agents on *The Carey Formula CD Library.* I have spent my lifetime building these contacts and have made them available to the public for the first time so that you will not have to research and spend the time and effort that I had to do in building contacts and relationships.

Another great product idea came from my commitment to keeping in shape. The year was 1994; the day was January 1. I woke up that morning and turned on the TV to watch QVC. They were selling every exercise machine imaginable by pitching a new year, a new day, and a new YOU. I was instantly captivated by all the energy because I had recently gone through my own metamorphoses of getting into shape, after Rich Jr. was born, by changing my simple everyday habits.

I turned to my family and said, "I can do this." I lost weight and got into shape by visualizing myself in my new look. I could bring my system to the viewers of QVC. But how? The image I had created of my new look had inspired me to achieve it. I knew that a lot of people didn't stick with diet or exercise programs, because it took too long for them to see results. If they weren't getting positive results or feedback, they got discouraged and quit their program. What if I could make a product that would allow people to actually see themselves as they would look in the future while staying on a healthy nutritional program that included daily exercise?

Then the idea came to me. I would make a mirror that you could look into and see yourself leaner and thinner, like a fun house mirror. My new Motivation Mirror would distort your image and make you appear slimmer (see image page 282). The way I created this was by placing a mirror in a frame that is slightly too small causing it to bend and giving a slimmer reflection. No tooling! I would also sell it as a set with a cassette tape called Escape Your Shape that would talk about the habits of a lean, healthy person. All I had done to lose weight and get into shape was to change my habits, visualize my new shape, and remain motivated to change. My mirror would help accomplish the last of those three, making it easier for people to do the first two.

The next day, January 2, I found a frame maker who could do the entire operation turnkey. He was in Southern California and I made an appointment for January 3 to visit him. I told him the exact specifications of what I wanted and the image I was trying to get from the mirror. He had a perfect prototype waiting for me the next day for the meeting. This is the type of vendor I like. Dennis McGee from DS McGee Enterprise, Inc. was hungry for business and prepared and excited to be on my team. Not only did he want my business, but he also wanted to check my credit. No problem there except I had none—this was before Hairagami® had become such a big success, so I had no proven credit track record. Every time we talked, he asked me for credit references. Even though I really wanted him as a vendor, I knew I had to hold him off on this crucial bit of information. Each time he asked me for references I told him I would be happy to provide them if I selected him as a vendor, and I had not yet done so. My strategy was to build a relationship with him and to get down the road far enough that he would do business with me, credit references or not. And how was I going to do this? Through a process of being a person who does what they say they are going to do.

When I told him I was going to call him at 1:15, I did—exactly at 1:15—not 1:16. When I told him I would send him an e-mail of the packaging at a certain time, I did. He told me he could make up to 5,000 pieces for my first order. My goal was to sell 5,000 units. When I met with a QVC buyer, she loved the idea. When the QVC buyer asked me for the price and the minimum order quantity, I told her she could buy as many as she wanted on the first order up to 5,000 sets. I also told her that for the first 5,000 sets the introductory price would be $35.00, but subsequent orders would be sold at $45.00 each. She said she would take all 5,000 at the introductory price. We both got a good deal. I got the order for the quantity I wanted and QVC got a great discounted price to introduce this new item. I negotiated three-day terms—when they got the mirrors, they'd pay me within three days of receiving them. I specified that the funds should be sent directly to my bank not to me. I did this because I had something in mind for later.

After the appointment with the buyer I faxed an order for the full five thousand pieces to Dennis. He was impressed. So was I. I had told him what I was going to ask for in the meeting and each deal point was addressed and detailed on the purchase order. At this point, Dennis knew I was a person who did what she said she was going to do.

When the time came for him to ship the product, he asked me again for credit references. I still had none. But I was prepared, since I knew it was just a matter of time before this issue would arise. I pulled out a piece of paper that instructed my bank to pay Dennis first, before me, as soon as the QVC check came in. I then pulled out the purchase order that showed the payment terms I'd negotiated—specifically how the funds were going directly to my bank account. QVC's payment was to be made in three days. How good was that? I essentially was creating an escrow account. Usually, you were able to negotiate thirty or sometimes sixty days from your manufacturer. Thirty-day terms for Dennis were good, but ten-day terms (seven days to ship and three days to get paid) were fabulous. I handed over both documents to Dennis and told him that I understood his need to get paid.

I also told him that I had created a situation that not only should make him feel safe, but also would have him paid in far less than his normal requirement of 30 days. I also suggested that based on the payment process I created, he should do a credit check on QVC, not me! He smiled and shook my hand and appeared quite pleased with the situation. We shipped the product. We got paid in three days. Ten years later I still know Dennis. His business has grown substantially and I would do business with him again in a heartbeat. And I believe he would do business with me too.

Barbara Carey's Simple Secrets of Success:

- Understand what it is that you can't do personally and surround yourself with people who can do what you can't. Concepts TV Productions is the expert for two-minute hair accessories commercials, so I hired the company to produce the Hairagami® spot. I would have been lost and ultimately unsuccessful without Concepts TV.

- Know your customers intimately. After speaking to so many of my customers I was able to profile them and tailor my communication to them accordingly. I knew my Hairagami® customer was a woman between thirty-three and forty-two years old. Typically she had three children and, most the time, two of her children were girls. Approximately thirty-two percent of the time she had long hair. She purchased the product between four and six P.M. while she was doing homework with her children or cooking dinner when she saw the commercial. Amazingly, thirty-eight percent of the time her son wanted a Hairagami® for her. He saw it on Nickelodeon and twenty-one percent of the time her son had memorized the catchy jingle I used in the commercial. I even knew how often she highlighted her hair. Why? Because I asked. You can seldom market something to someone when you don't know who that customer is. It is still amazing to me that Hairagami® was so successful. There was so much wrong at the beginning of the campaign. I literally dissected everything about the commercial to get it ticking. I analyzed the cost and the offer and the music and the pace. It was a fascinating project and a challenge that I will never forget. A Hairagami® type project does not come around often, but the process works exactly the same for success with products on a lesser scale, and this process could still create one of your big hits.

- Hairagami® had all the components of a successful product. It was inexpensive, had no tooling costs, had a high margin, high perceived value, magical transformation, dynamic packaging, a national self-funded marketing campaign, and it was easy to use.

- Building a strong relationship with a manufacturer or designer can pay huge dividends as it did with Dennis in creating Motivation Mirror. By stalling him on the credit issue, I was able to build trust that allowed me to create the deal even though I had no credit and not much of a track record. The main thing with Dennis was always doing exactly what I said I was going to do. Being a person of my word made him trust me and bend with me when I needed some help getting Motivation Mirror off the ground.

- Don't be afraid to take chances and persevere. It would have been easy for me to be satisfied with the initial success of Hairagami® through QVC. I had a larger vision, and though I went through some dark days with the television campaign and with one supplier, I hung in there, and in the long run earned millions more than I would have if I'd lost faith or sold the idea to someone else.

Preparing for and Getting a Sales Meeting

If you haven't figured it out by now, here's something you need to know about me: I never give up. Sometimes this perseverance has created good fortune for me. I'm also not someone who feels the need to always play by the book. In fact, that's why I'm writing, publishing, and marketing my own book. I've taken a lot of risks over the years, but as you're about to see, sometimes I have tested limits to such an extent, I could have gotten myself into a whole lot of trouble.

When I was first marketing Hairagami®, I knew that I needed to get Kmart on board because of its 2,000 stores nationwide. So I did what I usually do. I set an appointment with the hair accessory buyer, got the cheapest last minute flights (it took three of them) to Kmart headquarters in Troy, Michigan, and showed up for my meeting. Following my usual *modus operandi*, I arrived at the headquarters a half hour early. I sat in a reception area and glanced over some notes, leafed through a magazine, and tried my best to get into my mental "selling zone."

When the receptionist told me that my buyer was ready for me, I was more than ready for her. I was delighted when I saw that the buyer had long luxurious auburn hair splayed loosely over each shoulder from a neat center part. She was the perfect candidate for a little Hairagami® magic. Unfortunately, after we exchanged a few pleasantries, I reached into the hat to pull out a rabbit but came up empty. I was only halfway through my explanation of Hairagami® when I watched the buyer's face cloud over. I hadn't had that happen in any of my meetings for Hairagami®, and I was a bit thrown off. The young woman smiled and shook her head.

"I'm sorry, Barbara. I don't want to cut you off prematurely but I have to tell you. I don't buy everyday hair *accessories*. I'm the hair fashion buyer. I'm so sorry."

"I am, too. I'm not certain how this happened." What I didn't say to her was that this was even worse for me. Her department was way in the back of the store in a low traffic area. Hairagami®, a hot new concept at the time, needed to be displayed where it would attract attention. I had already had success elsewhere with front of the store placement. I wanted, and needed, that greater exposure.

I wasn't happy about the mix up, and as I sat in the conference room, I talked with the buyer about how this could have happened. I told her I'd done all of my usual research. Before setting the appointment I had checked out a store in California to make sure I had the correct department and the correct buyer. I told her the location of the store I visited and where I saw the hair accessories.

Her eyes lit up when she heard the location. "Barbara, not all of our stores have the same layout. I'm afraid the one you visited isn't a match with the majority of our stores. That explains it. You did the right thing, but just happened to pick the wrong store."

The fashion hair department was well in the back in most stores. That location certainly did not suit my purposes. In addition, she told me that the Kmart fashion hair department only bought new products every eight months and had just completed its buying cycle the previous month. If I wanted into Kmart's fashion hair department, I'd have to wait seven months. Since Hairagami® was a hot product, I didn't have seven months to wait. Still, I filed away that scheduling information in my brain for future reference.

On the positive side this buyer was very nice and loved Hairagami®. She suggested that I needed to see the "As Seen on TV" buyer. The buyer in that department would currently have the ability to buy and have access to front-of-store locations to prominently display Hairagami®. Since the various departmental buyers were on different floors, she didn't know the name of this other buyer, but she offered to check for me. As luck would have it, Kmart did not currently have an "As Seen on TV Buyer". They were looking to hire one. So what's a girl to do?

Well, I had a plan. I had to get in front of a Kmart corporate executive with my product. But I couldn't just walk into the corporate offices because they had tight security, and I had no appointment. As the buyer and I were walking out of the building, I was supposed to exit left out of the corridor I was in and go back to the reception area. She and I had hit it off and were talking, as we walked, about kids and juggling work and family. We got to the junction where four different hallways intersected. The corporate offices were to the right. I held out my hand, and she took it. I stepped in a little closer and said softly, "I'm not going back to reception. I'm going there." I inclined my head toward the double glass doors that led to the executive offices.

"You're not allowed back there." Her eyes were a big as saucers.

"I know. Don't look."

Her worried look was replaced by a smile. She winked at me and said, "Okay. Good luck, but I don't know anything about this."

As I walked down the corridor my heart was pounding like crazy because I knew I was about to do something that was totally against the rules. But in my mind I was on a mission to get Hairagami® into Kmart. Even if I got in trouble I had it in my mind that I was doing this on Kmart's behalf. I was sure that Hairagami® needed Kmart and Kmart needed Hairagami®. It was a perfect partnership. As I turned right I saw security guards dressed in blue blazers and gray slacks. They were about 100 feet to my left. I made the split-second decision to hike up my skirt, grab my briefcase, and run like hell toward the executive offices. (This was before 9-11. If you did this today you might get arrested on the spot.) I had a 100-foot head start on the blue coats, and I could hear them running behind me. I ran as fast as I could down the corridors. The offices were getting nicer and nicer as I went deeper into the area. I was scared, out of breath, and almost hyperventilating.

When I could run no further, I slipped into a wood-paneled office that had a large executive desk and a conference table. There was no place to go but under the executive desk. After I got under the desk, I pulled the leather executive chair in to camouflage me. In just seconds the blue coats were right on my tail. They burst into the room, and I could hear them talking on their walkie-talkies. They were saying, "I think she came down here, but I don't see her. " It was obvious at that point that many people were looking for me. I started to cry. I was scared out of my wits. In my mind I could hear my husband wondering, "What did you get yourself into *this* time?" I had to ground myself and justify what I was doing, so I started thinking about how much Kmart needed Hairagami®. Suddenly there was silence.

I thought the blue coats had left the room. I stayed under the desk for three or four minutes until I thought it was safe to come out. I started to crawl out and when I looked up I saw the person who belonged to this office looking down on me. He had a look of shock and horror on his face as if to say, "There is a girl crawling out from under my desk!" I don't know who was scared the most, he or I. At that point I stood up, brushed myself off, and adjusted my clothing like a lady. I was terrified and began desperately to try to explain my presence in this man's office. All I could say was that the blue coats were after me and that Kmart desperately needs Hairagami®. He could see how distraught I was, but he couldn't understand a word I was saying.

I finally asked him for a glass of water so I could calm down and explain why I was there. He gave me the water and we sat at the conference table while I explained myself. Just as I finished, the door flew open. The blue coats appeared and yelled, "There she is!" I was busted. But this nice man, who just happened to be a Kmart vice president said, "Pardon me. We are in a meeting. Please remove yourselves from my office." I couldn't believe it! I thought I was going to jail, but this nice man covered for me.

I kept telling him I needed to see the president of Kmart because there is no buyer currently for Hairagami® and Kmart NEEDS Hairagami®. He said that the president was out of town but he would see what he could do to find an alternative buyer who could meet with me the next morning. He took my number and said he would call me if he could set up a meeting. He suggested I should calm myself by going to a nearby mall and doing some leisurely shopping. I thanked him, and he escorted me back to the reception area. The woman behind the desk did a classic double take, just shook her head, and looked amused. I walked out of the building and into the cold and took in a deep breath.

What had I just done? I decided that I owed it to the VP of merchandising to take his advice and go shopping. Even though the mall turned out to be beautiful, I just couldn't get into shopping. I went to Baccarat and looked at the beautiful crystal, but I just couldn't get my mind off of needing to meet the president of Kmart.

The Kmart vice president called me back on my cell phone. He was touching base to see what my schedule was for the next day. But my fear was still that he would hook me up with a buyer who had no authority or no real interest in buying Hairagami®. I *knew* I had to see the president, whose name was Andy. Since I couldn't get interested in shopping, I headed back to my hotel. I was a California girl without a coat walking into what had turned into a snowstorm. I was still wearing the same skirt that I had on during my Kmart fiasco and I was freezing cold. As I was going through the revolving door into the hotel, I ended up in the same partition of the door with a well-dressed man in a large warm coat; he was heading out I was heading in.

I heard someone yell "Andy." Instead of going into the hotel I stayed in the revolving door with the man and went out with him. I yelled out, "You're not Andy, the president of Kmart are you?"

He turned slowly and with a shy grin said, "Why, yes I am."

I opened my arms like I had found a long lost relative and wrapped them around him. I told him how I had taken three airplane flights to get here only to find no buyer for my product, Hairagami®. "I have been looking for you all day long," I said. "I ran from your security guards and almost got arrested—all so that Kmart can have Hairagami® to sell."

Blinking through the snowflakes, he asked, "What is Hairagami®?"

I could tell he was totally confused, but also captivated by my positive energy.

I said, "I have one with me. Do you want to see how it works?" He said, "Yes, but let's go back into the hotel. You will freeze to death out here."

We both went back into the hotel, I placed my briefcase on a wing-back chair, and turned around. Then I put the Hairagami® in my hair, rolled it up and "poof," it did its magic. By this time there were four or five people who turned out to be other Kmart executives gathered around Andy. They all were impressed when the Hairagami® transformed my wind-blown hair into a perfect bun.

The next day I left Michigan with a purchase order for more than $300,000. Kmart reordered Hairagami® weekly for an extended period of time. It was fortunate for me that I was in the right place at the right time and that Andy was a visionary—a visionary without a bodyguard, to be more precise. He knew a saleable product when he saw one and he knew what it could do for his company. I was also fortunate not to get arrested for what I did. You might feel that I was lucky to find Andy, but luck only played its part because I was fully prepared for opportunity.

I can't exactly recommend you take the same actions I did in this instance. Instead of achieving great success, I could have been subjected to a battery of questions by the Troy Police Department. However, the thing to remember is if you put your mind to it, you can achieve your goals. I simply would not quit, and unlike my other Kmart experience with the disguises where I had to make a sale in order for my company to survive, this experience came after my company was successful. What really helped me in this situation was my energy-driven sincerity. I truly believed that Kmart needed my product; not to ensure they got it would be doing a disservice to everyone involved. You have to care about your clients because if they aren't successful, you won't be either. I was willing to get arrested to obtain my goal. I don't recommend this attitude to anyone.

My failure here was in not thoroughly researching the Kmart buyer. I should have known who I needed to see. Had I reached the correct buyer, I would have sold Hairagami® without the dramatics. It's just common sense that if you see the right buyer for the product you are selling, you have a dramatically better chance of success. In this case I was lucky on several fronts, which allowed my perseverance to pay off handsomely. But depending on luck is certainly *not* part of *The Carey Formula*.

In the pages that follow, I'll show you how you can do the right kind of research, network, and build relationships with buyers well in advance of meeting them, appear (and be!) knowledgeable and professional, and approach buyers with a win-win scenario that will assure profitability for both parties. Here are a few key points to keep in mind:

- Many people think that successful business people are successful primarily because they have special connections in some way with those who are their clients. This has never been the case with me. In fact all of my early business was literally from out of the blue. (I do get referrals now, but not very often because there are so many changes in the buying staff.)

- Before you can sell your product, you must initiate a sales meeting with someone in your target company who can make the final decision. Dealing with people who can't say "yes" is simply not productive.

- Selling a new product begins with researching the companies who are most likely to benefit from your product. You can get a quick start on your search by looking up your targeted customer's phone number in the 100-Top Retailers list in *The Carey Formula CD Library*. It is designed specifically to be used with this book.

- Attitude is everything. I believe that if the company benefits, I benefit. I try to focus on what my product will do for the company I am pitching rather than what that sale will do for my bank account. I am convinced this approach frees me to do what is best for both my buyer and for my company.

Befriending the Buyer

Some people love to romanticize the notion of the little guy storming the castle. They have visions of these major chain stores as armed fortresses with moats and cannons aimed at you, the seller. Not true. Keep this simple fact in mind: the reason why these people are called "buyers" is that it is their responsibility to *buy the products* their company can then sell through retail. You are not the enemy. You are a buyer's ally. Many buyers would prefer to work with entrepreneurs rather than with large corporations, with their teams of lawyers, contract managers, order expediters, etc. Play up the fact that you are a one-stop shop for all their needs. The personal touch can and does work wonders. While *I* may have stormed the castle at Kmart, I didn't have to. Have faith in your product and know its value to their operation.

Don't Just Research, Me Search

Many people roll their eyes at the idea of doing research. I guess they have visions of going to the library and scanning through books to find again (re-search) what someone else has discovered. That's helpful in some instances, but if I am going to sell to a chain store that has branches in my neighborhood, I will walk the aisles of that store to find the best possible place for my product to be displayed. Then I look for a secondary place just in case I don't get what I need from the buyers and merchandisers who handle my item or items. While casing stores is not an exact science, it usually works—my Kmart Me Search being the most obvious example when my Me Search was not as successful as it could have been.

Once you have determined the appropriate sales opportunity for your product, put a call in to that company's headquarters and ask for the appropriate buyer. Buyers purchase products for a specific department in a store. In most cases, the department your product belongs in will be fairly obvious. Even if it's not, once you make contact with one buyer, even if they aren't the right one for your product, they will likely steer you in the right direction. If they won't tell you who the buyer is or the department that might handle your product, try to get an e-mail address. The best-case scenario, of course, is to get a phone number, a contact name, and an e-mail address. Leave a phone message that you are sending an e-mail with detailed information on your product and why it is a good fit for the company. Then send the e-mail. Remember: as an entrepreneur you need to be persistent and creative. Don't be discouraged if you encounter initial interference in getting through to a buyer.

The Key to the Kingdom

What I am about to tell you is one of the most important parts of *The Carey Formula*: I start the sales process the moment I decide to launch one of my inventions. Getting orders is a process, not a one-time event. I call well in advance of the selling season for a particular product. I introduce my product and myself and inform the buyer that if I do certain things, I would like an appointment in the future. In fact, my first call is only an introductory call, and I put no pressure on the buyer whatsoever. I don't even ask for anything, except a future appointment. The same is true if your first contact is via e-mail. One thing you must do at the end of your e-mail is to ask point blank for a future meeting when you are ready to demonstrate your product. If you don't *create* the sales meeting, you can't make a sale.

I also tell the buyer that I will schedule the appointment only if I hit certain milestones—that I have a works-like prototype ready in three months, for example. I then fill in the several month gap with monthly contact. I always alternate e-mail contact with phone contact. I make a series of conversations consisting of "this is what I am going to do and this is what I did." I always say, "I am looking forward to meeting you when I am ready with a full and complete program." I keep my contact brief and directly to the point. Buyers are very busy and the last thing you want to be is a pest. This technique helps you in more ways than just getting the appointment.

Many times the buyer will respond to you and give you valuable marketing information so that by the time you do see the buyer you are on track. Frequent contact also allows you to build credibility and a relationship with the buyer. When I launched Hairagami®, I called my CVS buyer and told him I was not ready for an appointment, but instead I asked him what was important to him in a program. I asked him what margin he needed to have a successful product. I asked whether he bought and merchandised based on planogram or if he saw my product fitting into a promotion. He told me that because I asked specific and intelligent questions, he didn't have to educate me about all parts of the business. He was willing to share information with me because my questions were appropriate and would help me tailor my product, its packaging and pricing, etc., to his needs. He knew that when I walked in, we wouldn't have to go around and around the proverbial mulberry bush like a monkey and a weasel. We'd get down to negotiating a price and order structure that worked for him. In short, don't have them teach you how to do your business; allow them to educate you about theirs.

Planograms

Most retailers use some form of a planogram to structure their buying and selling of merchandise. A planogram is really a slightly more sophisticated yearly calendar. As a rule of thumb, I use eight months in advance of sale to figure when I will schedule a sales meeting. The reason I use eight months and not a year (which would seem logical since these are yearly planograms) is that most retailers re-evaluate their planogram six-months into the program. At that time, they may pull some of the merchandise that is not selling well and they will be looking for replacements.

No two retailers, and no two departments, are on the same schedule. For example, Wal-Mart, Kmart, Target, and CVS don't all designate the first week in March as the "buy hair accessories" period. That is why I build relationships with buyers and keep detailed notes of our conversations. They will typically tell you when they buy for their department. In addition to a planogram, buyers also acquire products that they sell "on promotion," for example, items marketed specifically for holidays and special occasions. Seasons of the year are typical categories for promotion. For example, May-June is sometimes known as "Grads and Dads." Those promotional periods often correspond to designated areas in the stores where the items will be displayed. As you saw with my Halloween mask sale, there is generally greater flexibility in the selling time with seasonal items than there is with the more rigid planograms.

In either case, getting information from buyers about these two programs is essential. On *The Carey Start-Up CD*, there is a planogram and promotion fill-in-the-blank form that is custom made so you can chart the buying schedules of the buyers with whom you're working. This is an excellent organizational tool.

So in the case of Hairagami®, in the next several months after initial contact I did exactly what the buyer wanted. By the time I saw him, I already had communicated with him at least eight times. I had established a relationship with him based on a foundation of respect. I gave him the program *he* wanted and got the order *I* wanted.

I started this technique with my very first invention, the Time-Out Watch. I knew I had a year to develop the product. I spent the year researching partners as well as building relationships. I told them exactly what I intended to do. I did it and showed them that I did. After a year, I was the epitome of a girl who did what she said she would do. I got appointments with every single watch manufacturer I targeted.

An Almost Certain Dead End

Another reason why I developed this strategy of directly contacting a buyer is that I am able to short circuit the system many companies have in place to "encourage" sales. Some accounts, like Wal-Mart, have a new products division. If you contact them about your product, you will be sent a form to fill out and you'll be given an address to which you send your product for evaluation. You don't get to have a face-to-face meeting with anyone; you don't get to do a demonstration of your product. You are literally just a number to them, and my guess that the number of successful sales through the new products division is about one in 100. Think of the time, effort, and expense of going through the motions of sending out a prototype that you will likely never get back and compare that to my suggestion that you dial for dollars, instead.

Strategic Dialing: Getting Your Finger in the Door

When I was first selling this book (before it was finished, of course), I decided to approach QVC. I had done business with QVC in the past but my last show with them was, ironically, September 10, 2001. QVC is based in the East and I was stranded there for a week after the Twin Towers fell. After much soul searching and research, I decided that QVC would be the perfect place to launch sales of this book. It would be *"The Carey Formula* on QVC." I called my Hairagami® buyer, but she had left the company. Having no other current contact, I dialed the number for QVC, then randomly dialed four digits when the automated system prompted me for an extension number. When a producer from QVC answered, I said, "I'm sorry. I have the wrong number. I would like to speak with the book buyer." She answered, "Here, let me transfer you to Doug's extension." Of course, I wasn't lucky enough to have Doug pick up the phone, but he did leave the number of an assistant on his message. I immediately called and said I wanted to send Doug an e-mail and asked if she could give me his email address. I quickly e-mailed Doug, introduced myself, told him my story, and why the book would be a perfect fit for QVC. It turned out Doug was in his office, he just wasn't taking calls. Not five minutes later I got the most gracious e-mail thanking me for reaching out to him. He also asked, "Would you be able to deliver by January?"

At the time, the book wasn't ready to be delivered on that schedule, but I had a serious buyer for when my book was ready. You have to be savvy and develop great people skills to get the contact information you seek. If you dial the main number to Target and say, "Can you put me in touch with a buyer?" chances are you aren't going to get very far. If you ask for a specific department's buyer, your chances of getting through increase slightly, but your chances of getting additional information increase greatly. You may be put in touch with the merchandise administrator. This person is your best friend. The reason: the merchandise administrator is both gatekeeper and keeper of valuable information. He or she works with the buyers, and though the merchandise administrator doesn't have the power to do a deal with you, he or she knows all the details about all the other deals that are being done, what the needs of the buyers are, the current status of the ordering process, etc. Treat that person with respect—chances are, as an administrator they do a lot of grunt work and the buyers get all the credit—and you will go a long way.

Other tips and tricks on making first contact include calling the switchboard and asking for the accounts payable department. They can be a treasure trove of information. I have even gone to a store, seen the competitor's products that are similar to mine, and called them up to ask what buyers they worked with. While I don't always get an answer, because most companies keep their contacts confidential, you'd be surprised how far a pleasant phone voice and a warm, professional demeanor can take you. You might not get the cell phone of the buyer, but you just might get pointed in the right direction. That's what networking is all about.

It's taken me twenty years to learn all of these things. Now that I've shared them with you, you are a quantum leap ahead of where I was when I began. A little creative risk taking, solid Me Search, and thoughtful relationship building will get you the appointment. In the next chapter we'll talk about how to handle that much anticipated meeting.

Barbara Carey's Simple Secrets of Success:

- Be persistent.

- Have faith in your idea and product.

- Do good Me Search.

- Establish a relationship with your buyer early in the process.

- Ask intelligent questions to show that you know your business; this will encourage the buyer to tell you about his.

- Be on time! Deliver the promises you made and earn your meeting.

Selling Yourself and Your Product—A Recap

One of things you have to be willing to do as an entrepreneur and inventor is examine yourself as if you were a product being offered up to a seller. What competitive advantage do you have over your competition? What are your selling points? What kind of margin can you provide buyers? Over the years, I've come to realize that I have two particular strengths. The first is that I've been smart enough and had enough experience to develop *The Carey Formula* in order to maximize the advantages of low upfront costs. Second, I've come to understand what my strengths and weaknesses are. For instance, I know now that I know how to sell. In the previous chapter, I demonstrated my tenacity and creativity in getting sales meetings scheduled. Well, to be honest, as important as that step is, as every salesperson will tell you, it's the ability to close a deal that separates the wheat from the chaff—and, if you'll pardon the dated expression, it's the wheat that you use to make the bread. On every sales force the world over, someone is designated as the closer, and you can develop some of the skills that a closer has.

In this chapter you will learn some of the tips and techniques that closers employ to seal the deal. Here is where you will rely most on your people skills. I've spoken with a lot of inventive and creative people, geniuses of a kind, and for many of them, no matter how wonderful their invention, this is the step in the process that is a struggle. If you've chosen the path of being a one-person operation, then you have no choice but to improve your skills in this key area. Personally, I love the opportunity to go out and sell. The process energizes me. Additionally, I don't think I can ever hire someone who will be as passionate an advocate or as knowledgeable about my product as I am. We can all go out and hire salespeople to take on this task, but I recommend you do that only as a last resort.

Think about it. Can a so-called "hired gun" ever have the same passionate commitment to the success of your product— *your creation*—as you do? Will that person invest as much time and energy as you can in doing your homework in preparation for your meeting? This is no knock on the many people out there in sales. I'm simply speaking in terms of the amount of resources (time, energy, focus) that they can bring to any one product when they are representing many products at one time. I believe that it is best to surround yourself with people who have strengths complementary to your own. As I've said, I'm not great with accounting, so I hire an accountant I can trust explicitly. Selling your product, the result of your sweat equity, is a task best left to you. Only you can do the work necessary to establish the crucial emotional branding for your product and your company. I have learned not to hire reps to get me into an account. I will only bring on a rep to maintain an account if need be.

That said, I do have a list of manufacturers' representatives that you can consult and who you may choose to hire. This list is available as a part of *The Carey Formula CD Library*. In addition, this *CD library* provides you with a list of retailers, representing over 30,000 locations, and contact information for them. This valuable resource is a product of my twenty years in the business. I really believe in information sharing and helping prospective entrepreneurs get over what many perceive to be a major hurdle— access to buyers, vendors and manufacturers. As I mentioned before, many people think that successful businesspeople are successful because they have special connections in some way with those who are their clients. This has never been the case with me. In fact all of my early business was generated from my own contacts. I called companies cold and took it from there. While the *CD library* can't make the cold calls for you, it does provide you with timesaving shortcuts to the information you most need to set up meetings and begin working your connections.

Now let's turn to some additional thoughts on sales meetings.

Know Your Buyer

Buyers come in a few varieties, with distinct work styles. In order to make your sales meeting as productive as possible, it is best to have a sense of who you may encounter. Below are the types of buyers, as I've identified them.

One of the first types of buyers you may set a meeting with is the Company Buyer. While this isn't a job title, it is a name I give to the type of person who plays strictly by the rules. They will want to follow every procedure to the exact letter of the company guidelines, and they are generally inflexible when it comes to most aspects of the negotiating process. Over the years, I've worked with some wonderful buyers who fall into this category. Once you get a sense that you are dealing with someone like this, it's important to go into your meeting as prepared as possible. Know that company's procedures and stay within them. I won't say that these people are no-nonsense, but they do tend to be the type who get down to business as quickly as possible. Save your comedy routines and anecdotes for another time and another type of buyer.

The second type of buyer you will encounter commonly is the Merchant Buyer. This type is my favorite. A word of caution here: you are likely to fall in love with this type of buyer because they are so pro-active and want to acquire new products and are willing to take risks the Company Buyer may not. As a result, they tend to be very successful and, therefore, valuable to other companies—that means they move from job to job, whether through promotion or through taking jobs with other retailers. These men and women are true visionaries. You can come in with your product and a plan and they can instantly see it and share your vision or refine it in such a way that it will be even more successful. My CVS buyer, Gary Marcott, who helped me greatly with my efforts to sell Hairagami®, is a wonderful example of a Merchant Buyer. More than just supporting me, he ran interference for me. He wasn't afraid to take on the task of being my advocate in dealing with management. His self-confidence was infectious, and he backed up his cheerleading by being a great player on the field as well. He made his company a lot of money with Hairagami®.

The third most common type is the Careful Buyer. As an entrepreneur, my instincts run completely counter to this type of person. In a way, they are the typical corporate animals. Only they aren't predators—they're the prey. They are so frightened that they are not willing to take a chance on anything that has even the faintest aroma of risk associated with it. They will go after the sure thing, and the sure thing only. What's topmost on the minds of these buyers is the annual review their manager will hold with them. They want safety above all else, so that end of the year when their manager looks at the sales results for the products they brought in, they will have a strong sell-through percentage. Like any kind of wary animal, these men and women need to be approached cautiously. You can't come on too strong or ask too much of them too soon, or you'll frighten them away.

Guaranteed Sales— A Guaranteed No Thank You

One of the terms that buyers will often try to get, and you must avoid, is the guaranteed sale. In my opinion a guaranteed sale really only guarantees one thing— that you will end up losing money. Under the terms of these sales, you provide your client with, for example, 10,000 units. They agree to offer them for a certain period of, say, six months. At the end of six months, they can either negotiate your deal again, or they can return any unsold merchandise to you. And by unsold, I'm not talking about boxed or crated bundles of merchandise, I mean every unit no matter the condition—well, maybe not in *any* condition, but certainly in a condition you wouldn't be able to resell elsewhere. But wait! That's not all! They also charge you a huge fee to return the goods.

Some buyers, particularly the real aggressors, will sense that they are dealing with a new vendor who is so eager to get a product on the shelves at their location that they're willing to do just about anything to make a sale. Don't fall victim to this. Remember that a guaranteed sale doesn't have to have those absolute terms I described above. You can negotiate with them and have a return policy that you will only take back unopened cartons, for example. If you do a guaranteed sale with an account you can count on only one party winning and that won't be you.

Think of your relationship with a buyer in the same way you would a dating relationship. You're both trying to figure out what the other wants out of the relationship and you both have something to offer. Don't sell yourself short. Keep in mind that when you are in a sales meeting, you are also buying something—the space in that buyer's store for your product. Be as careful in negotiating with them as you would for any major purchase.

Figuring Out Your Buyer's Type

Until you go through the process of meeting with buyers a few times, there's no way for you to know which of the types you will encounter. You'll likely develop better radar for this as you gain more experience. Sometimes first impressions can be misleading, but go with what your gut tells you. Some things that I look for in my preliminary assessment include:

- **Promptness of Response:** Do they get back to you quickly when you contact them or do several days pass between communication exchanges?

- **Level of Diction:** Diction refers to word choice and tone. Do they write very professional and formal sounding e-mails? Do they adopt a more chatty, informal tone in writing? You can also get a sense of the person based on their voice-mail message. Again, informal or formal?

- **Office Décor:** I've been in lots of offices over the years and they've ranged from the clinically neat to candidates for federal disaster relief funding. While there isn't a 100 percent correlation between a neat office and these types, I've run across very few Careful Buyers who didn't have spotless offices.

- **Corporate Mentality:** You can tell a lot about a company based not just on what its office looks like or where it's located, but on more subtle hints. For example, at Wal-Mart's corporate headquarters, you have to pay five cents for a cup of coffee. You don't put a nickel into a vending machine; you simply drop your five cents into a Styrofoam cup located next to the coffee pot. That sends a signal about their devotion to low prices. They're not spending their money on so-called luxuries for their vendors and employees. They're keeping their own costs low. I love that they do this and that they so blatantly displayed a message to me of what is important to them. Now, I can tailor my presentation to their needs and wants.

Another reason why I make it a practice to talk to buyers over a period of time is that I'm able to collect more data for my assessment of their type. Knowing their type helps me to tailor my presentation to their particular style and needs. All of that information I can use when I actually meet with the buyers face-to-face.

Pre-meeting Thoughts: A Checklist

❑ Define your goals. Do you want to close or are you building a relationship to close next time?

❑ List what you need to do, explain, or say in order to close the deal. Questions to consider:

- What is the margin of your product?
- What is the margin of the category?
- Who is your competition?
- Why are you better and what is your edge?

❑ Know what kind of incentive you can offer this account to avoid a guaranteed sale. Will you be willing to offer them markdown dollars? (If your product does not sell at the rate they want, they will still keep it on the shelves, but lower the price.) You can help them protect their margin by giving them markdown dollars upfront. They hold a portion of your monies owed to you from sales and release them when your product does sell. If it does not sell they use that portion to mark the price down. This is a much better option than getting product returned from a guaranteed sale. Another option is to offer them exclusivity for a short period of time only if they want to get behind your product by, for instance, taking in a large order with good payment terms.

❑ Have your item and vendor forms ready. Try to call the account in advance and have item and vendor sheets prepared. All accounts will need this basic information from you. The easier you make it for the buyer, the better the chance that they will work with you. *The Carey Start-Up CD* contains easy fill-in-the- blank forms for your reference.

❑ Bring your prototypes. Come prepared with a works-like and looks-like prototype that you can demonstrate.

❑ Be prepared with packaging. Bring looks-like mock-up packaging and displays.

❑ Get your UPC: Have a Universal Product Code (UPC) already registered; this is a must-have item. These are issued by the UPC council, and they not only identify your product, but the manufacturer as well. The application process is quite simple and an easy UPC number generator is in *The Carey Formula CD Library*.

❑ Line up your liability insurance. You won't get a written order until you have product liability insurance. Unfortunately, we live in society where lawsuits are common, so this is another must-have item. Many insurance companies and insurance brokers can help you buy a policy. Generally, I don't take out a policy until I have a solid verbal order. I provide a proof of insurability at the initial stages. Once the deal has been signed, I go ahead and take out the policy. Again, in *The Carey Formula CD Library*, I provide a list of insurance companies who can insure consumer products. Remember, you won't get a written order until you have product liability insurance.

❑ Bring business cards—or maybe not. This is up to you. With Hairagami® I chose not to invest in business cards until I hit the $10 million mark. (I don't always do things the conventional way.) I told the buyer at the beginning of the meeting, "I have no business cards, but fasten your seatbelt because I'm going to show you the very best program you have ever seen." By not having cards, I also sent this signal: I'm pumping all my funds into my products and not on meaningless extras. This also sets me apart. At the beginning of nearly every business meeting you open with an exchanging of the cards. I hope that by the time I walk into a room for a meeting, the participants will already have a sense of who I am. If not, then I'll be known as the woman without business cards. Stand out any way you can. I always write a follow up e-mail, which ensures that the buyer has my contact information and encourages continued conversation.

❑ Sell programs not products. You may only have one item. But talk about it like it is bigger than life. Show how you can do planogram programs and promotional programs. Show the buyer your vision on growth. Show them a peek into your vision of ancillary products or line extensions and even color combinations. Let them know you mean business and are a serious player.

❑ Let your buyers know *they* need *you*. Their job is to buy. Their job is to find the next hot item. Evaluate your buyer just like you would anyone in a healthy relationship. Remember everyone wants what he or she cannot have. It's not a bad idea to play hard to get, but do it with utter grace, respect, and dignity. You have limited inventory and you are going to place it in the accounts that really get behind it. Make your buyer want your product, but not by rolling over and playing dead. You buyer won't come to you if you look desperate. Be confident. Everyone wants a product that is solid with a plan to support it. They also want what is hot; since you have limited inventory, position your product as the type of hard-to-get item. Your persona should exude the aura of conviction. Don't let 'em see you sweat and always keep your composure. It is not a bad idea to throw in a bit of humor, but your timing must be impeccable.

❑ Know when to keep your ears open and your mouth shut. Many times you will be in a waiting room with other vendors who are there to meet with buyers, as well. I've sat in a lot of rooms and heard people speaking too freely about their products, their costs, and the like. As much as I believe in sharing information with you to help you get started, I don't want to give my competitors any advantage by revealing any of the specifics of my personal manufacturing costs, promotion plans, or of my particular project. You can learn a lot and get some great insights by listening, but you only stand to lose if you say too much.

Negotiating Points

Again, keep in mind that getting an order from a buyer is just one part of the entire process. Here's a quick summary of many of the major points you will want to discuss:

1. **Quantity.** Of course, you want your buyer to purchase a large number of items from you. Keep in mind, though, that your sell-through is crucial. Also factor in that the more they order, the higher your costs will be overall initially, though the production costs per item will likely be lower. If you don't get great terms (see #3), you may wind up having to pay out of pocket for your production costs. More than likely you will earn those costs back, but I would much rather not have that out of pocket expense, but instead I would want to use that money to advertise and promote the product in some way. As a rule of thumb, I usually work in round numbers based on a manufacturer giving me the cost per unit based on 100,000 units that would be purchased in one year. Then I order 10,000 units at a time, but at the 100,000-unit price.

2. **Price.** Even before you set foot in a buyer's office, you have to know what your costs will be and what profit margin you will need to sustain your operation; that means having the funds to do additional manufacturing runs, create, design and print packaging, and have additional monies available for advertising and promotion. You can work with your buyer to come up with a retail price that will get them the margin they need in their department (which you should already know and be able to exceed!), and what the competing products in your category sell for. Just as you would in any negotiation for a high-ticket item, such as a car purchase, leave yourself some wiggle room and understand that your buyer has some flexibility as well.

3. **Payment Terms.** The customary turn-around time for a retailer to pay you once you've delivered the goods is thirty days. For a new item they may want longer terms. This is also true of how you will be billed. Obviously, you'd like people to pay you more quickly than you pay others. I've been able to negotiate terms as short as three to ten days. Don't be talked into terms that are disadvantageous to you. While we are talking about each of these negotiations in isolation, they are all part of a package you put together with the buyer. Be willing to give a little on price if it will get you better terms. Losing a few cents per item won't be bad if you get your money weeks earlier and can put it to use promoting the product, paying your own bills, and avoiding late fees, or putting it in the bank where the magic of compound interest can do its thing.

4. **Promotion/Merchandising.** There are two main retail merchandising programs. The first is a promotional program. Promotions are typically seasonal such as an offering for Halloween or Back-to-School. Or they are done when a manufacturer has a special packaging offer. Promotions only last for a short and specified period of time. If you miss your ship date you will miss your shelf presence as well. It is really important to be on top of your promotional delivery schedule.

The second kind of retail program is called planogram. This is when the buyer reviews all products in a particular category, on a set schedule, and then sets the shelves for the next year, usually in a mock-up room. At midyear there is a second review to get rid of the dud products or to take advantage of a hot new product.

I always shoot for planogram. Then I present support programs to the planogram as promotional sales. I want to be on shelf the entire year, and I also want to use the promotional program to add sales dollars to both my customer and my company. For example, I try to work with the buyer to sell Hairagami® year around. I provide pastel colors for Easter promotion, glamour items for the fourth quarter, and promotions for the hot summer months. I try to stay away from specific Halloween or Christmas print or seasonal products because they don't go on the shelf well with the rest of my planogram after the promotion. Any way you look at it, returned product is costly.

5. **Cooperative Advertising.** Most retailers produce in-store fliers or do direct marketing to consumers through the mail—think of how much less bulky your Sunday paper would be without those sales inserts. Retailers don't often put your product in those circulars out of the kindness of their hearts. You can allocate a set amount of your profit to go toward paying for those listings in those advertising pieces. The same is true for premium placement in stores—end caps, front of store tables, window displays, etc.

6. **Markdown Dollars/Returns.** You can build in a cost structure that anticipates what will happen if an item isn't moving particularly well. By anticipating in advance what the markdown prices will be, you can preserve your margin, the buyer's margin, and sell more product—thus increasing the ever-important sell-through figure. Again, this is another flexible option you can use—a bargaining chip in negotiating other parts of the deal. The fill-in-the-blanks P&L in *The Carey Formula CD Library* takes into account these expenses.

7. **Exclusivity.** As you've seen, I've used this bargaining chip with retailers to help get advantageous terms for my products. There are time limits on the period of time you grant exclusivity, and you can also have more limited kinds of exclusivity, such as channel of distribution: for example, you may only make your product available in one grocery store, but leave it open to sell in department stores, etc. I'm reluctant to ever grant anyone absolute exclusivity, and it's rare that a buyer would ever demand such terms.

Anticipate and Solve Their Problems

When I went in to sell my newly developed jump rope package to Wal-Mart, the initial reaction was, "We already have jump ropes, why do we need yours?" My answer was, "Not only does my jump rope give your company a higher profit margin, it costs less, looks better, and it comes with a cassette music tape that is designed to use with the rhythmic motion of jumping rope." In short, my item clearly had added value for the Wal-Mart customer. By responding in this manner, I displayed vividly the added features that my product had over just any jump rope. If your product is well thought out and you truly understand the competition, you will be ready to meet any buyer objection head on.

Plan to Move the Meeting from Sales to Merchandising

We have discussed the importance of working with buyers to get good terms and the need to avoid a guaranteed sale. Now you need to know how merchandising plays a critical role in the sales performance of a product. The more you know about merchandising, and the more you include discussions of it in your negotiations with buyers early on, the better off you will be. Your decision on who to sell to shouldn't be based solely on who's going to take the largest order. You need to think about who is going to offer you the best program for selling your product through. Orders are great, but sales and your sell through percentage are your best gauges of success—for that product and for any future products you might want to sell.

Sell-Through

Sell-through is a simple percentage. To determine it, take the number of items shipped in and divide that by the number sold through. If you ship 100 items and there are 100 cash register sales, then your sell through is 100%. If you ship 100 items and you sell forty-five, then your sell-through is forty-five percent. Buyers calculate sell through by the week. Specialty stores work on a percentage as above, but food, mass and drug want to see how many units per door (location) per week are sold.

When Things Went Wrong at Longs

I once had a merchandising nightmare at my favorite drug store, Longs Drug. This is when I launched Dittie™ my "New, Fun, Feminine, and Fabulous Tampon" (see image page 284). I worked very closely with the buyers and merchandise managers to launch Dittie™ just in California. Longs was a very important account because they own the market in this region. What was difficult is that I could not get around their policy of promotional testing before doing a planogram program. This made getting strong enough sales to qualify for the planogram extremely difficult—especially for a feminine hygiene item. Tampons are a destination sell. Most women are married to a brand and simply walk into the aisle, pick up their favorite brand, and leave as fast as they can. A woman does not go to the aisle and say to herself, "Gee, I wonder what kind of new fun, feminine, and fabulous tampon they are offering today." Building a business with a retailer in this category can only work if your product has a permanent home in an aisle.

The challenge with Longs is that they use an outside distributor to do their promotions in scheduled locations in the store. What that means is that they cannot pinpoint the exact location of your promotion. Instead they just have a general idea where your item will be. I don't think the executive management has a full understanding of how ineffective this is, although the merchandising managers and buyers do understand the problem that outsourcing promotional programs creates.

For promotions to be effective, they have to be placed strategically. I also think that Longs Drug Store has been experiencing growing pains. When the chain was smaller, the store manager had independent control. This was great for entrepreneurs because we could go into ten stores, sell the managers on our product, get positive results, and then bring these results to company headquarters to secure a chain-wide distribution and sales program. In my opinion, to maintain a quality store with a great shopping experience, the store needs to have the same concept or look at each location. Target is effective because it follows such a formula. Target managers are given training and concrete guidelines to follow. The result is a quality shopping experience.

Over the years, I believe Longs' management has taken more of this independent control from the store manager. This is where the problem lies. You have old school managers wanting to do it the old way and new managers who insist on doing it the new way. Conflict is inevitable. When you talk to headquarters, they tell you they call the shots. When you go into the store, the managers tell you they call the shots. This would never happen at Target, because Target headquarters runs the company. They have a system and a procedure and all their employees are on the same page with the same goals. I believe there is no single message coming from the top at Longs to create and implement a comprehensive plan. In my opinion, Longs needs to do what Target already does. Longs needs to be able to delegate and implement a comprehensive program consistent to all stores—or let each manager independently operate his or her own store. You can't have it both ways. I get the feeling executive management does not like to rock the boat with the old school store managers and this might be why there is such a disconnect. I really miss their former President Steve Roth. Steve Roth was a leader in the truest form. Those were the days!

Since I had no choice, and since Longs was such a desirable location for the product, I agreed to this promotional program and Dittie, my tampon line, ended up in the hair removal section. Who is going to buy a tampon there? The answer is almost nobody. It was a disaster. While we had achieved success at our other accounts, Dittie™ wasn't long for Longs. It was heartbreaking because they are such a great account. I also have a special feeling for Longs Drug Store. I grew up with Longs and my office is seven minutes from their headquarters. In fact, when the Longs estate went up for sale in my hometown I came really close to buying it. They have supported many programs of mine and they did a fantastic job with my son's Water Talkie program. My buyers with Dittie™ were true merchant buyers with their hands tied. When the program did not work we worked together to pick up the pieces and I feel I will always have a relationship with this account.

Ask for the Order

One summer when we were on the road driving to another Kmart meeting, Rich Jr. and I were engrossed in a life discussion. Rich Jr. was eight years old and we were talking about selling products. He said to me, "Mom, just how do you do it? Whenever I am with you, you always get the order." I said, "Well, Rich Jr., first I never ask for the order unless I know the answer is yes." I added, "It's like kissing a girl. You should never kiss her unless you know it is OK."

Soon we arrived at our appointment and I was called in to see the buyer. I was selling an amphibious vehicle that had paddles on the wheels that I called Water Wheels (see image page 279). It was designed after a 1960's vintage Ferrari. The product was rather large so this time we had a conference room. I set up Rich Jr. at the table and gave him his Teenage Mutant Ninja Turtles coloring book and crayons to keep him busy. The presentation started like any other. The buyer had been buying the "ride-on" category for many years. I started my pitch by reviewing the current items on the market, the sell through, and the profit margin he could achieve with my product. I was really into it. The presentation was flowing amazingly well. Soon I realized my young son had stopped coloring and was on the edge of his seat. The buyer's eyes were wide open. Both of them were totally engaged with my dream of riding on water. I was in the zone. But just when I thought it could not get any better, Rich Jr. blurted out with unadulterated enthusiasm, "Come on Mom, ask for the order; ask for it NOW!"

The room went silent. For the first time in my life I did not know what to say. My son just sat there, stunned at what he had just yelled out. Then we both turned to the buyer to see what his reaction was and he said, "It's OK, go ahead and ask for the order." We both had a sigh of relief and I was beaming because for the first time ever I became aware that Rich Jr.. had "it" in him. The "it" is the instinct of knowing when it's OK to close a deal. This is an instinct you can definitely learn and improve with awareness and practice. If you are one of the rare people who have a natural instinct for the sales process, you really have a gift. You know when it is OK to ask for the order and when not to. How? You can just feel it.

In the next chapter, we'll put all the pieces of this puzzle together and take a closer look at Dittie™ and the special challenges I faced in bringing this product to market. While it necessitated varying slightly from *The Carey Formula*, it will serve as a wonderful case study and review of everything you've learned so far.

Barbara Carey's Simple Secrets of Success:

- If your product is not merchandised in the correct place or displayed consistently where your end users can find it, you won't do well in a retail atmosphere. You must insist on specific product placement and to do that you must know how the stores in a particular chain are laid out. Strive to get your buyers and merchandisers to display your product in a year-round planogram program so your customers can find it with ease and go back for repeat purchases.

- Avoid a guaranteed sale like the plague.

- Know your buyers and what motivates them to make a decision.

- Be prepared for your sales meeting and know your specific goals.

- Dissect your total package or total offer to your buyer and negotiate each detail.

Passion of PINK—
The Dittie™ Story

As an entrepreneur you come to think of many of your projects in almost the same way as you would if your project were your child. You experience some of the same emotions in bringing a product to market as you do or would do in raising your child. You want to see them do well in the world, and when they do, you take a great deal of pride in their accomplishments. Of course, with your physical children all the sensations are more intense and the stakes so much higher than they could ever be with a product. I'm pleased to be able to say that my son, Rich Jr., is a success beyond all measure as a person. No matter how else anyone can judge me as a woman and as a business-woman, or frankly how I may judge myself, nothing compares to the feelings I get through his presence in the world. You know a little bit about Rich Jr. and the role he's played in my life and the success he himself enjoyed at a young age.

What I'm most proud of is that he's a wonderful and solid person to be around. Rich Jr. has achieved a lot, and before I get to a story about one of his formal accomplishments, I want to give you a better sense of the kind of person he is. Even after all his success at such an early age, he remains very grounded and his integrity and strong moral compass have never led him astray. When he sold his company, together we made a decision to place all his money (reserving $435.00 so he could buy a surfboard) into a trust fund that he could access when he was thirty-five years old. At the time, he appeared on NBC television's *The Today Show*. One of the co-hosts, Matt Lauer, was stunned by our decision. He asked thirteen-year-old Rich Jr., "So what happens when you're eighteen and you want to buy a car and all your money is sitting there in this account you can't access until you're thirty-five?"

Rich Jr. looked at the camera and said without hesitation, "I'll get a job."

I firmly believe that we did the right thing in raising Rich Jr. this way and treating his money the way we did. Money can do strange things to people, and we were careful to guard him against the too-much-too-soon syndrome that robs some people of their sense of proportion and purpose. We never gave Rich Jr. everything he wanted, but we did the best we could to give him everything he needed. My cousin, Kathy, once pointed out to me that we can sacrifice our wants but we can't sacrifice our needs. I think that is really good advice and true. Most often, Rich Jr. had to work for what he wanted. I can't stress how important that is to families. Kids need to learn to work for things. When you hand a child something frivolous on a silver platter, you are essentially destroying his or her self-esteem. In a way you are saying to them, "I don't think you're capable of doing this any other way, so here." We couldn't do that to him. We did not want to rob him of the sense of satisfaction and self-worth that comes from accomplishing things himself. Those of you who have children or have been around children probably are familiar with how kids are when they are in the "me-do" phase of life, you know, how they want to exert their independence and how they desire to do things for themselves? Imagine what kind of children we would produce if we never let them get to that "me-do" phase in their teens and young adulthood.

And how have we been rewarded for the choices we've made in raising Rich Jr.? Well, one incident from back in the days of Water Talkies should give you a pretty good sense of that. One of my proudest moments in life came in June 1998, when my son was awarded the prestigious Entrepreneur of the Year Award from Ernst & Young—the accounting and business consulting giant. Here's how the company describes the award:

> *"The Ernst & Young Entrepreneur Of The Year® program celebrates the pioneering men and women who are unafraid to take risks, stay dedicated to their companies throughout the inevitable cycles of business, and create the products and services that support our communities and enrich our lives. We salute their vision, leadership, social responsibility, and achievement."*

You've already read about his Water Talkies, but what I haven't shared with you, until now, is something that he said in his acceptance speech. When he got to the part about thanking his parents, he said, "I especially want to thank my mother for being unburdened with reality." Everyone laughed. I didn't. I remember sitting in the banquet room of the Fairmont Hotel in San Francisco struggling to keep my smile from turning into a baffled look of confusion. I didn't really know what he meant by "unburdened with reality." My reality feels very "real" to me. Did he mean that I was somehow out of touch? Did he think that I existed on a plane different from everyone else around me? Had I somehow jumped the tracks and was living in the *I Love Lucy* world I so admired as a child?

I'm not one to leave a stone unturned, so later that evening, I asked him what he meant.

"Mom," he said, "everyone has dreams. You dream things and then you make them come true no matter what. Your dreams *happen*."

I was so touched by his sentiments. His words echoed those of fellow entrepreneur and mentor of mine, Tim Draper, who had said, "When Barbara envisions a company, she wills it to life."

A Post Script

Back in chapter one, I told you about Mr. Bruzzone, the wealthy developer who allowed me to board my hard-earned horse on his property. I had told Rich Jr. this story many times as a kind of parable about hard work and its rewards. In 1996, Rich took it upon himself to write to Mr. Bruzzone, to let him know how much of an influence he had been on me and subsequently on him. We had no way of knowing what an impact that letter had on Mr. Bruzzone and his family until Mr. Russ Bruzzone passed away.

As one of the community leaders and most prominent citizens in the area, his passing was newsworthy and sad. We received a call from Mrs. Bruzzone inviting us to attend his funeral, and Rich Jr. not only attended, he sat next to the widow, Joan, the entire time. At one point in the service, she rose to speak. Here is what she had to say:

"May I present to you a young man who I have not had the pleasure of meeting until tonight. His name is Richie Stachowski. Despite the rigors of finals week he has volunteered to share a letter he wrote Russ in 1996 when he was 11 years old. That meant so much to both of us at that time that

we have kept and cherished the beauty of it all these years. As I re-read it yesterday, its words are so enduring that it still leaves a special place in my heart as when Russell and I together first received it. It is incredible that one so young should show such a depth of compassion and the fact that he has so graciously volunteered to honor a man he has never met shows an enduring maturity his parents must be proud of.

Richie started his entrepreneurial career at such an early age, it makes the mind boggle—the fact that he was so successful is even more special. The wisdom of his nurturing gives one cause to contemplate. What an extraordinary fine young man."

Following this section is a copy of the letter my son wrote and then read at Mr. Bruzzone's funeral.

I bring this up, not so much as a doting mother showing off her child, but to reinforce a lesson about good business practice and good human interaction. Certainly Mrs. Bruzzone could have easily afforded to pay for the toys that Rich Jr. gave her. Certainly in the grand scheme of things, Rich Jr.'s giving them to her didn't put much of a dent in his bottom line. Certainly, Mr. Bruzzone didn't need to collect his monthly fee from me. In all our financial transactions, we were doing more than exchanging goods and services for money. We were involved in a more intimate kind of human transaction that transcends dollars and cents. We were teaching and learning about good will and good works. For all I've said about inventing and entrepreneurship, I'm most proud of my record and the visible legacy of decency that my son and his actions exemplify. Good business practices start with good people.

1996

Dear Mrs. Bruzzone:

I had so much fun making these Water Talkies. I want you to have some for your grandchildren. When I was working to make these my mother told me a story about when she was a child. I want to tell you this story:

When my mother was young, all she ever wanted was a horse. Every day all she could ever think about was horses. She could not afford to have a horse because it was so expensive to keep up a horse. One day she met a man who was very wealthy and he owned a lot of land. My mother asked if she could keep a horse on his land. This man had so much money that he probably could afford to let her keep her horse for free on his land. Instead of giving her free rent, he made a deal with her. He said she could keep her horse on his land for $20.00 a month. This amount of money was huge for my mother, but if she worked really hard she thought she could do it. This amount of money was tiny for the man. Every day while my mother's friends got to play, my mother would clean out horse stalls so that every month she could give this man $20.00. My mother's dream came true...she got to have a horse.

My mother got something else that she did not bargain for and did not expect. She got a gift that was worth so much more than $20.00 a month. What she got was a sense of tremendous accomplishment for doing very hard work and she learned that if you work really hard you can do anything you want.

The gift this man gave to my mother has now been given to me. I too felt a great feeling of accomplishment by doing this project. I too used my own money for my project. Please tell your grandchildren that this man was Mr. Russ Bruzzone, their grandfather. My mother says, "Richie, look at how much difference one person can make in another person's life. Mr. Bruzzone and this story will be part of our family for generations to come!"

Have fun with the Water Talkies. I hope I get to meet Mr. Bruzzone one day!

Sincerely,

Richie Jr.

Richie Stachowski

In writing this book, I tossed the notion of being "unburdened with reality" around in my thoughts some more, and I realized Rich Jr. was right in lots of ways. After much consideration, I decided I'm gratified I don't have any kind of grip on what may be considered reality. After all, if I had chosen a career where a realistic, pragmatic approach to business would have worked for many people, I would have been stifled and frustrated. I once saw a bird with an injured wing and took it home to care for it. I identified with its inability to be what it was born to be; it was a creature unable to soar freely. I had once felt that way when I worked for IBM early in my career, surrounded by a plastic wall which defined the limits of my movement while I looked at my calendar and dreaded the approach of another meaningless meeting. If I had a firm grasp of what is considered reality, I wouldn't have met the many challenges an entrepreneur faces. Perhaps the old expression about ignorance being bliss applies here, but I'm not certain that a lack of knowledge about the risks involved in what I've chosen to do would have deterred me—especially if I had known the rewards would be so great.

I am also reminded of the Ernst & Young speech story for another reason. Shortly before thanking his parents, Rich Jr. said that he wanted to thank the community for supporting his efforts and for being so kind to him. He pledged that he would give back to the community in thanks and in appreciation for the love and support that has been given to him. All I can tell you is those words pleased me more than anything. Even at that age, he had developed a sense of community and purpose: passion and profit coming together for a higher meaning. My eyes welled with tears of joy. Rich Jr. has made good on that promise. He has sat on the board of various organizations including Tim Draper's Biz World, Made by Kids for Kids, and the National Gallery for Young Inventors, among many others. He has given back to his school community through everything from funding the feeding of a classroom snake to purchasing and donating books on entrepreneurship for young adults to our local library, and giving talks in classrooms to inspire other kids to "go for it". The two of us share this passionate commitment to give back in ways large and small.

I tell this story about Ernst & Young for another reason. Their description of the award and the criteria they use to select the winners dovetails very nicely with my own philosophy of what it means to be an entrepreneur. I can't think of a better way to begin this chapter in which we take a look at all the steps in *The Carey Formula* in light of what many might consider my most risky venture yet. I loved working on every project I've been involved in, but the work I have been doing for the last two years has a special place in my heart. The Dittie™ Company and an associated venture called vendPINK™ have been the most rewarding and challenging enterprises I've been engaged in. There are many reasons for that, but none more important than the components that Ernst & Young promotes through their award—risk taking and social responsibility.

I mentioned very early on how important it is to give back to the community, that the profit motive can only take you so far. After all, there are far easier ways to make big dollars than being a David going up against Goliath every day. There are some rewards that go beyond bank balances and creature comforts. Giving back is the primary reason why I chose to write this book. Rising to the challenge and being the underdog is why I chose to form the Dittie™ Company. But there's far more to it than just that. Because of the success of Hairagami® and other products, I don't have to do what I do for a living anymore. Hairagami® and most of my other products was about putting food on the table for our family. I don't have to worry about that anymore. When I select a product idea to pursue, my main motivation now isn't how much money I can make, but how much will I be contributing to the greater good through these efforts. For me, Dittie™ has never been about building a better tampon. It's about making a difference in the quality of the lives of those who use the product, buy the product, and hopefully in the lives of those who distribute it. Here's a unique story—which I hope will inspire and instruct—about a little company that can.

Let's face it, talking about tampons and a woman's menstrual cycle isn't the usual topic in a business book. So let's get to the heart of this matter as quickly as possible. I never minded buying tampons at the grocery store, as long as I was filling my cart with a whole variety of things—bacon, eggs, fruit, tampons, and the like. Buying tampons solo was another matter. Standing in line with a box of tampons made me feel like I had a neon sign over my head that flashed, "Look everyone, this girl is bleeding now!" I don't know if my reaction was triggered by my conservative upbringing, but buying tampons was simply embarrassing. So my husband agreed to get them for me.

This arrangement worked fine until one day when my husband was off on a fishing trip in Mexico. I was on the 680 Freeway in Walnut Creek, California, and suddenly I felt the unmistakable whoosh/flow. "Oh no, not now," I was thinking. I was in a tampon emergency. I immediately exited the freeway and headed directly to Target. I had not been in the tampon aisle for at least ten years. When I located the section, I couldn't believe my eyes (see page 283). To me Kotex packaging looked like Dr. Scholl's wart remover; Tampax looked like Lactaid; and Playtex looked like Benadryl. Sure, I'd seen the boxes my husband had brought home, but to see them all lined up together like a wall of shame was almost too much for me to believe. The national brands from the major manufacturers looked so medicinal! I was thinking, "What is going on here? I'm not sick. I just have my period." Standing in that aisle, staring with my jaw dropping, I must have looked a little unhinged, but I didn't care. That's because simultaneously with that look of horror, a light went off in my head.

That's it, I decided. The world needed, and I needed, a new brand of feminine protection, one with a feminine flair. I grabbed boxes of Kotex, Tampax, and Playtex in addition to boxes of Dr. Scholl's wart remover, Lactaid, and Benadryl. Head held high, I made my way to the checkout line, and instead of being embarrassed or uncomfortable, I stood with all those products feeling like a woman on a menstrual mission—so, okay, I was looking like a lactose intolerant, warty woman with sinus trouble, and a menstrual mission. I happily plunked down my cash and headed to the car bearing my new-found red badge of courage.

So that was the beginning of the ideation stage. I was inspired by a need that I felt, and I was convinced that I wasn't alone in this need. I also knew that I wasn't Donna Quixote out to tilt at windmills for the sake of nothing better to do but act out my delusions. I put *The Carey Formula* to use and realized that tampons were a relatively low cost item and that I wouldn't likely incur tooling costs because I could buy them instead of starting my own tampon manufacturing plant. What I was faced with was a re-packaging challenge, and I knew I could do something more dynamic than the anemic efforts of my competitors. So far, so good.

From the beginning, Dittie™ was about more than just a product. I wanted to create an emotional brand for the product that was fun, feminine, and fabulous—a brand that would be empowering. I also saw well beyond the tampon to a larger mission. I knew that I could make a real difference in the lives of women if I could somehow devise a strategy that allowed women to bridge the gap between the stay-at-home mom and working mom. I also knew that I wanted to make a difference in the lives of women who were affected with breast cancer. Before all these visions crystallized, I also wanted to do a reality check to make certain I wasn't too wrapped up in my own crusade to see clearly.

When I went home I told Rich Jr. my idea. He was seventeen at the time, and his first reaction, predictably enough, was to raise his hand like a traffic cop.

"Mom, STOP! Don't talk to me about that."

I resisted the urge to ask him why he didn't hold his index fingers up in front of him in the shape of a cross to ward off the vampire. Instead, I said, "Okay." I waited another beat or two for him to put his hand down and for his face to lose the "eeew!" look.

"But really, you have to look at this." I rifled through the shopping bag and pulled out the boxes. I don't know if it was because he didn't have to look me in the eyes or what, but Rich Jr. transformed himself from a seventeen-year-old to a seasoned appraiser in a matter of seconds. He picked up the boxes and arranged them side-by-side. I could see the wheels turning in his entrepreneurial mind, "You know what, Mom, I think you have something here. They all look like medicine."

I figured if a seventeen year-old boy gets the idea, that's a good thing. Clearly though, he wasn't the target market. But he had a pipeline to a group that I thought would be an ideal source of market research information—high school girls. So I asked Rich Jr. "Can you bring me girls from school tomorrow?"

I already had a plan formulated in my head. I figured I had to make this as non-threatening an event as possible. I put my creativity to good use. By three-thirty the next afternoon, I was ready. Rich Jr. came to my office about a half hour earlier. He was going to be the waiter and serve pink lemonade. I was the one with waiting problems, however. I kept looking out the window wondering when these girls would finally show up. I should have never doubted the need for young women to want to get involved in the business world. First one car pulled up and four girls piled out of it and came up the path, laughing. Another followed that first car, and just as we heard the knock on the door, another car pulled up. By the time I'd ushered all the girls into the conference room and Rich Jr. had made the rounds with pink lemonade and the girls had helped themselves to Krispy Kreme donuts, we had a total of thirty high school girls. Rich Jr. excused himself after his duties were done.

I explained to the first focus group what I was considering doing and that I was hoping I could get their honest opinions about "feminine protection." I didn't need to be so concerned about terminology or whether the girls would feel comfortable talking to me. They were remarkably candid and willing to share their feelings. We shared period horror stories, and we talked about the packaging and how it made us feel. I would put the other brands' packages on the table and I'd just sit back and listen, occasionally asking a question, but mostly just listening. The first thing we learned was that the girls hated the word "tampon." One of the girls even pointed out that it is a French word meaning "to plug up." They didn't consider the word to sound very feminine and most agreed that they were embarrassed to ask for one by name. Several pointed out what I had concluded about the medicinal look being unappealing.

I knew right from the start that I needed to replace the word "tampon" with something better, softer sounding, and more fun to say. That first group was so successful, that I held a dozen more get-togethers that we called "PMS Parties." Rich Jr. was a trouper throughout the process, and it was somewhere around party number five that he said to me, "You know, Mom. This is my favorite product of yours. How else could I always count on having a room full of girls on a regular basis?" The parties also proved to be productive. Soon I was receiving phone calls from random boys from the three high schools in our area asking to be waiters for our PMS parties. We had so much fun with just the girls we soon decided not to allow the boys at all. We put a sign on the door for our parties that said "Dittie™ Club: No boys allowed!" After many focus groups we settled on the word "ditty" to replace the word "tampon." "Ditty" means a little statement or song. Our unique selling feature is that each individually wrapped Dittie™ would have a mood-lifting message on it: applying a different twist to the fortune cookie concept. We also wanted to soften the word up a bit, so we changed the spelling to "Dittie™". Somehow, changing the 'y' to 'ie' made it more fun to read. "Do you have a Dittie™?" was much more fun to say than, "Do you have a tampon? "

In the world of feminine protection, women have a lot of choices and most express clear preferences for the type of product they use. After surveying the girls, we found out that more than ninety percent chose to use a plastic applicator tampon. With such a clearly expressed preference, it was an easy choice to make Dittie™ a premium quality applicator tampon and to make the applicator pearlized plastic. With that product selection complete, we could now go out and compare our product to the two top sellers in the national marketplace: Playtex Gentle Glide and Tampax Pearl.

By the end of the sessions with the young women, I was fairly well set with the direction to go. The pearlized plastic applicators and a premium quality product were both good things for the bottom line. Rather than go with a cardboard applicator, which would have cost less, and consequently meant a lower retail price, the premium quality product had a higher price point. That gave me greater flexibility when it came time to negotiate with buyers. Although it was smart to start with a premium product it was part of my dream to eventually have a full line including a natural cardboard option.

Before I could do that, I had to complete two other essential tasks. Since I was going to be buying rather than making tampons, I had to find a manufacturer who would sell them to me, and I had to get to work on creating a sensational package for the product. The first step proved easiest in some ways, and it best illustrates the key point in *The Carey Formula*—have low tooling costs. I don't have an exact figure, but a tampon-manufacturing machine would have to cost at least a million dollars. While some of the biggies like Proctor & Gamble or Johnson & Johnson could afford those costs, I couldn't. Or I should say, I didn't want to incur them. So, I contacted the few private label tampon manufacturers in the US. Of course, they listened to me and wanted to meet with me since I represented a business opportunity for them. Most of the manufacturers were on the East Coast, so I flew to New York to meet with them.

The response was uniform. "Barbara, we love the idea. We love your enthusiasm and your spirit most of all. We can see the wisdom of your approach, but you'll never get the shelf space. You can't compete with the giants here. But we're hoping you'll prove us wrong. You get the orders, we'll make the product."

Well, I have to give them some credit; they understood *The Carey Formula* without my even having to tell them what it was. They wanted me to go out and sell before I had a product. So, no "works-like" or "looks-like" prototypes this go-round and no real commitment from a manufacturer like I'd had every time before. I was going to have to be flexible. I was also going to have to be even more persistent than usual. I was going up against some of the big guns, and I had to accept that some people were going to be skeptical. I was used to having more people sharing my vision, but this product's success mattered to me in ways that most others didn't. At this stage, I couldn't clearly articulate what the reason was for my passion, but I had a plan formulating that went even beyond empowering women with positive messages and overcoming the stigma associated with our menstrual cycles. But it all depended on getting those orders, and I'd stretch myself past the breaking point if I had to in order to get them.

I'd have to rely solely on storyboards to do the selling with me. I normally liked to go into a meeting with a buyer while being armed with a commitment from a manufacturer. I'd have to face this challenge—and it was a formidable one— all alone. I had to get orders. I had no expectation that I was going to fail; after all, my Golden Rule had always been to get the orders first.

I did my usual thing and began cold-calling buyers. I'd not sold into this category before, however I was surprised to learn that most of the buyers that I was targeting were men. Another obstacle. None of the men buyers that I left messages for would return my calls. When I did contact the few women buyers and

gave them my initial pitch, they were very receptive to the concept. After all, we shared a similar experience and perception
about most tampon makers' packaging and communication of
the product. We women shared a frame of reference and a perspective with each other that the men and I did not. Most of the
women I spoke with agreed with the notion that emotional
branding and bringing a more feminine approach to the product
was a needed concept; enthusiastically, they agreed to appointments. But I had a problem. A big problem. The male buyers
were not calling me back.

I was in a real predicament. I thought to myself, "How
could I get these guys to call me back? What would my father
advise me to do?" Well, I knew one thing. My father taught me
NOT to chase boys. He said, "You let boys chase you". It took me
about ten seconds to figure out what to do. I picked up the phone
and began leaving voice mail messages to get appointments to
present Dittie™. In the most sultry and sexy voice that I could
muster, I would say, "Hello, this is Barbara Carey and I am
launching a national brand of feminine protection. Please give
me a call because I would like to get on your schedule and come
show you my titties!" Yes, that's right—that was not a typo. I said
"titties," not "Dittie™s". And guess what? They all called me
back, and fast. They would sound a bit flustered and say to me,
"Barbara, Barbara what do you want to come show me?" And I
would say, "My Dittie™s! Trust me you don't want to see my
forty-four-year-old titties. They were kind of cute twenty years
ago but really you don't want to see them. But thank you kindly
for calling me back to set an appointment. Please allow me to tell
you about my 'Passion for PINK.' When would a good time be
for me to come visit you?"

I overcame their reluctance with my humor and little bit of
embarrassment for having called me back because of my "titties"
voice mail. They listened to my story and all made appointments

with me. Lanny Lewis, another smart buyer at CVS, thought the approach was so clever that when I visited him six months later he still had my original message saved. Warning: I only recommend using techniques like this if you own your own company. If you are working for someone else, this approach will probably get you fired. Also, I always try the professional and sensible approach first. But I must admit that if it does not work, I am a savvy girl, and I will dig deep into my bag of feminine tools to create something that does the trick. And some advice to you men: don't ever underestimate the power of a determined and smart business-woman. *She knows exactly what you respond to and she is not afraid to use it!*

Defining Your Sales Approach: How I Made the Sale

My "tittie" approach got me appointments. Sure, it was a stunt that could have backfired, but what did I have to lose? I was willing to take the risk, not just because I thought it would be a creative way to approach these men, but because I really believed in this project, and I had greater plans in mind down the road. As I've said, I've always been committed to developing products to improve the lives of women. Dittie™ certainly qualified in that regard, and I was planning to build on that proposition even further. My master plan depended upon getting Dittie™ to market, and before I could take any additional steps, I first had to get the orders. I focused on that challenge.

Two questions need to be addressed when developing a product. Why would consumers buy my product and why would retail buyers want to carry it in their stores? I had a good handle on why Dittie™ was unique and why the end user would buy Dittie™: Dittie™ is the first premium brand of feminine protection with diva-worthy style that is easily affordable.

Retail buyers decide to carry a product for a number of reasons. First and foremost, of course, is profit. If I priced Dittie™ appropriately I could present a case to the retailers that for every box of Dittie™s sold, their cost would go down and their margin up. I also could present a case that because we are appealing to a younger audience we could bring the young shopper into the store, thus increasing store traffic. Increased store traffic inspires supervisors and upper management, but not most buyers. When you bring a new shopper into the store they will not only grab a box of Dittie™s, but other items, as well. For this reason you need to get upper management involved in the buying decision—they have a better sense of the store's big picture, while departmental buyers have a slightly narrower focus.

If you can't pitch to upper management directly, you will need to train and coach your buyer to pitch your product to management for you. If your buyer isn't able to involve upper management, you will have to figure out a way to do it yourself. Be smart. Pitch your product on parallel paths to all the accounts at once. You can then speak about your product in terms of performance in distribution channels—drug stores, grocery stores, convenience stores, etc. The last thing a buyer at Drug Store X wants is for their competition, Drug Store Y, to have a popular item that is not on his or her own store's shelves. Define the profile of your end user to your buyer and use your marketing program to tell them about how you plan to drive that person into their store. Profit is king and queen.

Since I was moving into a new product category, I had to educate myself about pricing and margins. I am going to share with you the strategy I employed to get my information and some of the general numbers involved. To get a sense of the market, I figured the best place to go would be to a reputable buyer with a strong track record of success. I heard from a number of people that Lanny Lewis at CVS was a smart buyer and he'd be a good resource for me. I had planned to eventually sell to him, but my initial rollout was going to be primarily in California. Most of the 5,200-plus CVS stores are on the East Coast, so he had little to lose in sharing information with me. He let me know where I needed to be in order to cost average his margin up. He did this in a professional way without sharing confidential information, but by clearly letting me know what it would take for Dittie™ to be competitive at CVS.

Women tend to be brand loyal when it comes to feminine protection. They find a product they like and they stick with it. They don't stand in the tampon aisle and browse. They tend to go to the shelf, get the product they are accustomed to, and move on. Price incentive was only going to be one factor in getting them to switch. Of all the products I've brought to market, Dittie™ has the shortest profit margin. The best I could do to make the venture work was to price them ten percent lower than the competition.

Why was I willing to slice that already thin margin? Because unlike Hairagami®, Dittie™ is a repeat purchase. You may buy one Hairagami® and then a few months later, you may buy another because you want one in a different color. With Dittie™, I could count on women needing to replenish their supply regularly. The more product I sell, even on a very short margin, the more profit I can generate over time.

With that in mind, I refined my sales presentation. Because I didn't have a prototype to show, I relied on storyboards and focus group data to help make the sale. When I held the PMS parties, I had asked the participants to answer a questionnaire. I didn't bring in all 650 forms; instead, I compiled the results to show the trends to support Dittie™ as viable in the marketplace. Now, the major manufacturers are able to do the same thing—even on a larger scale. Also, store managers and corporate buyers have access to reams of data about purchasing patterns, etc. The great thing was that my surveys were different and the information

I collected shed light on aspects of women and their purchasing decisions and preferences and desires that these others didn't have.

We asked very creative kinds of questions. For example, we asked women if their tampon could be like someone, who they'd want it to be like? And the answers were Oprah Winfrey, Angelina Jolie, and Sheryl Crowe. Strong, powerful women. From the very first focus group, I learned that women shared a similar sense of embarrassment about their periods. So I asked them if they needed to borrow a tampon, how would they go about it? They told stories of whispering to a friend and clustering together to shield anyone's eyes from what they were fishing for in their purse and then passing it on like they were doing a drug deal or something. When I asked them how they'd feel if they had a tampon in a bright polka-dotted pink wrapper, they told me they'd toss it across the room to give it to someone in need of one. They didn't like how the national brands' medicinal packaging made them feel, and they loved the idea of having a fun, feminine, and fabulous product that made them feel confident.

I also invested $250 for an independent survey, as this would provide very good marketing information. (Survey resources are on the marketing CD in *The Carey Formula CD Library*.) I wanted to demonstrate the emotional side of the purchase decision. I wanted buyers to understand how women felt about tampons and how the products currently available on the market made them feel. I also wanted teens to respond to the concept of a more girl-friendly product and package. The results came back exactly as I'd hoped; girls were enthusiastically in favor of a new brand with this type of approach. I also shared with the buyers a few of the empowering and upbeat messages that were printed on the wrappers like, "A real friend doesn't talk behind your back unless she is playing with your hair" and "In my next life I want to be me."

I also knew that the tampon industry generated $800 million annually, and that they could get a larger portion of that money if I injected even a little more competition into the arena. As I did with all my other products, I also demonstrated that I could deliver. In telling my Dittie™ development story, I demonstrated that I was well informed about the industry and category and was a person who did what she said she was going to. I built trust, I demonstrated professionalism, I exuded passion and enthusiasm, and they already knew I had good sense of humor and would go to any lengths to get my Dittie™s out there.

A Picture is Worth a Thousand Words

As impressive as my data and anecdotal information about the PMS parties was, what really helped to sell buyers on Dittie™ was the product comparison graphic (see image page 283). In my opinion it showed what the competition looked like compared to other medicinal products. I also explained that each individual tampon would come in a high-grade wrapper, that the box itself was of a high quality, and was printed in four colors and had a cellophane window in it so that women could see the product and its wrapper. The key here was that I didn't just have an idea for a new or better or more absorbent tampon. I had taken a new approach to the packaging, communication, sales, and marketing of a product that was not different from the competition in any appreciable way. By that I mean the tampon itself was produced on a machine that made millions of other similar products. Dittie™s get a different wrapper and a different box, but the essential characteristics of the tampon itself are almost identical to others already on the market.

But when the buyers looked at those packages side by side, they could see that something was clearly different about Dittie™. They were sold. In a twenty-three day span, I went to every account I could think of: Target, Wal-Mart, Kmart, CVS, Safeway, Vons, Fred Meyer, Ralph's, Raley's, Nob Hill, Bel Air, and Longs Drug. I got a sale at every one of them. I had to do some convincing to get them to bend their usual procedures of buying chain-wide because I wanted to rollout in only California, Washington, and Oregon. I knew this was a major challenge, and I had to see the regional results before I tried to go national. Many of the accounts said that their western region meant all states west of the Mississippi, but I wouldn't relent. I got them to concede. Not only that, but at most locations I got a one-year shelf space commitment. I was honest with them and said, "I'll tell you right now; my sell-through isn't going to be great initially. In six months, it still won't be up to national level. So if all you can offer me is six months, don't do this program."

In addition, I got thirty-day payment terms across the board and I never had to accept a guaranteed sale. No returns. None. Nada.

I also made sure to let certain buyers know who else I already had in pocket. The buyers didn't want to be left out. That's one of the great sales strategies. Sometimes you can make a sale by letting someone know they can be the first to have a product—those are your willing-to-take-a-risk buyers. But many buyers will cave to the pressure of being left out. What if the product is a huge smash hit and they weren't in on the action? Visions of their supervisors and those end-of-the-year reviews will rear their ugly heads.

I had bigger plans for Dittie™ than I even let on to those buyers. I knew the big companies were watching my every move. They had to. I had no doubt that they would copy me, but at least not until I'd established some traction. How they were going to keep up with me was their problem, not mine. They might be big and mighty, but I was nimble and could turn on a dime. I confirmed that I was on their radar when one of the executives of Proctor & Gamble contacted me shortly before launch in the spring of 2004. He wanted to congratulate me on Dittie™. He had seen the design elements of the packaging and loved it and just the name of the product itself was intriguing to him.

I said, "That is so kind of you to call me. Why are you paying attention at all to what my little start-up is doing?"

He seemed a bit flustered by that question, but recovered to say, "We just think it's a great concept."

Staying in the voice of the Dittie™ brand I replied with a smile in my voice, "I think I know why you're calling. You're thinking that you had better be super nice to me because one day you may be working for me!"

He laughed and once again congratulated me. I was a bit relieved that the conversation was over. I must say he was a true gentleman and had a lot of class.

With firm orders in hand, I scheduled a launch for April 2004. Now I could go back to the manufacturers and work out the best deal possible. I eventually worked with a company by the name of Rostam. Boy, am I glad that I chose them. Two people in particular, Haim Ezer and Bosmat Levi, in their customer relations department were, and remain, absolutely wonderful to work with. Because so much of the success of Dittie™ depended upon their detailed support, we had to get every detail right, and the two of them worked tirelessly with their home office in Israel to make sure that the printers, box makers, etc. all got the job done spot-on. I couldn't be happier with the quality of the product and with the cooperation I received from the people at Rostam. We also received amazing support from our pantiliner/thong-liner vendor Hospital Specialty Company. Without the dedication of both Beth Richman and Bob Levine and support from their President Bill Hemann, our line would not be complete.

Because of the nature and use of tampons, I was concerned about product liability insurance. I had my business insurance in place, but I wanted to find out about any additional complexities involved in insuring a feminine hygiene product. Fortunately, I didn't have to worry at all. Rostam had already received approval from the Food and Drug Administration to manufacture the product. In addition, they indemnified the retailers and me. That means that if anyone filed suit against us, as the manufacturer, Rostam would be the one considered liable. We were fully protected.

Moving On to Marketing

I was psyched about getting the orders. I knew I was only part way up the mountain I had to climb. Still, it was important to take a few deep breaths and enjoy the view from this point. I contacted Don Kingsborough, the former president of World of Wonder toys (the makers of the famous Teddy Ruxpin bear) to let him know what I was up to and to see if he had any additional input. He e-mailed back a really sweet reply, and he said, "You really are the Little Engine That Could." I appreciated those sentiments greatly. I knew that the big guys had heard about my efforts at this point, and I knew that the mountain was only going to get steeper. If I were in the competition's shoes, I would have done the same thing they were doing—sitting and watching and waiting to see if my ideas about the emotional branding of this product proved true. In a sense, I was doing free market research for them. I wouldn't be the first or the last entrepreneur to have that experience. What they did not know is that I had plans. Big plans.

From the beginning, I conceived of Dittie™ as more than just a product. To me, Dittie™ was about creating a network of women teaming together in full support of one another. We've had that as our mindset and our mission from the very beginning. The emotional branding, the notion that women should care about and love each other, was what really mattered. I'd seen too many depictions of catty woman backstabbing one another in books, in films, and on television. I also saw an opportunity to ride a wave of a cultural zeitgeist. *Sex and the City* and its message of sisterhood among a close group of female friends was at its height of popularity during the development of Dittie™. Women were reading a new kind of romance novel for a younger generation, represented by books like *The Divine Secrets of the Ya-Ya Sisterhood*, which were flying off shelves. The moment seemed ripe for a change. And if the big guys capitalized on my efforts and changed their packaging, too (which they ultimately did), that was okay, too—especially if it meant that women got the message. Getting the message was, to me, as important as getting the sales.

I know that sounds a little Pollyanna-ish, but it really is not. After all, one way the women were going to get the message was by buying the product. And in terms of the mood-lifting messages (see image page 284), at first, we tried to collect as many inspiring quotes about women as we possibly could to print them on the wrappers. BORING! We didn't need the tried and true; we had to have the wild and new. I wrote some of the messages, and I quickly realized that task could take up almost all of my time. I hired a writer, a member of the Girl Power generation, to craft these empowering, inspirational, and entertaining messages. She saved me. In three days, she wrote more messages than I could have in three years. We made our print deadline, thanks to her genius.

Reality intervened in another, though not unexpected, way. When we rolled out in April, our initial results were stronger than I expected, but sell-through still lagged behind that of the major national brands. I was prepared for that news. But most importantly we established a baseline of data so we could test and evaluate different marketing approaches. A brilliant friend of mine, Michael Cookson, once taught me to record baseline sales (sales before you apply marketing) so that when you apply marketing you can analyze the effectiveness of your campaign. This bit of advice ended up being a simple secret to my success as a consumer product entrepreneur and inventor. And it is for this reason alone that I was able to rework the first under-performing Hairagami® commercial and turn it into an award winning program.

Marketing that Matters

I wasn't about to just rely on hope. I had been planning a promotional and marketing campaign all along. I wasn't going to spend $100 million on a TV campaign—since I'd gotten into the business the costs had skyrocketed to that degree. I knew I couldn't compete with the big guys dollar-for-advertising-dollar. I had to come up with a more innovative grassroots campaign. I also had to individually tailor it to a particular market segment, geographic area, and retailer. I had the kind of flexibility that the giants lacked. While they could put their giant footprint down, I could run around like an ant in the spaces they didn't bother to cover.

In this regard, Wal-Mart and Target are absolutely the best. Because they really want to help their suppliers succeed, their information systems allow their vendors to see daily results of sales. Target even gave me special clearance to generate reports daily and that is just what we did. Now, I could see if a marketing idea was paying off immediately. With that kind of feedback, I wasn't wasting time and effort on things that weren't working. I could immediately implement changes. And those changes produced results. For Dittie™, I had four SKUs—one each for a regular tampon, a super tampon, a pantiliner, and a thong liner. With each of my accounts together we set up a target goal for Dittie™ based on the number of units per door (per store location) I was expected to sell initially—and then grow that number from that point.

I'd established a group of guerilla marketers, a program for young women that we called Dittie™ Life, to go out into the community to do outreach for the brand. These young women were phenomenal. They did amazing work for Dittie™ at various events. (see image page 284). For example, we realized that a lot of young women would congregate at concerts, so we "bought" the restrooms at a Jessica Simpson concert. In all the restrooms at that venue, we transformed them from ugly, drab sinks and stalls into salons we dubbed "Dittie™ Lounges." We put in perfume tables, offered nail polish, and we plastered the walls with Dittie™ Girl posters.

We placed "tampon fairies" at each end of the sixteen stalls in the restrooms. Every fifteen minutes, a fairy at one end of the stall rows would announce, "Oh my gosh, I just got my period. Does anyone have a Dittie™?"

The tampon fairy at the other end would say, "I do."

She'd then passed a box of Dittie™s under the stall to the girl next to her and say, "Have a Dittie™ and pass it on." Of course, having the girls in the middle see, hear about, sample, and touch the new product was key here. We were after exposure and we were determined to try every measure we could think of to make an impact on these young girls at the concert.

Pink was our color and we added splashes of it everywhere with rugs and soaps and we even had a pink bucket for those girls who over-indulged in alcohol. We were there to support women and establish the brand, even if that meant their exposure to Dittie™ consisted of a story they'd later share that went something like—"Remember when we went to that Jessica Simpson concert, and I threw up in that Dittie™ Pink bucket?"

We wanted to create a positive association between them and Dittie™. So, maybe if you were sitting in a classroom at the Wharton School of Business, you wouldn't read a chapter that mentions puke buckets, but I'm talking about a real world experience here. I am talking about a brand experience. And the results of these efforts were blockbuster. I couldn't do too many concerts because of the expense, but anytime we did an event, like a meet and greet at a local Target, the sell-through jumped. In one case, we did an event at a local Target and in six hours sold over 168 boxes of Dittie™s. We used the Dittie™ Life Street team to sample in Wal-Mart neighborhoods and schools. In twenty-nine weeks our sales grew by 760%. That kind of positive feedback kept us going, even if we weren't reaching those national brand sell-through standards throughout the entire chain of stores. It was clear that Dittie™ struck a nerve in these regional marketing outreach efforts. When women learned about it, they bought it. The trick was, of course, how to get the word out without breaking the bank through television advertising.

Marketing in the Potty

The concert experiment was so successful that I wanted to repeat that success without the expense. As a result, I came up with the idea that our message, our voice needed to be in restrooms at all kinds of different locations and not just concerts. I first checked into advertising in restrooms with signage. You've probably seen these ads in the restrooms of a club or restaurant. The cost to buy one of these ads is about $200 per restroom per month. This type of advertising is strictly for the local advertiser, as the cost structure really does not work for a small company in need of a national campaign. Let's say I wanted to be in 100,000 restrooms—a fraction of the number of homes a TV advertisement would reach—then I would be shelling out $20,000,000 dollars a month. Let's face it, that's an unheard of amount to dedicate to advertising for a small entrepreneur. Well, I may be a small entrepreneur, but I have big ideas. I knew I needed to get Dittie's presence into the restrooms, but I had to find a way of doing it without it costing any money. Better yet, what if I could figure out a way for the restroom to support women and our bottom line at the same time? Now that would be revolutionary.

I really haven't explained completely as of yet how this all unfolded. Do you remember the story of the Trojan horse? Well, the truth of the matter was that for me, almost from the outset, Dittie™ was merely a delivery mechanism—it was the horse that housed the real soldiers who were going to go into action to make a difference in the lives of women. I knew from nearly the start that I wanted to find a way to get Dittie™ into the hands of women through some creative and unique means. That meant inventing new distribution channels—or at least drastically altering an existing one.

All of you women out there know that in some restrooms there are tampon dispensers. They used to be far more prevalent than they are now. Most of them are these corroded and chipped remnants of another era. They look more like hand towel dispensers than anything else—and not particularly sanitary ones, at that. I thought, what if we were to put Dittie™s in their own dispenser, but in the voice of Dittie™. At this point in time, most tampon vending machines dispensed cardboard applicator tampons. I wanted to vend a premium quality pearlized plastic applicator tampon, and it was clear that I would have to custom-design a machine to vend our Dittie™s.

I found vending dispensers and had them painted pink. I had special Dittie™ two-packs made up and customized the machine to handle this kind of product. I placed them in restrooms near a Target store where Dittie™ was on sale, and much to my delight in the weeks following the installation of the vending machines, the sell-through at that particular store went through the roof. Something else happened; we started receiving web orders and lots of them. After fully understanding the impact of each machine (revenue from vended tampons plus revenue from on-line orders) it was clear that each machine was as powerful to our bottom line as an individual Target location. Again, further proof that if women knew about the product, they'd buy it. I liked the idea of a vending program so much that I wanted to find a way to cut my costs on this operation even further. The first vending machines I used were expensive, and they needed modifications to work. Both those factors cut into my profit margin. I also still had another plan circulating in my brain.

In the process of researching tampon vending, I learned that in order for a tampon to be vended by any kind of machine, it had to be packed in a tube so it could roll through the machine. I thought, no problem; I'll look into getting automated equipment that can do this. Well, the equipment to tube a tampon cost $875,000. Now, I'm not to keen on investing in expensive fixed assets, so I had to find an alternative.

If I couldn't buy a fully automated machine, I thought I'd find someone who could make an efficient, cost effective, yet simple jig to do what I needed it to do. After a round of calls, I found a manufacturer in China who could create a tubing "assist" machine. I had to set up a free trade zone to legally and cheaply import tampons into China then export them to me in the US. The tubing jigs cost $500 each, and I bought six of them at a savings of $872,000 less than the cost of the automated equipment. So, in that regard, three thousand dollars is a low investment in comparison to what it might have been. We set up the jigs and tubed Dittie™s off shore. Now, with the tubing problem solved, all I had to do was to custom design a vending machine to vend a plastic applicator tampon.

This part was very easy. I found a manufacturing source for vending machines and after speaking with them they, too, had the Passion for PINK and agreed to amortize the tooling over one year. That was all great, and I was now ready to bring out my grand idea: vendPINK (see image page 285).

I have an absolute passion to support women, and most of the products I've developed had specific applications for women—whether it was to save them time and effort or boost their self-esteem.

But that wasn't enough. I remember how conflicted I felt when my son was born. I wanted to work, but I wanted to be with him full-time, too. That's why I took him with me on those sales trips when he was young. That's why I took the red-eye back and forth from the West Coast to the East Coast and then back again. All so I could be with my son. We have all heard about the "Mommy Wars" which is the conflict between the working mom and the stay at home mom. I have talked to thousands of women from both groups. The working mom thinks she is so smart that she must work and puts down the stay at home mom. The stay at home mom says she is more committed to her child and family because she is willing to sacrifice her career to stay at home.

After I talk with these women, the one common element I consistently hear is that both groups would prefer to work part-time. But the opportunities are quite slim and limited at best. Women should not have to make a choice between work and family. To be honest, I knew that for the majority of mothers in America it wasn't an either/or choice, but a very definite BOTH. They had no choice but to work. I wanted to figure out a way that they could earn the money they needed and still be home as much of the time as they could for their families. I wanted to develop a fun, rewarding passionate choice for the new "hybrid" mom.

That was the inspiration for vendPINK™, the world's first pink (we established the color pink as the trade dress and trademark of the Dittie™ Company for product dispensed) tampon vending distributorship program that supports women with breast cancer. What I decided to do was to empower people who would be responsible for seeking out the locations to place the vending machines, keep them stocked, use the proceeds to replenish their stock, buy more machines if they desire, and make a tidy profit to boot. I had plans for this independent contractor. This person would also become our brand ambassador.

The amount of time the vendor operator spends on the project varies. They can do it part-time as a secondary source of income—while the kids are in school, for example—or they can do it as a source of retirement income. And of course they can vendPINK™ full-time. How they choose to run their own company is up to them. I wanted them to have a choice about what to do, who to involve, and how much time to spend on vendPINK™.

You may be asking how difficult it is to get business owners to agree to allow a vendPINK™ dispenser in their place of business. Surprisingly easy, if you explain to them that if *their* customer has a tampon emergency and she has to leave their establishment, that's profit walking out the door. And on any given night, especially with the regularity with which women get their periods, they could be losing customers. Framed in that context, how could it hurt them to have a vendPINK™ dispenser on hand? The establishment is not responsible for stocking it or maintaining it and it improves the restroom experience for their customers, while contributing good will to a cause.

Helping Women in Need

We've just launched vendPINK™ as I write this, and the initial results are strong, with most of the first container of machines being sold before they even left China. (Remember the Golden Rule of *The Carey Formula*: sell your product first.)

VendPINK™ is a vending program preceded by none. We introduced vendPINK™ by offering start-up kits. Each start-up kit comes with enough tubed refill Dittie™s to pay for the machine. Imagine that, once your refill inventory vends, you have paid for the machine. Now you just collect quarters for the life of the machine. Of course you need to purchase the Dittie™s, but you as the owner of the machine make a 200% profit on each vend. You keep the quarters and I make the donation to the Y-Me organization. To be a vendor operator you can purchase ten start-up kits at a whole-sale price. We only place one vendor operator per zip code. What is unique with the vendPINK™ program is that our vendor operators make money two ways. First, by the vended tampons and, second, by on-line orders for boxes of Dittie™s. We call this our Dittie™ Delivery Program where anyone can order boxes of Dittie™s shipped directly to their door with FREE s&h (see image page 285). Each time we get an on-line order we match the zip code with the zip code of the vendor operator and the vendor operator earns credit for a new machine. This is how they grow their business. Vendor operators have access to a secure site where they can check the status of their "Dittie™ Dollar" account, order posters, download ads, and get product at wholesale prices to do their own guerilla marketing and promotional efforts. Vend-PINK™ is like the game of Monopoly—the more locations you have, the more money you make. In addition, our potential vendPINK™ operators can order a sales kit and pre-sell (the Golden Rule again) their locations before they buy machines from us. By expanding the brand awareness, they are helping the Dittie™ brand and they are helping themselves. This is a unique proposition in vending and I have filed a patent application protecting this business architecture. I'm proud that this innovation will help women on many fronts.

What I envision is that there will be 100,000 Dittie™ vending machines across the country and a lot of satisfied vendor operators. I also foresee that at no additional cost to the vendor operators, after a period of a year or two, they will substantially increase the number of machines in their control. This will increase their profits, and add substantially to Dittie™'s mission of supporting women. What could be better than that?

Well, it can be. I have made a pledge for the Dittie™ Company to donate twenty percent of its profits on all vended Dittie™s to a breast cancer outreach organization called Y-Me. Sadly, I know that cancer has touched everyone's life. Just a few years ago, I lost the aunt after whom I'm named to breast cancer. In the course of writing this book, just a few weeks ago, I also lost my beloved Aunt Doreen to this terrible disease. There are many wonderful organizations out there who have earned sterling reputations for the work they do in funding research and care. We selected Y-Me because their mission parallels Dittie™'s. They offer support to women who have breast cancer. Twenty-four hours a day, seven days a week, they have an outreach hotline that women can call to speak to another woman who's experienced cancer personally. In twenty languages, a toll-free call can assure any woman at any time that she is not alone. (Please visit www.y-me.org for additional information.)

So, as the sales of Dittie™ increase, as the brand gains awareness through its placement in vending machines around the country, we are making a substantial difference in the lives of those women who have enrolled in vendPINK™, as well in the lives of the millions of women who have been diagnosed with breast cancer. That's why I'm thrilled about the reception that Dittie™ and vendPINK™ have received in the marketplace. Those increases in sales reflect an increase in the funds going to a very worthwhile organization dedicated to helping women cope with the reality of their disease.

In Dittie™, I've merged my personal passion—my desire to help women—by meeting a need I felt personally and shared with many other women. In taking on the big guns in the feminine hygiene protection category, I've had to stretch, learn and employ creative efforts across the full spectrum of the process. I've put my trust in professionals who can do their jobs better than I ever could. I've innovated and struggled, but throughout, if there's been one guiding force in all of this, it has been the PASSION OF PINK. I hope that someday you'll find, or perhaps you already have, the project that ignites your passion, fires your creativity, and launches you into an orbit that provides you with a new perspective, a wealth of lessons, and the sense of satisfaction that only comes from meeting a challenge head on and with integrity.

Coming Soon!

The results for Dittie™ and vendPINK™ are not yet fully in, but I plan to share them with you in my next book. In *Going Up Against the Big Boys*, we will look more closely at what vendPINK™ has meant and what the results of my application of *The Carey Formula* in this arena have meant in terms of success. I know that

I'm not the only one who is watching and waiting to see the numbers showing how Dittie™ and vendPINK™ are performing.

In *Going Up Against the Big Boys*, I'll also share some of the insights and observations that I've made about a subject that has come up time and time again in the last few months. It seems as though everyone who learns about Dittie™ and vendPINK™ wants to know the same thing: weren't you afraid to venture into this territory? As you know already, I am truly passionate about helping women, and I really believe that the model I've set up for vendPINK™ can make an enormous difference in women's lives—giving them the freedom and flexibility to work and to mother that most women seem to desire. But more than that passion, the one other attribute that has helped me the most is the ability to embrace my fear and to rise to the challenge of this project.

I do feel fear, but somehow through years of experience I've developed a mechanism that allows me to channel that fear into positive momentum that helps me move forward in a focused manner. Sometimes that mechanism was triggered by overcoming obstacles and challenges on my own. Other times, it was developed through the caring of others; for instance, I remember when I was nine years old and I was taken on my first ski trip with my father's colleague and friend Jack Rominger and his family. He was an engineer and entrepreneur and one of the most accomplished, kind, and confident men I know, and he became an enormous influence in my life.

He helped me get to the top of the steepest, tallest expanse of snow that I'd ever seen in my nine years. I stood at the top of that precipice with my eyes wide and my breath catching in my throat. I looked around, and tiny bundles of insulated down and wool surrounded me on the bunny hill. It didn't matter to me that I was on the bunny hill—I was scared. Jack Rominger was a calming presence. He wheedled, cajoled, encouraged, and escorted me down the hill. I flopped and rolled and eventually rode the remainder of the way down the hill on the backs of his skis. You would have never known that was my route down based on what Jack said to me and what he told everyone else about what a trooper I'd been. He made me feel like I'd conquered Everest. A few years later, but while I was still very young, he taught me how to drive an off-road four-wheel-drive vehicle (on private property) with the same tenacious tenderness and compassion as he did on the slopes.

I grew up surrounded by people who encouraged me and nurtured me. They helped me overcome obstacles and conquer fears, always with an eye on moving forward. It's my hope that this book generally, and this chapter specifically, have been instructive and inspiring. Fear is just like any other obstacle you may face in your attempt to live your dream. There are multiple ways around, through, and over every one of them—with a little inspiration and creativity you can discover those avenues yourself.

I also have provided you with another resource to help you overcome any obstacle you may encounter. *The Carey Formula CD Library* that is available online at www.TheCareyFormula.com will help you with specific questions like what distribution channels are best for your product or how you can discover secret channels that others may not have considered for a product in your particular category. While I have never been to China, I have manufactured over 100 products there. I provide contacts to all my manufactures and the secrets to how I find new manufacturers. Also included are the links to over 30,000 retail locations that I present and sell to. I have invested a lifetime of work to create this resource guide so you don't have to start at the beginning like I did.

I offer these invaluable lists of contacts, forms, and other information because I believe that knowledge is power. I believe in equal access to information at an affordable price. I want to put the power of *The Carey Formula* in your hands, so that you can make a difference in your own life, and hopefully in lives of others, as well.

"After fifteen years of running Intouch Group, a music technology company, we have made a strategic decision to launch a consumer products division. I have known Barbara Carey for over fifteen years. Her CD Library has been an invaluable tool, and has saved us an immense amount of time by being able to go right to the source in several categories with no fuss. I recommend Barbara's CD Library to any entrepreneur. Most companies keep their contacts as confidential business information. Barbara has made them available so that your road to success is easy and direct.

Josh Kaplan
President/CEO
Intouch Group

I started off this chapter talking about my son's statements about the relative strength of the grasp I have on reality. Well, the truth about reality is that we all create it for ourselves. If you are interested in creating a new reality for yourself, I want to provide you with the tools and resources you can use to do so. That's the great thing about America. I know that the American Dream has become such a clichéd term as to be almost meaningless. Or it is so different for everyone as to be almost impossible to classify. But to me, that dream has always been an expression of our relationship to reality. In many places in the world, the reality you are born into is the one from which you will exit when your life ends. In America, we're blessed with an abundance of opportunity. No resource is greater than the opportunity to reinvent ourselves, transform our life circumstances, and create a new and better reality for our loved ones and ourselves. It is almost as if we are all the directors of the movie of our lives. We can control and shape the outcome, so that the story can truly proceed anyway we choose.

Of course, I am an optimist. To me the glass is almost always half full, but I also have two empty glasses that I want to fill up. I am aware that we all experience many tragic losses along the path of our lives, just as I did with the painful loss of my two beloved aunts to breast cancer. I am going to keep working until both of those two glasses are full. I hope that you'll join me on whatever personal crusade matters to you. I promise you that it will be an interesting and fulfilling journey.

Zen and the Art of Balance

As I mentioned earlier, one of my all time favorite books is Robert Pirsig's wonderful work of nonfiction called *Zen and the Art of Motorcycle Maintenance*. I love it for a couple of reasons. First, Pirsig does a remarkable job of telling a thrilling story about a cross-country motorcycle journey with his son. On this journey, they retrace steps Pirsig took many years before. There's an element of mystery to this journey strand of the book, and its resolution is emotionally charged and poignant. While I'm not a big fan of motorcycles—cars are more my thing—I love how Pirsig uses the motorcycle and its upkeep as a metaphor for a number of key points he's trying to make. One of those points is that our lives are way out of balance. Writing in the 1960s, he understood that even then, most of us were too busy to really understand new technologies. Because we lacked understanding, when those technologies didn't work, we got angry and frustrated. Still today, his point holds. Most of us fear what we don't understand, and how many of us can say that we fully understand the multiplicity of technologies available to us? We just want them all to work seamlessly when we want them to work, and leave the understanding up to the geeks.

Where I grew up, shade tree mechanics used to be commonplace, but cars have become so sophisticated that unless you're an electrical engineer, you may not be able to do much of anything in case of a breakdown. How many times in your life has even the simplest gadget failed and your frustration level risen to near-breaking point? I've heard horror stories about important presentations going up in flames because some piece of technology failed. What's the point of PowerPoint, if you can't make your point without power?

One of the points that I keep coming back to in this book is that knowledge is power. You may have had an idea for a wonderful invention but felt overwhelmed and thwarted by the next steps. Hopefully, especially now that we've gone through *The Carey Formula* in its entirety, you are feeling better about your prospects for realizing your dream because you know what steps to take next. Pirsig felt much the same way about knowledge. He took the time to learn how his motorcycle operated, so that in the case of an eventual mechanical breakdown, he wouldn't suffer a mental breakdown. I think we feel most frustrated and angry when we don't know what steps to take. I hope that this book will serve as a kind of owner's manual for you to consult so that if you get stalled anywhere along the way, you'll be able to refer to this book to get you back on the road as soon, and as economically, as possible. Knowledge can offset and overcome those feelings of helplessness and hopelessness that we have all experienced when those strange noises start emanating from underneath the hood and we begin to hear the death rattle of the starter playing a duet with the chattering of our own teeth.

I wanted to include a chapter on balance in this book for a number of reasons, and I've given you one of the main ones already. With this book and the accompanying CDs you can purchase, I've made available to you many of the tools necessary for success as an inventor/entrepreneur. If for some reason you should find that you have somehow wandered from the path to success, you can consult this book and find your way back. Most importantly, though, I believe that this book can serve as a rich resource that will enable you to restore balance in your life. Why is balance so important to an entrepreneur? Well, when you think about it, you are a kind of one-person team, a jack-of-all-trades, if you will. You'll be expected to fill many positions and juggle many responsibilities. You're also no doubt competitive, and if you can't find another solution to a problem, you're likely to hyper-focus and try harder, work longer hours, and give even more of yourself than you did before you encountered the obstacle. How do I know this? Let's just say that I have seen the image of that person in my own mirror.

Balance as a Buzz Word

If you recall, I wasn't a traditional student. School seemed to stifle many of my best traits, but I do recall a few concepts from those days. One of them is a term I remember from biology—"homeostasis." Homeostasis refers to the body's ability to "maintain internal equilibrium by adjusting its physiological processes." In other words, the body is constantly regulating itself to maintain a proper balance. That balance could be internal temperature, the acidity level in the blood, heart rate, blood pressure, and a thousand other different processes. We don't even have to think about the homeostatic efforts of our body—they happen at a subconscious level. The only time we really think about the acidity level in our body is if our stomach acts up. We react to those stimuli of pain and discomfort. Well, truth be told, we'd be a lot better off if we were more in tune with ourselves—if we were more fully aware of our body's innate sense of balance, knowing it has the capability to anticipate problems. We would then proactively take measures to avoid feeling the pain and discomfort of one of our systems not functioning properly.

Pain is the body's way of telling us that something is wrong, but wouldn't you rather avoid feeling pain? And how many of us have developed the ability to block out pain and discomfort in order to get the job done or finish some task? How many times have you been at work, at home, or at the office and only at the end of the day do you realize, after finally finishing some task, how sore your jaw is from having clenched your teeth for so long? Or how many of you have sat at your desk and at the end of the day felt as if a small burrowing mammal had worked its way under the skin of one side or another of the back of your neck and had gnawed away at a shoulder muscle? Or even worse, how many times has your day been so busy that when you finally do take a break, you have this painful tightness in your midsection and you suddenly realize your bladder is in imminent danger of bursting? That's a life out of balance. We'll discuss some of these physiological symptoms later. First, I want to take a look at the big picture, to show you how important it is to have the Big "B" Balance working for you rather than against you.

Build a Balanced Foundation

I remember as a youngster thinking that I wanted to be my own boss. I knew that my independence was worth more to me than most anything else in my life. Autonomy was worth having even if it meant that I would lack a sense of financial security that comes from working for someone else. Autonomy was worth having even if it meant that I would have to take full responsibility for every setback I faced. Somehow I knew, even then, I would have to figure out a way to maintain my balance. Imagine for a second that you have a seesaw in front of you. On that seesaw you have to place an orange and a peanut and you have to get them to balance. Can you figure out a way to do it? Well, it may not be easy, but by placing that orange as close as possible to the fulcrum, or balance point, on which the seesaw rests and the peanut as far to the end of the opposite side, you should be able to accomplish this balancing act.

Being an inventor/entrepreneur requires you to be a skilled balancer—of time, energy, money, emotional capital, and a whole host of other things. You won't be good at balancing unless you have a steady and substantial fulcrum on which to place the plank of your seesaw. In other words, instead of balancing that seesaw on a narrow point, it's better to have a larger, broader, more stable surface. For me, at least originally, independence did serve that invaluable function. My desire to not work for anyone else and to invent my own rules for my own game was so powerful, that I found a way to balance the many demands and frustrations of the work I'd chosen. Over time, that desire has evolved and branched off in several different directions. You know about my passionate commitment to women and the bettering of their lives, you know how important it is for me to give back to the community, how demanding I am of myself to insure that I am fully present as a parent to my son, and that I live my life with integrity and honesty.

Before we can begin to talk about the many ways balance impacts your life as a person and as a person engaged in an enterprise, you have to understand one thing: without that fulcrum, that steady substantial place on which to rest the many demands life imposes on us as individuals and companies, you will be doomed to eventual failure—either personally or professionally. I'm no engineer, but even I know that unless you build something on solid ground and have a stout foundation, whatever dreams or designs you conceive will topple. On a personal level, that means truly and completely doing the self-assessment work we talked about much earlier in the book. There's that old joke about how to run a million-dollar business—start a multi-million dollar business and wait. Without balance and vigilance, that scenario can become the truth all too easily. I've alerted you already to the dangers of a single-minded devotion to money and the pursuit of financial profit alone. We'll take a look at that issue again here, more specifically in terms of balancing the profit motive with other goals and desires. Even better, when we build upon our intrinsic values and deeply held beliefs, we'll have an even more substantial foundation than if we worked from the profit principle. In this chapter, we're also going to take a look at negotiation and other business practices and how they are all part of a balanced business and personal life. Before we get to these ideas, however, we're going to start with some of the other basics—how we care for our physical bodies, our emotions, and our spirits.

A Pace of Grace

Linda Kavelin-Popov has written an excellent book about maintaining balance in our lives. A former high-powered New York executive turned speaker and leader of a wonderful not for profit organization, The Virtues Project, she now travels the world as a much in demand workshop leader. In her book, *A Pace of Grace*, she talks about being stricken with polio as a child and her eventual recovery. She went on to be a hard-charging, do-everything super mom who pushed herself to such a degree that later in her adult life her disease recurred, sapping her of every bit of energy. In the book, she relates the many lessons she's learned and offers guidelines so that we too may find our own pace of grace. She doesn't advocate dropping out or ceasing completely, but setting up and maintaining proper boundaries so that we don't get caught in the cycle of do-every-thing and be-everything for everyone else. Women are especially vulnerable to the very real dangers of becoming caretakers of the world's ills. Popov reminds us that if we run ourselves into the ground taking care of everyone else, then when we are truly needed, our fuel tank will be empty and we won't be able to be of service to anyone.

She also offers some essential tips on taking care of the body. While we all have heard most of these, they bear repeating.

Drink Water

Experts estimate that anywhere from twenty-five to forty-five percent of Americans are either borderline dehydrated or are fully dehydrated. This isn't because of any drought or lack in our water supply. It's because of a lack of awareness of what is taking place in our own bodies. Hard to believe these statistics, especially when water coolers seem to be a ubiquitous presence in most offices. I'm aware of these numbers, but many times I've found my energy flagging, my attention wavering, and I've real-ized that an hour or more has passed since I had a drink of water. Let me also remind you that soft drinks and coffee are both diuretics—they actually lower the fluid level in your system by causing you to eliminate fluids more frequently. The guideline to drink sixty-four ounces of water (eight eight-ounce glasses) daily remains a useful target. Doctors will also tell you that it is best to spread that consumption out over a long period of time, rather than slug down thirty-two ounces of water in one big gulp moment twice a day.

What I've found most effective is to keep a small mug of water at my desk rather than a large bottle of water. Why? Well, with the smaller mug, I'm likely to take in smaller quantities more frequently. As an added bonus, I have to get up from my desk more often to walk to the water cooler, the sink, or the drinking fountain to fill it. What's the advantage of that? Well one of the other things that Kavelin-Popov and others stress as important is the taking of frequent breaks and stretching opportunities during the course of the day. Many cultures thrive on the siesta system, yet we in the states seem reluctant to even get up and stroll to the water cooler. Not good.

A Good Deep Breath

One of the other body functions that Kavelin-Popov and so many others claim that we ignore is breathing. How can that be? After all, every few seconds of every day, we take in oxygen to feed the approximately 75 trillion cells. That's right, 75 trillion cells, and every one of them requires oxygen to function properly. Most of the time we don't think about our breathing at all and we take in shallow gulps of air. Even if you spend five minutes each morning before you begin work doing deep breathing exercises—using your diaphragm to help expand your ribcage to draw in a greater volume of air—you will find that your mind is clearer, your focus more acute, and your energy level higher. Essentially, what you're asked to do is to become more aware of your body and attuned to your levels of tension and stress. Breathing deeply and fully oxygenating your cells is the surest and one of the fastest and easiest ways to reduce your stress level.

In addition to focusing on your breathing, many books and magazine articles are available to demonstrate how you can partake in mini-stretching/yoga breaks while seated at your desk. These two- to four-minute breaks are amazingly restorative. Even those walks to refill your water container or to empty your bladder (the number one complaint of those who find the sixty-four ounce consumption guideline too punitive) can serve the same general function. Get out of your chair, move around, increase your circulation, and allow your body to move. I have a friend who, when he works, frequently gets so engrossed in what he's doing that he doesn't realize he has the habit of resting one elbow on the desktop with the hand of that arm flopped over at the wrist, fingers dangling lifelessly in the air like a drooping flower. He can hold that position for hours, completely unaware of its lifeless presence until the painful sleeping sensation penetrates his consciousness. It makes you wonder what really fell asleep. Most of us live our lives not fully present in our bodies, not working at nearly the full capacity we're capable of because we don't have enough body awareness, or we've become so numb to our usual state of being that we think of being depleted as "normal."

A good friend of mine tells me the story of a former college classmate who is married to a wonderful man. He's a terrific provider, a generous father to their two sons, and a constant source of worry to his wife. Why? He gets up everyday at four-thirty in the morning to go to work. He feels he can get more done early in the morning before he has to attend to the deluge of e-mails, voicemails, and meetings that cram his daily schedule. He also wants to be home in time to spend a few hours with his sons before they are off to bed—an entirely admirable goal, right?—so he prefers to arrive early rather than stay late. Still, he is convinced he has to be at work until at least six each evening, so his usual routine calls for a minimum of a twelve-hour workday. He's been doing this fairly regularly for the last fifteen years. His diet consists of coffee and a donut on the train ride to work, a bag of pretzels and a diet soda at his desk while he works through lunch, and then a big dinner at home (usually after eight) to make up for the huge calorie deficit incurred during the day. Of course, with this schedule, there is very little time left for exercise. He violated nearly every principle that nutritionists expound, and it's no wonder that his weight ballooned.

Only when his father died suddenly of a heart attack, did he hear the wake-up alarms his wife had been sending out. He began to eat smaller and lighter meals throughout the day, started to work out more frequently, and dropped the thirty-five pounds he needed to without any kind of fad dieting. He simply decided he needed better balance in his work life, trimmed his hours and his intake slightly, and couldn't be happier. He has more energy than ever and is even able to coach both of his sons' youth league baseball teams. He's more driven and focused than ever, but is enjoying his work more, and with a few simple alterations in his diet is healthier than he's been his entire adult life. He found the balance that was right for him, imposed his considerable will on a new goal, used the knowledge he gained in the wake of his father's death, and made a positive change.

Mind and Spirit

You've probably heard the wonderful expression that, "We are not physical beings having a spiritual experience; we are spiritual beings having a physical experience." For most adults the majority of our waking hours are spent at work. It stands to reason, then, that we would want those hours to be spent in a way that fulfills us and not just our bank accounts. I know that I've made this point elsewhere in the book, but I hope that you've been able to witness my own personal evolution as you've read about my experiences, culminating with the work I am doing currently with vendPINK™.

I admit that early on in my career, I was more interested in building empires than I was in building a karmic bank account. Call it ego, call it ambition, call it survival, call it stubbornness, or what have you, I wanted to succeed. I wasn't a very process-oriented person in the beginning stages of my career. I was much more concerned with the bottom line results. That's why I was so devastated by the lack of success with the Time-Out Watch—to the extent that I locked myself in a darkened room and was determined to seal myself off from the rest of life until I felt presentable again. And how was I going to become presentable? The only way, of course, was by having some demonstrable evidence of financial success or at least a viable plan to show how I could make large sums of money. Over time, the empires got erected, the cash flowed in, and all the outward, and many of the inward, trappings of success were mine. Was I happy? Absolutely. Was I content? No way. Not because I wanted more or better, but because there was something inside me that was evolving, something that didn't have a unit price attached to it, something I couldn't really put on a traditional balance sheet or a profit and loss statement.

In a way, what my early successes taught me is that I could succeed on my own terms—that I could create companies and products and still be a full-time mother. I could sacrifice (though I didn't necessarily think of it in those terms) by taking red-eye flights and foregoing overnight hotel stays so that I could be home with my son as much as possible. In other words, my early successes made me aware that I could find my own personal balance, independent of anyone else's perceptions of me or what was "right." Just as I had to learn to be sharper, more flexible, and more agile to compete with larger companies, I had to apply those same lessons to my personal life, to attend to the larger mission of becoming a successful person, wife, mother, and citizen of the world. I know that sounds a bit highfalutin, but I was reminded of this idea while watching the recent Academy Awards broadcast. In her acceptance speech for winning Best Actress, Reese Witherspoon quoted June Carter Cash, the woman she portrayed in her award-winning role. Ms. Cash's response to the question, "How're you doing?" would frequently be, "I'm just trying to matter."

Another way to phrase that would be to say, "I'm just trying to make a difference." Whether that difference is in the lives of my family, friends, community, or the world at large, that is what I'm trying to do. As my successes mounted, the spheres I targeted for success enlarged. I knew that I was making a difference in the life of my immediate family—we were spending more time together, taking more frequent vacations—and once their needs were being met, it was easier to look outside that inner circle to see who else I could aid, either directly or indirectly. I incorporated that aspect into my personal mission statement. Sure, I still wanted to make money, but my mission included making a difference as well. Money became a means and not an end. I could do more to help women through vendPINK™. But vendPINK™ was built with dollars earned by Hairagami® and other products—and not just with the dollars, but with the lessons learned, the relationships built, and the confidence inspired by those successes.

Balance with Business

In addition to vendPINK™ and the breast cancer charities associated with that venture, I've found other outlets for the important balancing act of giving back to the community. I've recently been asked to deliver the keynote address at the National Gallery for America's Young Inventors' induction ceremony in Akron, Ohio. If you recall, my son Richard was a student board member for this organization. I believe wholeheartedly in the organization and its mission to celebrate the learning, insight, creativity, and workmanship of America's student inventors by recognizing and preserving their accomplishments for the inspiration of future generations.

One of the reasons why I am so committed to this organization is because of the pressing need for America to retain its place at the head of the global pack. Much has been written recently about the rise of India and China as research giants. Many of the best minds from those countries have come to the U.S. to receive their college education and post-graduate degrees. In the past, many of those students stayed here in the United States, working at cutting-edge research facilities. Now that their nations of origin have become more advanced economically, many of those students are returning home to gleaming new research facilities. This kind of attrition is but one effect causing what some see as a potential science gap. Fewer and fewer American students are enrolling in rigorous science and technology majors or graduate programs. Our educational system lags behind many other nations', and while our government cuts back funding in crucial areas such as education and research, requiring the private sector to fund what other countries' governments do, America may soon lose its global competitive edge. Nearly every single major innovation of the last century—from the microchip to Teflon—was the result of American ingenuity. We can't assume that our domination of the intellectual capital markets will continue forever. That's one reason why I offer you, the reader, the opportunity to purchase this book from me directly online or through my call center. When you do, we will ask you if you would like to donate one dollar to this amazing organization, The National Gallery for America's Young Inventors. If you do, I will match that donation dollar-for-dollar. It is my hope to raise $600,000 to help offset their operating expenses to ensure that the organization will remain viable. While I've no problem with outsourcing work to other countries when appropriate, and I do the bulk of my manufacturing overseas because of lower costs and availability, I do have a problem with the idea that other nations may one day out-research us. We no longer face the challenge of Sputnik (the Soviet Union's satellite program that set in motion our efforts to reach the moon), but we do face challenges in the global economy. Whatever we can do to encourage and promote innovation and invention among our young people is a wise investment on any balance sheet.

Keeping It All in Perspective

One of the most difficult things any entrepreneur faces is balancing family life and work life. I know from personal experience how difficult that is. On the one hand, you feel as though what you are working toward is a better life for your family in the long run, but in the short term it is often far too easy to feel like those benefits may be too far in the future to really matter. I know that my extended family had to sacrifice a lot in order for me to succeed.

Remember, I said that autonomy and independence were essential values in my work life. Well, a lot of that also rubbed off into my personal life as well. I don't know how my husband endured some of my early antics, but I want to share another of my stories about when my life and the adventures I saw on *I Love Lucy* ran parallel to one another.

It all started because the California winter in 1986 was bleak—rainy and dreary in a way that just drained me. By the time spring rolled around, I wasn't feeling much better and the weather wasn't cooperating much either. In 1986, Rich Jr. was five years old. I knew I wasn't going to have another child. I was feeling maternal pangs combined with the weather-related blahs, but mostly I was feeling like I needed something new and fresh and exciting in my life. I wanted another baby, but I knew that was impossible, so I decided instead to have a lamb. I'd been happily involved with them when I was young and part of a club called Future Farmers of America.

One bright spring morning, I woke up and prepared for work; I put on my business suit, clasped a string of pearls around my neck, and checked my hair in the mirror. I looked at myself and said, "You know, Barbara, you've been fighting this feeling for weeks now. What's the point? You know you want one. Go get one."

I hopped into my car, and instead of driving the few miles into town to get to my office, I headed north. Forty-five minutes later, I was in the heart of Petaluma and its ranching country. Before I'd left, I'd made a couple of calls and found out that we were smack dab in the heart of lambing season and that many ranchers had lambs for sale or at auction. The first auction I attended was in a large indoor arena where the animals were led into a circular viewing area, not unlike where a rodeo event would be held.

I was only slightly self-conscious as I pulled and tugged at my skirt as I sidled across the grandstand toward an empty seat. I was the only woman. The grizzled ranchers could barely hide their annoyance and amusement as they had to shift onto one Levi cheek and slide a mud and sheep dip encrusted boot onto the bench to let me by. I didn't care. I wanted a lamb, and I was going to get a lamb no matter what I had to endure. When the announcer said over the public address system that the first entrants coming into the arena were lambs, I had visions of Little Bo Peep and her sparkling white lambs gamboling and prancing in the grass. What I saw instead was an ambling, darting, gray and wooly beast about ten times the size of what I had in mind. I wasn't going to be able to snuggle up to one of these beasts to bottle feed it. The things had to be at least eighty pounds and were barely controllable, let alone huggable.

What was the deal here? How could the little lamb of my imagination and memory be so far removed from this beastly and odorous reality? What I quickly learned was that I had inquired about lambs being available. Any sheep less than a year old could be called a lamb. The rest of the animals up for auction were going to be similar to the first batch I'd seen.

Wiser but no happier, I excused myself past the row of herders and ranchers and out to my car. I figured I'd gotten off on the wrong foot with my search, but that didn't mean that I couldn't pivot off that foot and change direction. I started to drive. The area around Petaluma was loaded with sheep farms. I'd just stop and ask at each farmhouse if they had any lambs. The first couple of stops weren't too successful. I was told that they had lambs, was led to a field and shown what I'd just seen at the auction. I learned to refine my question, "Do you have any new-born lambs. Any born within the last twenty four hours?" No, no, no. But I pressed on. At one point, I was driving down a long dusty access road toward a farmhouse. The road was narrow and rutted and I felt more like I was in a kayak in white water than a car. I eased to the side of the road when I saw an enormous stake-bed truck approaching. I looked out the side window of the car and saw sheep grazing contentedly in the field. I had a good feeling about this.

I flagged down the truck driver and he stopped. He got out of his cab and I got out of my car. He gave me one of those looks, the only kind of look you can give a woman when you are driving a truckload of sheep and a woman in a business suit driving a very suburban, conservative sedan, having the glazed looked in her eye of a lamb-lovin' city girl, stops you and asks you if you have any newborn lambs for sale. When she asks you, you say just about the only thing you can possibly say in that situation.

"Sure do, ma'am. Today's your lucky day. Just had twins born last night. They can be separated and the mother will still have one to nurse."

"Can I buy it?"

"How's twelve dollars?"

I fish in my purse for cash and come up with a few bills. "Will you take nine?"

"Sure."

Next thing I know I'm wobbling unsteadily in the field in my black pumps, picking my way carefully through the minefield, to get my lamb. It turned out to be the lamb of my dreams—mixed in with a bit of pre-godmother Cinderella. The lamb was as cute and cuddly as a pup, but was gray and ashy looking. I didn't care. I had my lamb. I practically floated back to the car. On the way back home, I stopped at a feed store for some sheep's milk, and then at Longs Drug Store for baby shampoo.

As soon as I got home, I brought the lamb inside and got a couple of bath towels to wrap it in to make it comfortable. Then I went on a reconnaissance mission to find the very softest and warmest blankets I could find. Essentially, I was looking for swaddling clothes; I pulled down and aired out everything soft I could find in the attic. Next, I took the lamb and filled the kitchen sink with warm water in preparation for her bath. Once bathed, she was the pristine white bundle I'd been dreaming of. I wrapped her up in the blankets and carried her around the house with me, feeding her and cooing to her just as I would have done with a human infant. I was lost in a reverie of maternal bliss.

That's when I heard a car pull into the driveway and my stomach dropped. I had to take in a few deep breaths to prevent myself from going into full-blown panic mode. I looked out the window and saw that Rich Sr. had picked up our son from school. Okay, I told myself, I can handle this. I'm an adult. I made a hasty decision, but hey, it wasn't the first time and this too shall pass and all of that. The problem, though, was that this really wasn't the first time I had made a decision like this without consulting my husband. In fact, only three days before he had sat me down and talked to me very calmly about my penchant for making too many executive decisions without consulting him. Now, how was I going to explain this lamb in the wake of my very contrite and very genuinely apologetic claim that I would do better from then on out? How could I, after barely seventy-two hours of diligence, gone off and made a major decision like buying a lamb without even thinking of calling Rich Sr. first? I was a terrible person, no doubt about it.

If I wasn't buying new furniture, moving other pieces around the house, buying and selling fixer-upper houses—all without consulting him—I guess a sheep wasn't so bad, but the size of the purchase wasn't the point, now was it? Even I could see that.

I ran around the kitchen trying to clean up—as though the sight of water spills and towels would arouse more suspicion than the four legged (and adorable) lamb cradled in my arms. I scampered toward the front door, and just as I was about to open it, I heard Rich Jr. crying. I yanked the door open, bent down to my son to cradle him while concealing the lamb in my arms and asked, "What happened?"

Through sniffling inhalations, he said, "I fell and hurt my knee!"

Without showing him the lamb, I said the first thing that came to my mind. "Would you feel better if you had a lamb?"

He immediately stopped thinking about his skinned knee and looked me in the eye and said, "Well, as a matter of fact, I would."

I looked up at his father, a guilty smile playing at the corners of my mouth. "Do you think he'd feel better if he had a lamb?"

My husband shook his head and smiled, "Oh, I'm sure he would."

"Rich, you're brilliant! Look, Rich Jr., your father and I bought you a lamb!" I opened the blanket and exposed the real-live lamb. Rich Jr. and I stood up and did a tiny dance. He totally forgot about his knee and spent the next hour feeding and playing with our new addition to the family.

I don't know if this was another of those moments when reality and I took a few steps back from one another or if it was just another in a series of Carey family treasured memories, but it didn't matter. Somehow, things seemed to resolve themselves. Our hearts were in the right places, and though I hadn't quite mastered the art of the bilateral decision and I'd still meandered into the clover of unilateral choices, we managed to weather that wooly storm. There were sure to be others; you know a few of the slings and arrows that have made up the bulk of my professional life.

Despite all the other major successes I had in business, this story means the most to me. Not just because I managed to think and to react quickly in my little crisis, or that I had low up-front lamb costs, but because I had surrounded myself with the right people who supported me no matter if my choices didn't fit within the parameters of some decision-making matrix. When you really think about it, a lamb doesn't make much sense logically. But that's not the point of owning the lamb, and that's not always the point of bringing any product to market. What would be the fun of doing business if all we did was crunch numbers and do data analyses to determine the relative profitability of a venture?

Sometimes you just want to have a lamb no matter what anyone else may think. Nothing else can replace the feelings that choice produced. I hope that you'll be able to enjoy your fair share of lambs on your journey and that you'll find others to share your vision and your passion. When you balance belief, desire, and the right kinds of information, you can't go wrong—just hold out hope that down the next dusty access road, you'll find exactly what you've been looking for.

Fun

Even though I'm fairly far removed chronologically from the days when those three simple letters were the be all and the end all of my days, I still find time every day for fun. I can't imagine living a life in which fun is something you've packed up and put away for safekeeping along with other cherished childhood mementos. Play is an essential part of what I do—whether its playing with ideas, marketing possibilities, or throwing a ball in a fiercely fun game of fetch with my dog, I take time every day to simply let loose and enjoy the abundance of pleasure that life provides us. I don't have to look very far or search very hard to find fun. Like an essential vitamin or other nutrient, we have to take in a healthy dose of fun every day. Just like some people take their regimen of vitamins in dull capsules and others enjoy Flintstone's Chewables, we all have a choice on how we respond to our daily environment and circumstances.

One of the reasons why I wanted to tell you my sheep story is so that you can see how impulsivity and pleasure have always been a part of my life. I have to be disciplined and judicious in so many ways as a businessperson, but I also have to let that other part of me have free reign. That's why buyers love it when I come calling. I treat those meetings seriously, but I don't take myself too seriously. Yes, I want the order, but I won't let that become the single-minded pursuit and outcome of that meeting. Business requires meeting new people and building relationships with them, which is, frankly, the primary source of fun in sales. I love to laugh and I love to make other people laugh. I don't think of a sales meeting as an opportunity for me to refine my stand-up comedy routine, but I love to inject humor spontaneously into any situation when appropriate. Timing is everything in this regard.

Take time to laugh, take time for fun. Build fun time into your daily routine. I don't know about you, but I feel like I went to bed when I was in the fourth grade and woke up this morning and here I am an adult. I still feel like that kid inside. I still want to run around in the sun and wind every afternoon around lunchtime. I still love the pit of my stomach feeling of a swing ride as it reaches its apex.

Remember the great Tom Hanks and Elizabeth Perkins movie *Big*? In it Hanks is a kid named Josh Baskin who gets mysteriously transformed into an adult and becomes an executive at a toy company. His child-like wonder and appreciation for the fun factor transforms Perkins and the other crusty business people. He helps them keep in perspective that essential balance between kid and adult necessary to stay sane and successful in business.

Just so you'll understand how important fun is and has been in my life, I want to share with you something I wrote a long time ago.

My Favorite Subject

My favorite subject is recess. Every day we get to go out to recess two times. I love recess. But then we work. And then we work—and we work—and we work work work. But I want to play. I just love recess because I get to play and play.

By Barbie Carey Kraft - 1968
First Grade - Mrs. Hoisington

The more things change, the more they stay the same.

Balance and *The Carey Formula*

In developing *The Carey Formula* over the last two-plus decades, I've come to realize that in addition to developing a plan to effectively create, produce, and market products, I've also developed a strategy for achieving balance in my personal and professional life. When you take a look at each phase of the program, you can see how balance is woven into each concept. For example, one of the founding principles of *The Carey Formula* is to select products that are inexpensive to make. That makes good business sense, but how does it make balance sense? Well, if the idea behind being a sole proprietor/entrepreneur is to remain as independent as possible, then not having to seek out investors to fund your project (and take a large portion of the profits down the line) keeps the balance of power always where you want it—in your hands. Secondly, by not having to invest a large amount of money into your operation early on (and preferably only investing profits at any point in the life of the product), you aren't forced by circumstances to make decisions from a position of weakness. For example, when you think about the Time-Out Watch experience I had, think of the number of dollars and hours I invested in that product. Each time I had to make a decision about whether to continue to pursue that goal or to stop, I had to factor in how much of a potential loss I stood to incur. That weight of potential loss is huge.

In the field of behavioral finance, experts study people and the decisions they make about money. What they've found is that while people's feelings differ, and as a result how much they influence their decisions about spending, all of us have an emotional response called "loss aversion." We hate to lose money. If you were to ask someone how they felt about losing, and here I mean physically losing $200 in cash that fell out of your pocket, versus how they felt about having purchased a product for $1,000 that fell far short of their expectations and often failed to work properly and required them to sink more money into repairs, most people would say that they felt worse about the $200 because it was a flat out complete loss. It doesn't really make sense logically, but that's how many people feel.

When trying to balance emotion and reason, most of us are not very good at the task. We're not like Mr. Spock, or other coldly rational beings who can simply detach themselves from a situation and operate purely on data. Though it is beyond the scope of this book to talk about money and our emotional attachments to it, let me say this—how we deal with money issues is as emotionally charged as how we deal with issues of sexuality and relationships. By keeping the emotional quotient low (having low costs initially), we can look more logically at our expenses and our experiences. I was devastated by the failure of the Time-Out Watch because so much was at stake. If my Halloween Masks hadn't succeeded, I wouldn't have been as devastated because I had so much less invested in terms of time and money. I could think much more clearly and make more level-headed decisions because the risk factor was lower.

Behavioral finance also talks about people and their relative levels of comfort with risk—generally about their investments—but we can extrapolate from that to talk about it in terms of *The Carey Formula*. By keeping your costs low initially, you are in a low-risk venture. You've seen the results of some of my products, and you know that they have earned high rewards. Why wouldn't you want to be involved in a low-risk/high reward venture? I mean, I'm an adventurous gal and I love the art of the deal as much of the next person, but I also love to win. Why not play a game where the chances of winning are far greater than they are of losing? That's another way to look at balance. If I have all the information I need (by doing the kind of market research and investigation *The Carey Formula* mandates); if I have very low up front costs and thus a low-risk venture planned; if I have both information and a strong chance of success on my side; and if my risk/loss aversion is very low on the emotional scale and my reason/rational skills are on the high side of the scale, then I'm entering this process with both feet firmly balanced.

We all love the notion of business ventures being like high-wire acts. We love the mavericks, the men and women who play high stakes Texas Hold 'Em poker and are willing to go all in even when the odds are stacked against them. We cheer on the underdog. But you know what? On balance, for every one of those successes there are thousands of people who've crashed and burned and lost it all. As I said before, I love the game, but I love winning more. The thrill for me comes not from seeing how close I can get to the edge before I tumble into the abyss, but from getting as far from that edge as possible knowing I've been appropriately wise and kept my mind so focused that I can't fail. Different strokes for different folks, but I get so much satisfaction out of being able to get an order before I've sunk any kind of serious cash into a venture, that words fail me. I haven't put myself at great risk. I haven't mortgaged my son's future. I haven't left my employees and their futures flapping in the breeze while I chased a vision willy-nilly to satisfy my own ego.

Believe me, it took me some time to get to that point of balance where—always and every time—I operate from a position of strength. Remember another key point of *The Carey Formula*—surround yourself with people whose strengths offset your weaknesses. You've heard me go on about accounting and numbers and my aversion to them, so I won't hammer on this point too much longer. But I use the word "hammer" purposefully here. I learned a long time ago that you need the right tool for the right job. Everybody knows that. But I've also noticed that some people are single tool kind of people. If they're a hammer, then every problem they encounter will look like a nail and they'll apply that tool to it. Not a smart way to go about doing things, obviously. Not every problem is a nail needing to be bashed. I love tools and gadgets and multi-purpose tools like the Leatherman or the various Swiss Army knives, and tools are almost as fun to browse over as shoes (I said ALMOST!). In business, it's not really possible for one person to be all things. Surround yourself with people whose strengths will help you keep your balance. Admitting your own shortcomings can be one of your greatest strengths as an entrepreneur. There's never any harm in admitting that you can't do something or don't know something.

The Carey Formula works to help you keep your balance and your balance sheet in order in many other ways. Recall that I didn't start investing in media to promote my Hairagami® line of products until I had generated enough profit to pay for it. I only invested in as much media as I could afford based on my most recent sales. I kept my marketing costs firmly in line. Again, behavioral finance has a lot to say about this issue. We've all encountered the "throwing good money after bad" phenomenon, and most of us have been put in a position where we had to do exactly that. How much we dislike being put in that position may determine if you're the buyer of a new car every two years type or the kind who believes that getting anything less than 200,000 miles on a car is a failure of the soul. By following *The Carey Formula*, at every step along the way, you will have checks and balances built into your program to avoid being in the "good money after bad" position.

One of the most difficult decisions you can make is when to abandon an idea. It hurts. But if you've not invested a great deal of time and money and other resources into the venture prematurely, you can be more levelheaded in your approach. As much as I hate throwing good money after bad, I hate throwing good ideas after bad. But the whole point of *The Carey Formula* is to not throw money around anyway. I can think of far better things to do with it than that. Besides, keep yourself in shape for another kind of pitching—crafting presentations guaranteed to get you an order.

Knowing how to prioritize and what to focus on is a balancing act that everyone needs to perfect. How can you possibly focus on a sales meeting fully if you have one eye on your diminishing cash reserves the entire time? I know a lot of people who pride themselves on being multi-taskers, but I'd rather have someone on my side who can focus on one thing to the exclusion of all else until that task is completed. In a very real sense, *The Carey Formula* breaks the process down into defined steps so that you or some other member of your team can focus on a specific task. One of the great things about entering a sales meeting is that you go into it with a distinct advantage over many other vendors. You have invested little money at this stage, so you aren't negotiating from a break-even point. In other words, a lot of times entrepreneurs will have an anchor point in their minds when they enter a negotiation. They know what they've already invested and at minimum they want to be able to earn that plus a profit. The "plus" may vary, but they've already established a baseline for what they must get. If you have followed *The Carey Formula* and have low up front costs, it will be easier for you to forget about those costs and negotiate from a position of emotional strength.

If you've done all the homework *The Carey Formula* has suggested, used the various calculators and profit and loss statements made available, then you are also operating from a position of information strength. Look for every advantage you can so that you can balance out your initial fear of not getting an order. Balance out that fear with knowledge of the type of buyer you are dealing with, being aware of what margins he/she generally prefers. Balance out that fear knowing you have the freedom to negotiate as aggressively as possible, because you have little invested up front anyway. This sense of freedom is similar to the

www.Hairagami.com

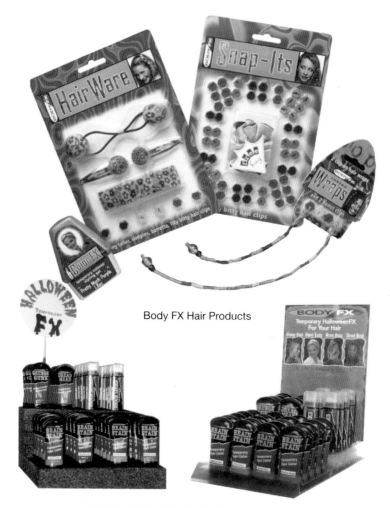

Body FX Hair Products

THE TIME-OUT™ WATCH
THE <u>TOTAL</u> TIME CONCEPT FOR CHILDREN!
THE *FIRST* INTERACTIVE VISUAL WATCH

Halloween Masks

Jump Rope

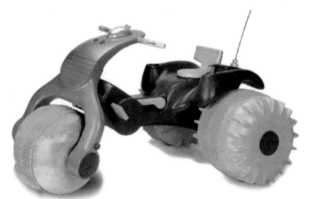

Water Wheels

Children's Books

Touch Tube

Closing the deal at Toys R Us with Chuck Miller.

Robert Miller & Rich Jr.

Today show with Danny Grossman, president of Wild Planet 1999.

1986   1992   1995

Ernst & Young Award, 1999.   Rich Jr. 2005

www.richstachowski.com

Motivation Mirror

Flax

Bloombra

"I'm not sick—I just have my period!"

Dittie—Trustworthy, reliable, fun *and* stylish!

www.dittie.com

⁘ DIMENSIONS
26"H x 7.5"W x 6.5"D
(7.5" wall footprint)

Grassroots Marketing!
www.dittie.com

Confessions of a dangerously premenstrual mind

Send and e-dittie!

FREE stuff!

Where have your ditties been?

Roadmap to SUCCESS

1 IDEATION

- Utilize a combination of re-search and "me-search."
- What do others need.
- What do you need.
- Examine your own hobbies and interests.

Will It Save Time?
Will It Make Users Life Easier?
Does It Have Added Value?

2 IDEAS

- Seek products that need improvement.
- Combine two products to create something new.

3 EVALUATION

- Meets a need?
- Has added value?
- Key features?
- Mass market appeal?
- Low unit cost?

Return to Ideation Phase.
Re-evaluate production
method and simplify.

◯ YES   ◯ NO

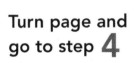

Turn page and
go to step 4

4 PRODUCT DEVELOPMENT

- Research manufacturers *(CD Library)*.
- Develop a strategic plan to get the most favorable terms.
- Research and implement a patent plan.
- Order sample materials and evaluate.
- Research buyers.

Consider:

- Do you need a prototype?
- Research and develop packaging.
- Using the Carey Formula Profit and Loss Statement, determine what your total costs will be (CD Library).

- Establish the retail price.
- Establish the wholesale price.
- Calculate the cost of goods sold.
- Calculate the profit margin (CD Library).

COSTS

- Research
- Production
- Legal
- Design
- Marketing
- Misc. support

5 PREPARE FOR SALES MEETING

- What category does your product fall into?
- Do you have multiple locations to sell your product?
- Develop relationships with buyers?
- Consider alternative distribution channels.
- What is the average margin for products in that category?
- Think like a buyer and figure out a way for your product to increase the department's margin.
- Will your product cannibalize sales of another product?
- Prepare for the cannibalize issue: If you can demonstrate sales at other outlets, your buyer won't want to be left out.
- Does your product have a lower margin than those currently available?
- Chart planogram and promotional schedules (CD library).
- Discuss merchandising and the unique needs of the account.
- Ask smart questions.

6 GET THE ORDERS

- Be energetic and informative.
- Lead with the perceived value of the product.
- Let buyer know that you have a marketing program and full product line vision.
- Negotiate favorable terms to benefit both parties.
- Get short terms up front and use exclusivity as a bargaining chip.
- Don't agree to a guaranteed sale.
- Ask for the order.

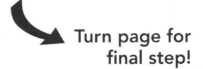

Turn page for
final step!

7 PRODUCE AND MARKET THE PRODUCT

- Negotiate terms with your manufacturer and use the power of the purchase order to pay them after you get paid.

- Set up an account to pay them from your bank directly if need be.

CAUTION: These terms are essential to your cash flow.

- Use proceeds from first order to pay for marketing and more inventory.

- Supplement the retailers' advertising and promotion efforts with your own.

- Employ grass roots and guerilla marketing efforts until sales justify other media buys.

- Communicate directly with consumers to build good will and get feedback.

- Use profits to fund marketing and promotion efforts

- Establish baseline of sell through success.

CAUTION: Test in pennies spend in dollars.

- Monitor sell through to stay on track.

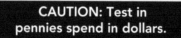

feeling I try to instill in friends when they are interviewing for a job. I always tell them, "You can only *get* something based on this interview. They can't take anything away—they can only give." That kind of balanced mindset that *The Carey Formula* provides is essential to being able to focus on the task at hand without additional layers of pressure (Oh my God, can we eat this week?) and risk recovery (Oh my God, will this order cover all my expenses?).

Clearly, the reason why I never go into production until I have a firm commitment for orders is to help keep my operations balanced. I want that money coming in to pay for my production and packaging and shipping costs. I want those comfortable homeostatic processes to work. It's almost like diet and nutrition. I want to make sure that I don't go into some kind of caloric deficit, have my blood sugar drop to near zero, be light-headed and dizzy and irritable, and be forced to make decisions while in that unbalanced state of mind, body, and emotion. *The Carey Formula* allows you to maintain an even keel, and level out of the inevitable highs and lows that are a part of the roller coaster nature of doing business. When it works at its best, however, *The Carey Formula* gets you off that roller coaster completely. You are not a passive rider on a course of someone else's design. You're not strapped in a seat, powerless to control the speed and direction of the car you're riding in. *You are in control.* You have a destination in mind. You can speed up and slow down and change course as you see fit.

Control. I guess what it comes down to for me is that I like being in control. I've called it autonomy, but perhaps at its simplest, my desire has always been to be in control. Isn't that what most of us want out of life—to be in control of our own destiny? You know, this book is a guide to achieving your version of the American Dream. For most of us, and for most of our history, that dream has been about freedom. As Americans, we love to be in control. We love automobiles because they give us the freedom to go where we want, to not be subject to someone else's schedule, to stop when and where we want, take whatever route we choose.

I hope that is how you will view *The Carey Formula*—as a vehicle that you control. I've simply done the design work for the vehicle. How you equip it, how you choose to use it, is entirely up to you. I wanted to design something that offered you enough choices and enough latitude so that you would feel comfortable operating it. I wanted to balance that with enough guidance and information so that you are empowered and equipped to begin. I hope that you see that you still have a great deal of freedom to employ these steps in ways that work best with your individual personality and work style. I hope that you will use this book as a tool for self-assessment, so that you can take a balanced look at yourself to learn what areas of your life and your skill set lend themselves best to a specific business venture. Most of all, I wanted to share with you my passion for this kind of work, the joy it brings me, and the rich rewards (financial, emotional, and spiritual) that come with success. I hope that you, too, will see how important it is to keep all aspects of this in perspective.

I know at times I've felt the adrenaline rush of excitement that comes from the belief that what I'm doing is nearly a matter of life and death. I know logically that it's not, but I let myself feel that it is. The difference between knowing and feeling could never be more pronounced than it is in those moments. I allow myself to get carried away, and I hope that this book gives you the push you needed to allow yourself to be "Careyed" away to pursue your passions with all the grace and integrity you can muster, mindful that success comes in many forms, and that as long as you keep trying to matter you will make a difference in your own life and the lives of an ever-widening circle of others. I'm grateful for the opportunity to share my experiences and insights with you, and I look forward to hearing from you about your own ventures in entrepreneurship. We'll be in touch again soon.

The Entrepreneur

As if brought to life by sheer will, the Entrepreneur must free himself from the common stone that entraps him. Blindfolded, he must trust his instincts, almost sensing his way through. Although wounded from missed strokes of the hammer and chisel, permanent reminders of his own mistakes, his progress has been masterful. But will his aggressive pace be his own undoing? His next stroke could be decisive. Will he free his leg to take that next giant step forward, or will this risky thrust be the one that cuts him off at the knees? His future rests solely in his own hands. But he would have it no other way.

I found this picture over a decade ago and it motivates me to persevere.

Acknowledgments

So many people contributed in so many different ways to the making of this book. Among those, two people deserve my special thanks:

Rich Stachowski Jr., I am so proud of you not only for your accomplishments but mostly for the fine man that you have become.

Rich Stachowski Sr., for a quarter century of rock solid support, my deepest gratitude goes to you.

Thanks and love to My Other Mothers: Rita Stachowski, Pam Kraft, Aunt Kakie, and Shirley Holloway, and My Other Fathers: Dave Stachowski, and Alan Holloway, a.k.a. "Alan the Great." Thanks to my brother Scott who has always given me positive encouragement. Thanks to Margaret Celis, Isabel Hamilton, Kathy Moldthan, Kathy Mitchell, Cheryl Panattoni, Margo Plummer and Anne Vrolyk for their unconditional love and sensibility. Bruce Canepa, you are the best race car driver I know. Matt Dawson, I love you, cousin!

Gary Brozek, your keen insight and hard work have made an immeasurable contribution to this book. Stew Nohrnberg, thank you for providing generous assistance and creative input. Nicholai Martinsen, you helped me keep my focus and gave me invaluable input and support, and you have my sincere appreciation. Karla Dominguez, thank you for your creative talent and positive inner game. Casey Adams, you have my heartfelt thanks for your tireless, quality-minded work and energy. Bill Gladstone, thank you for your contribution on multiple levels. Lisa Liddy, thank you for your detailed work typesetting *The Carey Formula*.

Many thanks for the kind insightful endorsements of *The Carey Formula*: Anne Vrolyk, Founder of Vrolyk & Company, Mark Hughes, CEO Buzzmarketing, and Eric Kolhede, for being the catalyst for my love affair with business.

I also would like to thank a host of others. Robert Miller, your positive attitude is what makes you successful and thank you for 15 years of fun, oops I mean work! Zephyr Manufacturing—special thanks to De Anne and D'Miles for our partnership. Tim Draper, thank you for your constant support of both my son Rich Jr. and me. Danny Grossman, you have been my role model of integrity and thank you for your wisdom. Scott Gorley, thanks for always being there to listen to and brainstorm with me. Michael Cookson, thank you for always asking me challenging questions. Gary Marcott, many thanks for teaching me great lessons—you are a brilliant man. Chuck Miller, you have a bright perspective on life—thank you for shining on me. Michael Rosa, I appreciate not only your smarts, but also your sense of humor and compassion. Josh Kaplan, you are a star, and thank you for giving me a small piece of your life. Collette Liantonio, thank you for sharing so many similarities with me, among them are our children and business interests. Thank you Patrick Seidler and Art Gunther. Sue Knight and Linda Voracek, many thanks for putting up with me over the years. Lisa Bowerman, you never let me forget who is in charge. Lori Preiss, thank you for your always insightful advice and for eating ice cream with me for breakfast. Thanks so much Dr. Ruefenacht. Nancy Steiner, I am looking for you and thank you for your support in my early years.

Many thanks to those who have made a difference in my life: George Asmus, Jim Balitsos, Ken Berry, Dave Capper, Harry Chang, Charlie Coane, Sabrina Denebeim, Sharon Dillon, Haim Ezer, James Gavney, Chis Hagestad, Mark Hastings, Don Hawley, Bill Hemann, Lew Hendler, Andy Hon, Michael Hsieh, John Juleson, Barbara Kee, Tony Kerry, Don Kingsborough, Francesca Kuglen, David Letterman, Bosmat Levi, Bob Levine, Sophia Lovre, Scott Luschen, Letty Montano, Jonathan Owens, Paul Rago, Beth Richman, Jack Rominger, Henry Saar, Rowland Schaefer, David Silva, Dana Smith, Ashley Stachowski, Jay Stakelon, Stephanie Stewart, Cameron Tuttle, John VanWassenhoven, Jennifer Winschittl. Also, if I forgot to thank anyone I sincerely apologize and please let me know my oversight.

Lastly, this book is in loving memory of Russ Bruzzone, Brother Giles, Doreen Hamilton, and Barbara Inman.

Index

A

A Pace of Grace 254
Adams, Casey 296
Asmus, George 297
"As Seen on TV" 165
Attitude 183

B

Balance 249, 251, 255
  and *The Carey Formula* 270
  mind and spirit 258
  with business 260
Balitsos, Jim 297
Behavioral economics 124
Behavioral finance 271, 273
Belsky, Gary 124
Berry, Ken 297
Bloombra 71
Book of Knowledge 133
Bowerman, Lisa 297
Bowler Mitchell, Kathryn P.
  128-131
Breathing 256
Brother Giles 101-102, 111,
  297

Brozek, Gary 296
Bruzzone, Joan 70
Bruzzone, Russ 95, 297
Bumper-Jumper-Paddle-Pumper
  69
Business formula 37
Buyers
  negotiating points 201
  types of 193-196
  working with 183, 193, 198
Buzzmarketing xiv

C

Canepa, Bruce 295
Capper, Dave 297
Careful Buyer 194
Celis, Margaret 295
Chang, Harry 297
Change, adapting to 146
China 160
Claire's Boutique 167-168
Coane, Charlie 297
College experience 97-99,
  101-102
Combining products 61

Company Buyer 193
Concepts TV 165-166, 172
Cookson, Michael 234, 296
Cooperative advertising 204
Copeland, Mrs. 82
Creative process 144
Creativity 12, 121
CVS 161-162, 167, 226

D

Daemon 23-24
David Letterman Show 66
Dawson, Matt 295
DCH Mask 54
Delegation 80
Denebeim, Sabrina 297
Dillon, Sharon 297
Diray TV 166
Direct response campaign 163
Dissatisfaction, job 17
Dittie™ 1, 136, 206, 208,
    211-212, 218, 225, 230,
    233, 235, 238, 243-244
    focus groups 221
    Life Street team 237
Dominguez, Karla 296
Draper, Tim 214, 296
DS McGee Enterprise, Inc.
    170
Dyson example 38-39

E

Empathy 135
Entrepreneur 25, 102
    characteristics 117
    differences with inventor 12
    key signs for 32
    personal worth 118
    self-improvement 118

traits 18, 110
Ernst & Young "Entrepreneur of
    the Year" 64, 66
Escape Your Shape 169
Exclusivity 49, 161, 204
Eye of a Turtle 65
Ezer, Haim 232, 297

F

Failure 48, 54, 72, 143
Flip Clip 162
Friendship Bracelets 1
Fun 267-269

G

Gardener, Howard 122
Gates, Bill 118
Gavney, James 297
Getting orders 185
Gibran, Kahlil 20, 22
Gilovich, Thomas 124
Girl Scout Cookies 29
Gladstone, Bill 296
Going Up Against the Big Boys
    244
Golden Rule 83
Gorley, Scott 296
Gresset, Jean 47
Grossman, Danny 296
Guaranteed sales 195
Gumption traps 87-88
Gunther, Art 44, 297

H

Hagestad, Chris 297
Hahn, Karen 157

Hairagami® 1, 149-150, 153,
   156, 158-161, 163, 165-168,
   172, 175, 179, 260
Halloween masks 61, 271
Hamilton, Doreen 297
Hamilton, Isabel 45, 295
Hastings, Mark 297
Hawley, Don 297
Hemann, Bill 232, 297
Hendler, Lewis 297
Hendrickson, Carolyn 157
Hillman, James 23
Holloway, Alan 295
Holloway, Shirley 295
Hon, Andy 297
Horse example 89-94
Hospital Specialty Company 232
Hsieh, Michael 297
Hughes, Mark xiv, 296

I

I Love Lucy 78-79
IBM 106-110, 112
   Sales Boot Camp 108
Idea evaluation 11
Ideation 43, 149-150
   stage 220
Incentives 31
Independence 12-16, 18, 139
Ingredients for success 12
Inman, Barbara 297
Intellectual property 155
Intrapersonal intelligence
   122-128
Inventors' Hall of Fame 66
Inventory of skills 117

J

Jay Leno Show 67

journal 134
Juleson, John 297

K

Kakie, Aunt 295
Kaplan, Josh 247, 296
Kavelin-Popov, Linda 254, 256
Kee, Barbara 297
Kerry, Tony 297
Kinesthetic intelligence 122, 126
Kingsborough, Don 233, 297
Kmart 53, 55, 57, 175, 178
Knight, Sue 297
Knowledge 136
Kolhede, Eric 103-104, 296
Kraft, Margie 13, 19, 21-22,
   82-83, 107
Kraft, Pam 295
Kraft, Ron 12, 83, 88, 94
Kraft, Scott 13, 84-87
Kuglen, Francesca 297

L

Lessons learned 49, 143
Letterman, David 168, 297
Levi, Bosmat 232, 297
Levine, Bob 232, 297
Lewis, Lanni 226
Liability insurance 199
Liantonio, Collette 166, 296
Licensing 49, 73
Liddy, Lisa 296
Linguistic intelligence 122-123
Logical-mathematical intelligence
   122-123
"Looks-like" prototype 154
Loss aversion 270
Lovre, Sophia 297
Luck, role of 145

Luschen, Scott 297

M

MacArthur Foundation 120
MacArthur Prize 121, 145
MacArthur, John D. 119
Made by Kids for Kids 64
Marcott, Gary 161, 194, 296
Markdown dollars 204
Market research 5
Marketing 237
  plan 167
  program 227
Martinsen, Nicholai 296
McGee, Dennis 170-171
"Me Search" 184
Merchandise administrator 189
Merchandising 205
Merchant Buyer 194
Miller, Chuck 63, 65, 296
Miller, Robert 64, 296
Mitchell, Kathy 295
Moldthan, Kathy 295
Montano, Letty 297
Motivation Mirror 1, 169, 171,
  173
Multiple Intelligences 122
  intrapersonal 122
  kinesthetic 122, 126
  linguistic 122-123
  logical-mathematical 122-123
Multiple Intelligences, *cont.*
  musical 122, 126
  spatial 122, 125
Musical intelligence 122, 126

N

National Gallery for America's
  Young Inventors 260

Negotiating points 201
  payment terms 202
New beginnings 54
Nohrnberg, Stew 296

O

Observation skills 132
Orders 5
  asking for the 208
Ordinary = Profitable 37
Orwell, George 18
Owens, Jonathan 297

P

Panattoni, Cheryl 295
Partnership for America's Future
  64
Passion xiv, 8-9, 12, 77, 139,
  211, 230
Patent It Yourself 155
Patents 61, 155
Patience 110
Payment terms 202
Perseverance 77
Persistence xiv, 9, 12, 74, 88,
  110, 140
Personal worth 118
Piaget, Jean 41
Pirsig, Robert 87-88, 249
Planograms 186-187, 203
Plummer, Margo 141-142
Plummer, Plummer 295
Points to remember 110
Preiss, Lori 297
Pre-meeting checklist 198
Pressman, David 155
Product
  development 5
  selection 43

Pre-meeting checklist 198
Pressman, David 155
Product
    development 5
    selection 43
    viability 36
Professionalism 230
Promotion/Merchandising 203

Q

QDirect 163
Quantum Leap 44, 51
QVC 156-158, 162, 169, 188

R

Rago, Paul 297
Reality 140
Recording your thoughts
    132-133
Research 184
Research and Development
    151-153
Respect 83
Retail lessons 96-97
Richman, Beth 232, 297
Role of luck 145
Rominger, Jack 245, 297
Rosa, Michael 167, 296
Rostam 232
Roth, Steve 208
Ruefenacht, Dr. 297

S

Saar, Henry 297
Sales approach 226
Sales meetings 5, 182
    preparing for 175, 182
Salmon, De Anne 296

Salmon, D'Miles 296
Schach, Dini 297
Schaefer, Rowland 297
School experiences 81, 110
Secrets of success 30, 49, 71,
    110, 172, 190, 210
Seidler, Patrick 44, 297
Self-assessment 123
Self-Confidence 140
Self-improvement 118
Selling recap 191
Selling your product 137
Sell-through 5, 201, 204-206
Shekerjian, Denise 121-122,
    144
Silva, David 297
SMH 46-48
Smith, Dana 297
Social Security Card example 25,
    28
Spatial intelligence 122, 125
St. Mary's College 101
Stachowski, Ashley 297
Stachowski, Dave 295
Stachowski, Rich Jr. 62-63, 65,
    113, 115, 151, 209, 295
Stachowski, Rich Sr. 102, 295
Stachowski, Rita 295
Stakelon, Jay 297
Steiner, Nancy 100, 297
Stewart, Stephanie 297
Supervision 18
SWOT analysis 104

T

Target 207
The Carey Formula CD Library
    152, 156, 168, 182, 246
The Entrepreneur 293

The National Gallery for America's Young Inventors 261
The Soul's Code 23
The Virtues Project 254
Thinking Globally, Acting Locally 143
Thomas Register 152
Thought Rate/Speaking Rate disparity 138
Time-Out Watch 41-42, 44-45, 47, 54, 59, 71, 74, 114, 187, 259, 270
Tooling costs 49, 71
Toys"R"Us 62, 65
Tuttle, Cameron 297

U

Uncommon Genius: How Great Ideas Are Born 121, 144
Universal Product Code 199

V

VanWassenhoven, John 297
vendPINK™ 218, 240-241, 244, 258, 260
Visionary 136

Voracek, Linda 297
Vrolyk, Anne 295-296

W

Wal-Mart 53, 114
Water Talkie 62-63, 66, 68, 70
Who Am I? mask 75
Why Smart People Make Big Money Mistakes and How to Correct Them 124
Wild Planet 64, 66
Winschittl, Jennifer 297
"Works-like" prototype 154
Writing example 138-139
www.Dittie.com 242
www.Y-Me.org 243

Y

Y-Me organization 242

Z

Zen and the Art of Motorcycle Maintenance 87, 249
Zephyr Manufacturing 158